WALKING
THE
TWILIGHT

Women Writers of the Southwest

WALKING
THE
TWILIGHT

edited by

KATHRYN WILDER

Northland Publishing

The text type was set in Weiss.
The display type was set in Weiss Italic and Castellar.
Cover and interior designed by Trina Stahl
Edited by Erin Murphy
Production supervised by Lisa Brownfield
Production by Rudy J. Ramos

Manufactured in the United States of America

FIRST EDITION
Second Printing, 1995
ISBN 0-87358-585-2

Library of Congress Catalog Card Number 94-28280
Cataloging-in-Publication Data
Walking the twilight : women writers of the Southwest / edited by Kathryn Wilder. — 1st ed.
p.   cm.
ISBN 0-87358-585-2 : $14.95
1. American literature—Southwestern States.   2. Women—Southwestern States—Literary collections.
3. Southwestern States—Literary collections.   4. American literature—Women authors.
I. Wilder, Kathryn, 1954–
PS566.W35   1994
810.8'09287'0979—dc20   94-28280

0560/5M/2-95

To generations:

my mother, Helen;

my sisters of blood—Terry and Peg—

and spirit—Rebecca;

and my sons, Kenney and Ty:

May your stories be told

in truth.

This is Coyote's country—a landscape of the imagination, where nothing is as it appears. The buttes, mesas, and redrock spires beckon you to see them as something other: a cathedral, a tabletop, bears' ears, or nuns. Windows and arches ask you to recall what is no longer there, to taste the wind for the sandstone it carries. These astonishing formations invite new mythology for desert goers, one that acknowledges the power of story and ritual, yet lies within the integrity of our own cultures. The stories rooted in experience become beads to trade. It is the story, always the story, that precedes and follows the journey.

—TERRY TEMPEST WILLIAMS, *Coyote's Canyon*

Contents

TO BEGIN

It is hard to walk back to a place I have forgotten.
There is no map. Only here. And there. If there ever was.
And if here is where I am to begin.

I know this: I do not want to start this journey.
My skin hurts. My bones ache. My eyes blur.
And my feet, ahhh, these feet are too large to fit in the footprints my life has left behind.
And they are old and flat. My feet are all wrong for this walk.

I hear a voice that says:
You know the way.

I hear a voice that says:
There is such a place; it is yours and yours alone.

I hear a voice that says:
No matter your feet; your heart will do the walking.

I hear a voice that says:
The place you've forgotten is called home.

I do not know if I believe this voice.
But I wonder about these heartsteps that will be mine.
I imagine I shall want to follow them after all.

—MARILYN TAYLOR

Introduction

Twilight:
the time when
day slips into night
or fall fades into winter
or one century cascades into another.
As we walk this time,
our silhouettes become defined,
we find our footing in the dark,
and our voices . . .

I T'S A STRAIGHT STRETCH of highway, almost any southwestern highway. I watch flat red rocky soil erupt into sky-pointing fingers, or rise and spread into distant flat mesas, or fall away into splits of earth snaking out across the world. Sometimes the red dirt begins to grow grasses, and the highway climbs gently toward sagebrush stubble, scrub oak or piñon pine, ponderosas on the skyline making their own monuments to the heavens. Other times the red dirt yellows, junipers recede, and prickly pear and saguaro stand guard while jumping cholla and ocotillo wave toward the sun. It doesn't matter—it's the straight stretch I'm after, and my hand moves across the seat to the stack of manuscripts piled beside me.

Months ago my words to the man driving the truck were, "Do you mind?" Now I say, "Can you stand it?" He knows what I mean, and I know he means it when he says, yes, of course. I select a manila envelope randomly from the pile as the black Ford with its steel-framed camper shell and river-gear racks pulls highway miles beneath its tires. Reading aloud, my voice blends with rubber on asphalt while story images merge with the terrain. I read; he drives; we listen, and see, and feel. When the road changes from straight to curvy I put the manuscript down and we talk, stories running through our conversation like the love of redrock and river, and the spiritual balance we find in these places.

The stories take me into parts of the Southwest I did not before know; they take me into human experience I have only imagined. And as they take me, so I have taken them—down highways, across skyways, downriver. Manuscripts in a canvas briefcase on the floor of the truck, or packed in a blue rubber dry bag and strapped to the rigging of a boat. Manuscripts read by the light of a campfire, the river's voice in the background; from a rock in the sun, water rippling at my feet; by dawn's light, from the warm depths of a sleeping bag; on straight stretches of southwestern highway. For months, these stories have followed me everywhere.

WE'VE JUST come off the river. The boats are de-rigged, the truck and trailer packed full, and the other members of our crew have headed off to town—Green River or Moab, we're not sure which—for showers and bar beer. I throw the last of the aluminum in the big bin kindly provided by the State of Utah at the take-out, and use the "facilities," sitting on a seat that doesn't pinch in a room with a door that closes people, and canyon walls, and the river, out. The privilege of privacy is not worth it—the walls in the square green building with its filtered light and meager ventilation close me in, and I wish that I were back upriver, sitting amid young cottonwoods with the water rolling by five feet away. I leave the facility quickly.

Knowing already where I will find him, I see my friend—driver, boatman—perched on a rock overlooking Swasey's rapid. I step into the water's edge nearby, feel the current pull against my calves, the river inviting me in, but I decline, bending instead to wash my face and hands one last time in the red silt-water of the Green. I pick out another rock, one flat and low and wet with river spray, and sit there, the river washing me with a mist as fine as any Female Rain. I look into swift waters and see five days of basic human experience—food and drinking water packed in, waste and garbage packed out; adrenaline and fear carried in, memories carried out. Five days is not enough. I dip my fingers into the river; I bring them to my face. River tears mix with my own.

Thank you, River, I say, for carrying me safely downstream; thank you for helping me shed, like old skin, towns and jobs, deadlines and money worries, needs for such things as electric lights and refrigeration and clean clothes; thank you for reminding me of what matters in life: water, food, shelter, and truth. My truth, his, hers, yours. On the rock by the river, I come to understand what my traveling companions for many months have in common, what these stories by southwestern women writers share—truth.

WALKING THE TWILIGHT, like many books, began as a random thought: As the Southwest is shaped so visibly, tangibly, audibly even, by fire-rock, wind, and water, so are its people. People are drawn here by erosion and timelessness; here, where the confluence of what was and what is can be touched and tasted, can be soaked into the skin, swallowed into the soul. Emotional erosion takes place here. And stories are formed, told, and passed on.

A random thought grew into specific questions: Does the Southwest as place influence its stories beyond the setting of cactus and canyon? Does it influence character and plot beyond leathered cowboys and classic westerns? Enough so that it becomes a style among a select group of people? Writers? Women? Like the writers of the New West, are there women writers of the Southwest?

Miles of stories later, I am satisfied by the answers.

I HAVE done some difficult things in my life, like learning to teamrope at twenty-five, be a mom at thirty, and run rivers at thirty-five, but selecting thirty-three pieces of short fiction from hundreds of powerful voices and strong stories is among the more difficult tasks I've faced. I kept the guidelines general, wanting stories by women who were either from the Southwest or who lived here for a significant period of time, and stories in which place was nearly a character. I purposefully did not define the region of the Southwest in my call for submissions, thinking that the submissions themselves would define it for me. Nor did I want to be too specific about the length of time a writer has spent here. I held the notion that the stories would identify the writers of the Southwest, as well as the region, for me.

And they did, which is why Texas, Oklahoma, and California stories are included in this collection. I learned that to some, the Southwest consists of New Mexico, Arizona, and Utah, and maybe Nevada and Colorado. But the submissions I received from the outer states expanded my editorial horizons; hence, the inclusion of three Texas stories (it's a big state), and "That Horse," set in Oklahoma. Having spent time in the Mojave Desert, I consider it part of the Southwest, and was pleased to find that that perception was supported by several submissions, of which Cathryn Alpert's "The Plain of Nazca" is one. I also wanted to honor Mexico's place in southwestern culture, which Ana Consuelo Matiella's "Angels" does hauntingly.

New Mexico, Arizona, and Utah stories flowed in like tributaries to the Colorado, but I did not receive a Nevada story, or one by a Nevada writer, until the very last minute, when Teresa Jordan's piece arrived in the mail. Although Teresa does not consider herself a Nevada writer—yet—and "Effie's Garden" deviates from even my most generous guidelines in that it is set in Wyoming, the essence of the story, and of the character Effie, is the barrenness of the high desert country of Nevada, of the Southwest. Teresa's family has been in Wyoming for five generations, but she acknowledges that "high desert images most truly capture the landscape of Effie's personality," images she would not have had if she had never left the short grass prairie where she was born. After living in Nevada, she realized the story was especially fitting to the Nevada landscape, but we chose to leave it unaltered.

Teresa Jordan's experience of having roots in Wyoming, living in six western states and frequenting as many others, is not uncommon, and raises the question of mobility. "Like so many westerners," she says, "I've moved and moved and moved." Most of the writers in this anthology have done the same, and because transience is such a component of southwestern culture I chose to include one story from a woman who has not, as yet, lived here. A Pennsylvanian, Lisa Chewning has visited the Southwest as much as possible over the past six years, and it is her intention to make it her permanant residence soon. In the meantime, she has let the Southwest into her soul and her writing, and she pays daily attention to the Albuquerque weather report. In her story, "Holy Dirt," Lisa conveys the heart-draw the Southwest has upon those passing through.

I have few disappointments, overall, in what I have compiled, primary among them being that I couldn't include all the wonderful stories I read. In addition, I regret that although an impressive number of timely issues are covered, AIDS and incest are not. As an incest survivor, I had a strong desire to see that issue developed in a story, but the only such story submitted was one of mine and it didn't make the cut. I received no AIDS stories, which could mean that that trauma has not touched the lives of these writers, or that we've not had time to incoproate those experiences into words. Either way, they're missed. I also hoped to have more Native American stories included, and more southwestern tribes represented, yet I am not surprised that the Navajo Nation, the largest Indian nation in the United States, has the strongest showing. And I wanted more ethnic diversity represented, as that would truly reflect the Southwest.

On the other hand, I am delighted with the variety of stories I have. The ages of authors range from twenty-five to sixty-three, and the ages of characters, infancy to old age. Two countries and seven states are represented, and the authors live in California, Pennsylvania, and many places in between. The selections come from widely published, award-winning authors as well as new, even unpublished, writers. And they all come from women brave enough to tell the truth.

TRUTH IS what matters, in life *and* in literature.

Like the Southwest, like the river, these thirty-three writers have worn away the unnecessary, exposing truth bare as stone. Their words are as raw and rugged as the redrocks of Utah, as deep and daring as the Grand Canyon, as fluid and cutting as the Colorado River, or the Green. Their stories cover the vast expanse of the Southwest, the breadth of human emotion, and the issues America's women, children, and men are facing at the end of the twentieth century. Like the story that precedes and follows the journey, it is the truth that precedes and follows the story.

TWILIGHT IS the time of the setting sun, when day shifts into night and sky-colors layer and pastel, crystallize, then fade away. It's a time of transition, of movement from one realm to another. A time of change—unsettling, spiritually renewing. Such is the way with these stories.

In one of the creative writing classes I took at Northern Arizona University from Ann Cummins (author of the story "Neutral Zone"), she told us something a professor of hers had told her: To make a story a story, the main character has to change. This much we all knew. A good story will change the reader, Ann said. Hmmm, we responded. But the best stories, she said, are the ones that have, through the process of the writing, changed the *writers*. Through my involvement with these women and their words—through my journey into the twilight of their truths—I have grown and changed. It is my prayer that this happens for you, too. It is my guess that the stories in this anthology have already changed their writers.

MY GRATITUDE extends beyond the deep canyons, redrocks, wild rivers, and twilit skies of this blessed country, the Southwest; it leaps to northern California, and my mother, Helen Park Bigelow, who was born in the same Berkeley hospital in which she had me, the same hospital in which her own mother was born. Birthplace, however, is not all we have in common. My mother was raised in the home of an artist who worked the erratic and temperamental schedule his need to make art demanded. I, too, was raised in such an environment, by a mother who made pots for a living. I attribute some of my creativity, and my need to form a life around it, to generations.

But it doesn't stop there. For a time my mother lived in Pennsylvania, where she found the winters and the clay too cold for her hands to continue giving shape to round earthen balls. She took to words. I was working toward my Bachelor of Arts degree in creative writing at San Francisco State University, and a new relationship formed, like a bridge, between us. We critiqued stories and essays through the mail and over the phone; rejections were commiserated, acceptances celebrated. If there were some things we could not discuss, we could always talk about writing.

And we did, until about two-and-a-half years ago when I grasped the throw-line of recovery and found that distance was what I needed. But recovery—like the river, like this book—is change and movement and growth, so when *Walking the Twilight* unfolded and I found myself suddenly sitting beside dozens of manuscripts without a co-editor, I accepted my mother's offer of help. Like her hands on clay, her sense of good story, artistic background, and familiarity with my literary tastes have lent strength and grace to this collection.

Others to whom I wish to express gratitude begin with the women who are courageous enough to tell their truths, *no matter what,* and who have faith enough in their voices to want their work read.

I'd like to thank the people in my publishing house whose efforts are far greater than the credit they're given: Trina Stahl, art director; Rudy Ramos, assistant art director; Katy Spining, editorial assistant; and Erin Murphy, editor, who not only opened a door for me but pushed me through it. And to the rest of Northland's staff: Your efforts have not gone unnoticed.

I'd like to thank Scott, now back in Montana, for his support of the idea of this book when it was just that; Mary Sojourner for her early involvement; Kathleen and Leslie at Aradia Bookstore for finding and lending (and selling) me books I needed for research; Rebecca Lancaster for her terrific typing skills; Ed Bigelow for all those computer-oriented long-distance telephone calls; Molly and Marilyn for their love of the spirit in me; and Teresa Jordan, Linda Hasselstrom, Cathryn Alpert, and Terry Tempest Williams for their words of encouragement, support, and sisterhood.

And to Mark, who spent many miles driving me across the Southwest—to Diamond Creek, House Rock Valley, Marble Canyon, Cottonwood Canyon, Moab, Kanab, Sand Island, Sand Wash, Green River, Dolores, Durango, Santa Fe, Taos and home, always home—listening while I read: Thank you, for taking me down the river, for stopping at sunsets, for walking with me in twilight, for listening.

I am most grateful to H. P. and N. A., for helping me find the miracle within.

Just Past Shiprock

LUCI TAPAHONSO

LUCI TAPAHONSO was born in 1953 in Shiprock, New Mexico. A member of the Navajo Nation, she now lives in Lawrence, Kansas, with her husband and children, but frequently visits her homeland. She is an assistant professor at the University of Kansas, and her work has also appeared in numerous journals, such as Beloit Poetry Journal *and* Guadalupe Review, *and anthologies such as* Sisters of the Earth *and* The Desert is No Lady. *She has published three books of poetry,* One More Shiprock Night, Seasonal Woman, *and* A Breeze Swept Through, *and a collection of poems and stories,* Sáanii Dahataał/The Women Are Singing: Poems and Stories

WHEN I WAS A child, our family traveled often to Oak Springs, Arizona. Oak Springs is on the eastern slope of the Carriso Mountains, about fifty miles west of Shiprock. My father grew up there, and we have many relatives in the area. Our family has a plot of land with a hogan and storage cellar there.

On one occasion, we were going to Oak Springs, and there were perhaps six or seven children in the back of the pickup and Mary, an older cousin. Mary's father and my mother are siblings, so she is considered our sister. She is considerably older than we are and did not take part in the noisy playing we were involved in. Since she was the oldest one in the back of the pickup, she was responsible for our behavior or misbehavior.

As we went past Shiprock, there were flat mesas, gentle sandhills, and a few houses scattered at distances. Mary pointed to a mesa as we rounded a curve and asked, "See those rocks at the bottom?" We stopped playing and moved around her to listen. The question was the opening for a story. The rocks she pointed at were

1

midway between the ground and the top of the rock pile. The mesa loomed behind, smooth and deep ochre. The rocks were on the shaded side of the mesa. Then Mary told this story:

THEY SAID a long time ago, something happened where those rocks are. When I was little, they told me that one time before there were cars or even roads around here, there was a family traveling through here on horseback. They had a little baby girl who was sick. As they came near here, the baby became sicker, and she kept getting worse. They finally stopped. They knew it was no use going on. They just stopped and held the baby. By then, she was hardly breathing, and then finally she just stopped breathing. They just cried and walked around with her.

In those days, people were buried differently. The mother and father wrapped her in a pelt of sheepskin and looked for a place to bury her. They prayed, sang a song, then put the baby inside. They stacked rocks over this place so that the animals wouldn't bother her. Of course, they were crying as they rode home.

Later on, whenever they passed by those rocks, they would say, "Our baby daughter is right there," or "She would have been an older sister now." They wiped their tears, remembering her. A lot of people knew that the baby was buried there— that she was their baby and that they still missed her. They knew that and thought of the baby as they passed through here.

So that's why when we come through here, remember those rocks and the baby who was buried there. She was just a newborn. Think about her and be quiet. Those rocks might look like any others, but they're special.

WE LISTENED to the story, and since that time we have told the story many times ourselves. Decades later, those particular rocks hold the haunting and lasting memory of a little baby girl. This land that may seem arid and forlorn to the newcomer is full of stories that hold the spirits of the people, those who live here today and those who lived centuries and other worlds ago. The nondescript rocks are not that at all, but rather a lasting and loving tribute to the death of a baby and the continuing memory of her family.

Cuatas

(for Chayo)

RITA MARIA MAGDALENO

RITA MARIA MAGDALENO'S relationship to the Southwest is focused on her Mexican-American heritage and her grandparents, Andrés and Maria Magdaleno, who migrated to Arizona in 1923. They lived in copper country in Miami, Arizona, where her grandfather worked as a minero for Inspiration Consolidated during the Depression. Rita was born in Augburg, Germany. She is primarily a poet, and her poetry has appeared in New Chicano Writing, *volumes 2 and 3;* After Aztlan: Latino Poets of the Nineties; *and* Named in Stone and Sky: An Arizona Anthology. *She lives in Tucson with her golden Lab, Pachita.*

Se murieron desde bebes. Creo que no nacieron bién. Solo hicieron una pasadita para ver la tierra. Se fueron de ángeles.

I think that some weren't born right because they died when they were babies. They only made a small stopover to see the earth. Then they went up to be angels.

—Dominga González Castellanos, from *Retratos y Sueños: Photographs by Mexican Children*, by Wendy Ewald

MY MOTHER LOST TWO babies in the same year—1940. Evangeline, who had been born in August, only lived for one hour. We don't remember her very well. I do know that it was summer when she died and it had been very hot, for days, in Grover Canyon. But the other one, Rachel's twin, Rebecca, was such a beautiful baby and I remember everything so clearly.

The girls were born on March 1st at 10:30 at night. We didn't know that my mother was going to have twins. It was such a beautiful night! One twin, Rachel, was as dark as anything. They called her *la prietita*. But the little ones couldn't say *prietita* so they always called her *Pepita* and that's how Rachel got her nickname. Now Rebecca, her sister, was very light. *Una buerita*. She had the most beautiful eyes and the longest eyelashes. Chuy, my brother, was ten years old and he really took to her. She was always full of light, like the sun, and it was so easy to love her.

My mother never gave her babies a bath when they were little. Mostly because it was so cold in the canyon. But winter was ending and it had been such a nice day. It was February, a Friday afternoon. So my mother decided to give both of the babies a bath. The twins ended up getting a little cold. It was nothing serious. But by Monday, Rebecca had bronchitis. All that week, my mother stayed by her side. Day and night. And Cuco, our little brother, stayed in the bedroom with my mother and Rebecca. He was always like that, very close to my mom.

It was Thursday afternoon when it happened. My father was in the kitchen and we, the girls, were helping him cook our dinner. Some *papitas y frijóles*, a few *nopalitos*. It was 4:30 in the afternoon. Suddenly, Cuco ran out of my mother's bedroom. "*¡Papá, está muriendo Rebecca!*"

My father dropped the small paring knife in his hand and cried, "*¡Corrale!* Go get the doctor. And get my *comadre!*" So Cuco had to run down the canyon road to the public telephone. It was a couple of miles from our house. He ran and ran. So fast.

Well, that night we had the wake. And the next morning, my father didn't go to work at Inspiration. Instead, he went alone to Miles Mortuary in Miami and he made the funeral arrangements.

That early Friday morning, I still remember the way my father hunched over our kitchen table. He said, "My baby never had a new dress to wear."

Lola Flores, the daughter of my mother's *comadre*, was there. She had a car. So she drove downtown to J C Penney's and got a pink taffeta dress for the baby. Also, Lola had a camera, so my mother asked Lola for *un retrato de* Rebecca in her new pink dress. My mother wanted to buy the film but Lola said, "No, I have a lot of film in my camera."

So we put the little pink dress on Rebecca and then we waited for my dad to come home. When he walked in, he was holding a little pink bonnet. He told us, "I found twenty-five cents in my pocket. I went to the five-and-dime, got this little *gorrita* for your sister. *Aquí está.*" Then he handed it to us and I put that little cap on Rebecca, tied the pink ribbon very carefully under her chin.

That afternoon, Lola took me and Rebecca into the yard where there was a lot of light. I was thirteen years old. And Lola took a picture of me holding my little sister. It was Friday and I remember our backyard full of light. So much sunshine and Rebecca's *carita*, all white, *como una ángelita*. And you know, I'm sure that my mother still has it—that little black-and-white snapshot.

My Lucy Friend
Who Smells Like Corn

SANDRA CISNEROS

SANDRA CISNEROS, 39, lives in San Antonio, Texas, where she is "nobody's mother and nobody's wife." She was born in Chicago, Illinois, the daughter of a Mexican father and a Mexican-American mother. Presently at work on a novel, Caramelo, *she is also a member and organizer of* Mujeres por la paz, *a San Antonio women's peace group, and an associate editor for Third Woman Press. The author of two short story collections,* Woman Hollering Creek *and* The House on Mango Street, *and two volumes of poetry,* Bad Boys *and* My Wicked Wicked Ways, *she is the recipient of two NEA fellowships for poetry and fiction and the Lannan Foundation Literary Award for 1991.*

LUCY ANGUIANO, TEXAS GIRL who smells like corn, like Frito Bandito chips, like tortillas, something like that warm smell of *nixtamal* or bread the way her head smells when she's leaning close to you over a paper cut-out doll or on the porch when we are squatting over marbles trading this pretty crystal that leaves a blue star on your hand for that giant cat-eye with a grasshopper green spiral in the center like the juice of bugs on the windshield when you drive to the border, like the yellow blood of butterflies.

Have you ever eated dog food? I have. After crunching like ice, she opens her big mouth to prove it, only a pink tongue rolling around in there like a blind worm, and Janey looking in because she said Show me. But me I like that Lucy, corn smell hair and aqua flip-flops just like mine that we bought at the K mart for only 79 cents same time.

I'm going to sit in the sun, don't care if it's a million trillion degrees outside, so my skin can get so dark it's blue where it bends like Lucy's. Her whole family like that. Eyes like knife slits.

Lucy and her sisters. Norma, Margarita, Ofelia, Herminia, Nancy, Olivia, Cheli *y la* Amber Sue.

Screen door with no screen. *Bang!* Little black dog biting his fur. Fat couch on the porch. Some of the windows painted blue, some pink, because her daddy got tired that day or forgot. Mama in the kitchen feeding clothes into the wringer washer and clothes rolling out all stiff and twisted and flat like paper. Lucy got her arm stuck once and had to yell Maaa! and her mama had to put the machine in reverse and then her hand rolled back, the finger black and later, her nail fell off. *But did your arm get flat like the clothes? What happened to your arm? Did they have to pump it with air?* No, only the finger, and she didn't cry neither.

Lean across the porch rail and pin the pink sock of the baby Amber Sue on top of Cheli's flowered T-shirt, and the blue jeans of *la* Ofelia over the inside seam of Olivia's blouse, over the flannel nightgown of Margarita so it don't stretch out, and then you take the work shirts of their daddy and hang them upside down like this, and this way all the clothes don't get so wrinkled and take up less space and you don't waste pins. The girls all wear each other's clothes, except Olivia, who is stingy. There ain't no boys here. Only girls and one father who is never home hardly and one mother who says *Ay! I'm real tired* and so many sisters there's no time to count them.

I'm sitting in the sun even though it's the hottest part of the day, the part that makes the streets dizzy, when the heat makes a little hat on the top of your head and bakes the dust and weed grass and sweat up good, all steamy and smelling like sweet corn.

I want to rub heads and sleep in a bed with little sisters, some at the top and some at the feets. I think it would be fun to sleep with sisters you could yell at one at a time or all together, instead of alone on the fold-out chair in the living room.

When I get home Abuelita will say *Didn't I tell you?* and I'll get it because I was supposed to wear this dress again tomorrow. But first I'm going to jump off an old pissy mattress in the Anguiano yard. I'm going to scratch your mosquito bites, Lucy, so they'll itch you, then put Mercurochrome smiley faces on them. We're going to trade shoes and wear them on our hands. We're going to walk over to Janey Ortiz's house and say *We're never ever going to be your friend again forever!* We're going to run home backwards and we're going to run home frontwards, look twice under the house where the rats hide and I'll stick one foot in there because you dared me, sky so blue and heaven inside those white clouds. I'm going to peel a scab from my knee and eat it, sneeze on the cat, give you three M & M's I've been saving for you since yesterday, comb your hair with my fingers and braid it into teeny-tiny braids real pretty. We're going to wave to a lady we don't know on the bus. Hello! I'm going to somersault on the rail of the front porch even though my *chones* show. And cut paper dolls we draw ourselves, and color in their clothes with crayons, my arm around your neck.

And when we look at each other, our arms gummy from an orange Popsicle we split, we could be sisters, right? We could be, you and me waiting for our teeths to fall and money. You laughing something into my ear that tickles, and me going Ha Ha Ha Ha. Her and me, my Lucy friend who smells like corn.

The Man Who Loved the Rain

MARILYN TAYLOR

MARILYN TAYLOR, 46, was born in Ray, Arizona, a place that exists today only as an open pit copper mine. Her father, who was also born in Arizona, and her grandfather lived as miners and ranchers in the deserts of southern Arizona. She moved to Flagstaff in 1974, and has worked there as a court reporter for the past twenty years. It wasn't until 1991 that she became interested in writing down her own words rather than the words of others, and through her writing she has found that she is forever drawn to the souls that survive in the desert, and the sweetness that tempers their strength. "The Man Who Loved the Rain" was a winner of the 1992 Syndicated Fiction Project and is Marilyn's first published fiction.

WHEN I WAS A child, I lived in a small town in the Arizona desert where there were few women, even fewer children, and lots of men.

I think that place was too stark and too quiet for me. I was scared of the desert with its rattlesnakes and scorpions, and I was scared of most of the men. These were hard, rough-skinned men who gathered to talk in small groups. Some of them would chew and spit, and occasionally one would nod his head, but I never ever saw one of them blink. It was a lonely place for a little girl, but it was my home.

Our house faced a dusty side road near the edge of town where there was an old corral. The fence around our front yard was all that stood between me and that road and that corral. Of course I wasn't allowed to play in the road or go near the corral, but I discovered the most wondrous thing. The fence that kept me from doing what I thought I wanted to do was real sturdy. It was made of thick posts, crossed with two-by-fours, and metal sheep wire was nailed to the wood. I could lace my fingers through the wire and lean against it and that fence was strong enough to support me. I could hang there all day if I wanted to and never get tired.

It was there, leaning on that fence, that I first fell in love, and as it happened, I fell in love with two men at the same time. One was called Cowboy Bill, or Willy, and the other was called Mr. Ming, the Rock Man. Both were ranchers.

Cowboy Bill was short and muscular with red sunburnt skin, and Mr. Ming was tall and thin with papery brown skin that hung in tiny wrinkles and folds. And Cowboy Bill was young and Mr. Ming was old, but they seemed alike in all the ways that mattered to me.

They both wore faded blue Levi's and sweat-stained work shirts. They both wore scuffed-up boots and yellow straw hats. They both rode brown horses.

The only difference between those two men that I could see was that Mr. Ming also wore a red kerchief tied around his neck. I thought that was real fancy. I figured that when Cowboy Bill got older, he, too, would probably wear his kerchief around his neck, but for now he kept it folded into a small square in his hip pocket and would take it out from time to time to wipe off the sweat.

I loved to watch him do that. He would take his hat off with one hand, reach in his back pocket for his kerchief with the other, dab at his face with that tiny bit of red cloth, tuck it back into his pocket, smooth his hair and then put his hat back on. I knew more about poems than poetry back then, but I can tell you that Cowboy Bill must have been what's nowadays called poetry in motion when he wiped that sweat from his face.

So I would spend my afternoons in the shade of the big chinaberry tree at the side of our house, drawing pictures in the dirt with a stick, waiting for Cowboy Bill to drive up in his blue pickup. That old truck would bounce and rattle when it hit that dirt road, and when I heard all that noise I would run over to the fence and settle in.

I would watch Cowboy Bill and Mr. Ming get out and walk to the back of the truck. Cowboy Bill would grab ahold of the cattle rack and pull himself up. He would hang on to the corner of the rack and work the pins out that held the gates together. He would fasten each side so the gates couldn't accidentally swing shut. Then he would hop to the ground and unhook both sides of the tailgate and lower it. Mr. Ming would rest against the side of the pickup while Cowboy Bill got the horses out. Cowboy Bill would yell, "Yeehaw, git, git on out of there," and wave his hat and flap his arms at the horses until they jumped out of the back of the pickup and walked over to the water barrel.

I used to think Mr. Ming didn't work as hard as Cowboy Bill, and I couldn't figure out why Cowboy Bill put up with it. It looked to me like all Mr. Ming did was lean against the fender of that truck and look at the sky.

Cowboy Bill would strip the horses of their load, haul everything over to the back of the truck, the saddles and blankets and bridles and bits, and he'd lay it all in the bed of the pickup. Then he'd go to the little lean-to next to the corral and throw some hay to the horses.

Finally he'd walk back to where Mr. Ming was standing and he'd put one foot on the running board and lean into the door and do that wonderful thing with his hat and kerchief, and the two men would talk.

Cowboy Bill would always say, "Well, oldtimer, quite a day, huh," and Mr. Ming would always answer, "Same as any other, I 'spect." And then nothing. Silence. Neither of them would say a thing. I tell you, I pressed as hard as I could into that fence to make sure I didn't miss a word, so I know that was all that was said.

Just about the time that wire was starting to make little triangular creases in my forehead and cheeks, Cowboy Bill would say, "Smells like rain, don't it," and Mr. Ming would tilt his head back and sniff the air.

"Can't tell," he'd say. "Those clouds could mean most anything. Might rain; might not."

Cowboy Bill would drop his head and swear. Then he'd say, "We need that rain awful bad. We need it now. We stand to lose it all if it don't rain pretty soon."

"Now, Willy," Mr. Ming would say, "you're forgetting your lessons. This is hard country. All your stewin' ain't gonna make it rain. You know that." And Cowboy Bill would pretend he was trying to kick something away in the dirt, but he was mad, that's for sure. I could tell when he got mad because he always kicked something, and he kicked pretty hard.

"Bud," he'd say— that was Mr. Ming's first name—"I put the last of my savings in them cattle. We can't be hauling water all over this blasted desert. It's got to rain. I mean it now. It's got to rain."

Mr. Ming would never answer Cowboy Bill directly. Instead—and this is the best part—he would point over to where I was pressed against the fence and say, "Willy, you see that pretty little girl over there? I'm thinking she looks like she might like a treat today. What do you think?" Mr. Ming knew how to work a crowd, the sun dancing in his eyes. "I fixed her a bracelet out of some of them Apache tears I polished the other day. Do you think she would like that?"

And Cowboy Bill would look over at me and smile and say, "I think she would. Shoot, if she don't like a pretty thing like that, she ain't worth much, now is she?"

Part of me knew that those two men knew I stood there every day and watched them at the corral and listened to what they were saying, but I pretended like it wasn't so and they did too.

So Mr. Ming, the Rock Man, would walk over to my fence. His old bones would be stiff after a day in the saddle, so he'd take his time. He'd check all his pockets as he walked and finally would find the small pouch he kept his stones in. He'd fumble endlessly with the drawstring. Then he would stop in the middle of the road and holler back to Cowboy Bill. "Willy," he'd say, "what did I teach you? What was your lesson today?"

Cowboy Bill would duck his head and I couldn't hear for sure what he was saying, but I know it wasn't nice words.

"Did you hear me, Willy?" Mr. Ming would ask. "You didn't answer me, young fella. What did I teach you today?"

Cowboy Bill would stick his tongue in his cheek, but he never could stop his smile. "You taught me about rain today," he would answer.

"Not good enough," Mr. Ming would shake his head. "What in particular did I teach you about rain today?"

I wanted Cowboy Bill to just tell him so I could get my bracelet. Even I knew the answer by heart. But he would take his time. It seemed like he looked at the ground and said those bad words under his breath forever.

Finally he'd throw back his head and laugh. "I'll tell you what you taught me about rain today, you used up, good-for-nothing old horse thief. It's raining someplace in the world today, that's for sure."

"That's right," Mr. Ming would say, "and don't you forget it. Now you go on and cool down those horses while I take care of this pretty little girl."

Mr. Ming would empty all the stones out into his hand. There were purple ones and pink ones, a few white ones, and my favorites, the Apache tears. He would tell me where he had found each one and how he had polished them.

And then I saw the tiny bracelet that I knew was for me. It was beautiful. It was shiny brass, about five inches long, with a hook so it wouldn't fall off, and each Apache tear dangled from a little metal cap. I could see the glue that held the stones.

I'd look up at him with my creased face and hold out my right hand so he could fasten it around my wrist. I'd turn my hand so the stones could catch the last light of the day and Mr. Ming showed me how to look into the smoky topaz to see the clear gold that was hidden within the soft brown of the stone.

Mr. Ming would hold onto my small hand for another second. I remember his dry skin. I'd look into his bright blue eyes and whisper my thanks. I was too shy to do much more than that. Then Mr. Ming would touch the tip of my nose and say, "Now, Little Missy, do you remember our lesson?"

I would nod my head and repeat the words he had taught me: "That man loves the rain. Cowboy Bill loves the rain."

"That's right," Mr. Ming would say, and for a second it would seem like he was going to cry, although such a thing was unthinkable.

"It's okay, Mr. Ming," I would say, to make him feel better. "It's not a hard lesson. I won't forget it. See, I can say it again: Cowboy Bill loves the rain."

Mr. Ming would kiss my hand and straighten up and look over to where Cowboy Bill was walking the horses. "It's a very hard lesson, Little Missy," he would say, "one that I wish I didn't have to teach you."

I would wait to make sure he made it back to the truck okay. He'd always turn and wave good-bye. Believe me, it took all my manners to wait until he got in that truck before I ran inside to show Momma what the Rock Man had given me.

I can't tell you how many afternoons I spent on that fence. I know at one time I had more pretty rocks than I could count, and I know I spent enough time on that fence that some days it actually did rain and Cowboy Bill was truly the happiest man alive.

But I outgrew the fence eventually, of course, and spent those hours giggling with other little girls and playing Red Rover Red Rover with the kids I met at school.

And there came the time when I not only outgrew the fence, but the town itself, and I went away to college. I left most of my town stuff at home—it didn't seem right somehow for the city—and I mostly forgot about my pretty rocks and bracelets and all the other gifts of my childhood.

I lost touch with Mr. Ming, but I always saw Cowboy Bill when I went back to visit, and now and then Cowboy Bill would call me on the telephone with some news from home. I'd always know it was him because as soon as I said hello, he'd say, "How's the weather, Missy? Any sign of rain?" and I'd laugh and we'd talk a bit, mostly about the weather. Mr. Ming had been right. That man loved the rain.

And there came the day, as I knew it would, that Cowboy Bill called to tell me that Mr. Ming had died and he'd left me a paperweight studded with some of his polished stones. He asked when I'd next be coming home so I could get it.

That was the saddest phone call I ever got in my entire life. I couldn't stop crying. I was so upset, I said the words before I could stop them. "Cowboy Bill," I said, "I've always loved you. You know that. Please just this once tell me you love me. I really need to hear it. Just this one time, please."

Well, the words were out and there they hung, somewhere in the air between the city and the town, between me and Cowboy Bill. But I'd done the asking, so I had to wait for the answer. I'd finished my crying before I realized Cowboy Bill hadn't said a word. In that long silence I heard Cowboy Bill breathing into the other end of the phone, and all at once I knew he was asking for what he needed, too.

So I walked over to the window where the sun was shining bright against the high-rise chrome and said, "Cowboy Bill, it's raining here and it's beautiful. You'd love it. I wish you could see these clouds. It might rain for days, the way it looks out there," and I told him everything I knew about the rain, the colors, the smells, the sounds.

When I hung up the phone, I leaned against the window and thought about the lesson Mr. Ming had taught me when I was a little girl. I finally understood why he had looked so worried back then. So I looked up, clear through that sky, past the sun and into his heavenly blue eyes, and told him straight out, "Mr. Ming, you were so right. It's raining someplace in the world today. And it's hard to be the daughter of the man who loves the rain."

A Mean Eye

BARBARA KINGSOLVER

BARBARA KINGSOLVER , 39, was born in eastern Kentucky and grew up "in the middle of an alfalfa field." Despite her family's regional roots, she moved to the Southwest in the early eighties, receiving a Masters of Science degree from the University of Arizona in Tucson. Pregnant and suffering from insomnia in 1988, she began writing the award-winning The Bean Trees *in a closet at night. That novel's sequel,* Pigs in Heaven, *from which the following excerpt is taken, won the 1994 Mountain and Plains Booksellers Association Award.* Pigs in Heaven *continues the exodus of Taylor and Turtle, the characters around which* The Bean Trees *revolves.*

Look up, Turtle. Angels."

Taylor stoops to her daughter's eye level and points up at the giant granite angels guarding the entrance to the Hoover Dam: a straight-backed team, eyes on the horizon, their dark, polished arms raised toward the sky.

"They look like Danny," Turtle observes.

"Biceps to die for," Taylor agrees. Danny, their garbage man, is a body builder on his days off.

"What do angels need muscles for?"

Taylor laughs at the thought of some saint having to tote around the overfilled garbage bags of heaven. "They made this back in the thirties," she says. "Ask Grandma about the Depression sometime. Nobody could get a job, so they had this WPA thing where people made bridges and sidewalks and statues that look like they could sweat."

"Let's take a picture." Turtle's tone warns off argument; she means Taylor will stand under the angels and *she* will take the photo. Taylor stands where she's placed and prepares to smile for as long as it takes. Turtle concentrates through the rectangular eye, her black eyebrows stranded above it in her high forehead. Turtle's photos tend to come out fairly hopeless in terms of composition: cut-off legs or all sky, or sometimes something Taylor never even saw at the time. When the pictures come back from the drugstore she often gets the feeling she's gone on someone else's vacation. She watches Turtle's snub-nosed sneakers and deliberately planted legs, wondering where all that persistence comes from and where it will go. Since she found Turtle in her car and adopted her three years ago, she has had many moments of not believing she's Turtle's mother. This child is the miracle Taylor wouldn't have let in the door if it had knocked. But that's what miracles are, she supposes. The things nobody saw coming.

Her eyes wander while Turtle fiddles. The sun is hot, hot. Taylor twists her dark hair up off her neck.

"Mom!"

"Sorry." She drops her arms to her sides, carefully, like a dancer, and tries to move nothing but her eyes. A man in a wheelchair rolls toward them and winks. He's noticeably handsome from the waist up, with WPA arms. He moves fast, his dark mane flying, and turns his chair smoothly before the angels' marble pedestal. If she strains her peripheral vision Taylor can read the marble slab: It's a monument to the men who died building the dam. It doesn't say who they were, in particular. Another panel across the way lists the names of all the directors of the dam project, but this one says only that many who labored here found their final rest. There is a fairly disturbing bronze plaque showing men in work clothes calmly slipping underwater. "Poor guys," she says aloud. "Tomb of the unknown concrete pourer."

"Working for fifty cents an hour," the wheelchair man says. "A bunch of them were Navajo boys from the reservation."

"Really?"

"Oh, yeah." He smiles in a one-sided way that suggest he knows his way around big rip-offs like this, a fancy low-paying job that bought these Navajo boys a piece of the farm.

The shutter clicks, releasing Taylor. She stretches the muscles in her face.

"Are you the trip photographer?" he asks Turtle.

Turtle presses her face into her mother's stomach. "She's shy," Taylor says. "Like most major artists."

"Want me to take one of the two of you?"

"Sure. One to send Grandma." Taylor hands him the camera and he does the job, requiring only seconds.

"You two on a world tour?" he asks.

"A small world tour. We're trying to see the Grand Canyon all the way around. Yesterday we made it from Tucson to the Bright Angel overlook." Taylor doesn't say that they got manic on junk food in the car, or that when they jumped out at the overlook exactly at sunset, Turtle took one look down and wet her pants. Taylor couldn't blame her. It's a lot to take in.

"I'm on a tour of monuments to the unlucky." He nods at the marble slah

Taylor is curious about his hobby but decides not to push it. They leave him to the angels and head for the museum. "Do not sit on wail," Turtle says, stopping to point at the wall. She's learning to read, in kindergarten and the world at large.

"On wall," Taylor says. "Do not sit on wall."

The warning is stenciled along a waist-high parapet that runs across the top of the dam, but the words are mostly obscured by the legs of all the people sitting on the wall. Turtle looks up at her mother with the beautiful bewilderment children wear on their faces till the day they wake up knowing everything.

"Words mean different things to different people," Taylor explains. "You could read it as 'Don't sit on the wall.' But other people, like Jax for instance, would think it means 'Go ahead and break your neck, but don't say we didn't warn you.' "

"I wish Jax was here," Turtle says solemnly. Jax is Taylor's boyfriend, a keyboard player in a band called the Irascible Babies. Taylor sometimes feels she could take Jax or leave him, but it's true he's an asset on trips. He sings in the car and is good at making up boredom games for Turtle.

"I know," Taylor says. "But he'd just want to sit on the wall. You'd have to read him his rights."

For Taylor, looking over the edge is enough, hundreds of feet down that curved, white wing of concrete to the canyon bottom. The boulders below look tiny and distant like a dream of your own death. She grips her daughter's arm so protectively the child might later have marks. Turtle says nothing. She's been marked in life by a great many things, and Taylor's odd brand of maternal love is by far the kindest among them.

Turtle's cotton shorts with one red leg and one white one flap like a pair of signal flags as she walks, though what message she's sending is beyond Taylor's guess. Her thin, dark limbs and anxious eyebrows give her a pleading look, like a child in the magazine ads that tell how your twenty cents a day can give little Maria or Omar a real chance at life. Taylor has wondered if Turtle will ever outgrow the poster-child look. She would give years off her own life to know the story of Turtle's first three, in eastern Oklahoma, where she's presumed to have been born. Her grip on Turtle is redundant, since Turtle always has a fist clamped onto Taylor's hand or sleeve. They cross through the chaotic traffic to the museum.

Inside, old photos line the walls, showing great expanses of scaffolded concrete and bushy-browed men in overalls standing inside huge turbines. The tourists are being shuffled into a small theater. Turtle tugs her in for the show, but Taylor regrets it as soon as the projector rolls. The film describes the amazing achievement of a dam that tamed the Colorado River. In the old days it ran wild, flooding out everyone downstream, burying their crops in mud. "There was only one solution—the dam!" exclaims the narrator, who reminds Taylor of a boy in a high school play, drumming up self-importance to conquer embarrassment. Mr. Hoover's engineers prevailed in the end, providing Arizona with irrigation and L.A. with electricity and the Mexicans with the leftover salty trickle.

"Another solution is they didn't need to grow their cotton right on the river-bank," Taylor points out.

"Mom!" hisses Turtle. At home Turtle whines when Taylor talks back to the TV. Jax sides with Turtle on the television subject, citing the importance of fantasy. Taylor sides with her mother who claims over the phone that TV has supernatural powers over her husband. "Just don't believe everything on there is true," Taylor warns often, but she knows this war is a lost cause in general. As far as her daughter is concerned, Mutant Ninja Turtles live in the sewers and that is that.

OUTSIDE THE museum, a foil gum wrapper skates along the sidewalk on a surprise gust of wind. A herd of paper cups and soda straws rolls eastward in unison. Lucky Buster sits on the ramparts of the Hoover Dam, trying to figure out how to save the day. People will throw anything in the world on the ground, or even in the water. Like pennies. They end up down there with the catfish. There could be a million dollars at the bottom of the lake right now, but everybody thinks there's just one red cent—the one they threw.

Lucky sits very still. He has his eye on a bright red soda-pop can. His friend Otis is an engineer for the Southern Pacific, and he's warned Lucky about pop cans. They catch the sun just right and they'll look like a red signal flare on the tracks. When you see that, you've got to stop the whole train, and then it turns out it's just a pop can. Bad news.

The people are all up above him. One girl is looking. Her round face like a sweet brown pie can see him over the wall. He waves, but she bobs behind the mother and they go away. Nobody else is looking. He could go down there now. The water is too close, though, and scares him, water is black, blue, pink, every color. It gets in your eyes there's so much light. He looks away at the nicer camel hump desert. Now: go.

Lucky drops down and scoots along the gray wall that runs along the edge. One side is water, fish-colored; on the other side you fall into the hole. He is as careful as the circus girls in silver bathing suits on TV, walking on wires. One foot, another foot.

A white bird with scabbed yellow feet lands in front of Lucky. "Ssss," he says to the bird, shaking his hands at it. The bird walks away fast, one spread foot and then the other one. Lucky is two steps away from the pop can. Now one step away. Now he's got it.

The bird turns its head and looks straight at Lucky with a mean eye.

THE SUN has dropped into the Nevada hills and rung up a sunset the color of cherries and lemons. Turtle and Taylor take one last stroll across Mr. Hoover's concrete dream. Turtle is holding on so tightly that Taylor's knuckles ache. Their hypochondriac friend Lou Ann has warned Taylor about arthritis, but this snap-jawed grip is a principle of their relationship; it won Turtle a nickname, and then a mother. She hasn't deliberately let go of Taylor since they met.

The water in the shadow of the dam is musky green and captivating to Turtle. She yanks on Taylor's fingers to point out huge catfish moving in moss-colored darkness. Taylor doesn't really look. She's trying to take in the whole of Lake Mead, the great depth and weight of water that formerly ran free and made life miserable for the downstream farmers. It stretches far back into the brown hills, but there is no vegetation along the water's edge, just one surface meeting another, a counterfeit lake in the desert that can't claim its own shoreline. In the distance someone is riding a kind of small water vehicle that seems pesty and loud for its size, like a mosquito.

Storm clouds with high pompadours have congregated on the western horizon, offering the hope of cooler weather, but only the hope. The Dodge when they get back to it is firecracker hot and stinks of melted plastic upholstery. Taylor opens both front doors and tries to fan cooler air onto the seat. The ice-cream cone she bought Turtle was a mistake, she sees, but she's not an overly meticulous parent. She's had to learn motherhood on a wing and a prayer in the last three years, and right now her main philosophy is that everything truly important is washable. She hands Turtle a fistful of fast-food napkins from the glove compartment, but has to keep her eyes on the road once they get going. The Dodge Corona drives like a barge and the road is narrow and crooked, as bad as the roads she grew up risking her neck on in Kentucky.

Eventually they level out on the Nevada plain, which looks clinically dead. Behind them the lake stretches out its long green fingers, begging the sky for something, probably rain.

Turtle asks, "How will he get out?"

"Will who get out?"

"That man."

"Which man is that, sweetheart?" Turtle isn't a big talker, she didn't complete a sentence until she was four, and even now it can take days to get the whole story. "Is this something you saw on TV?" Taylor prompts. "Like the Ninja Turtles?"

"No." She looks mournfully at the waffled corpse of her ice cream cone. "He picked up a pop can and fell down the hole by the water."

Taylor narrows her eyes at the road. "At the dam? You saw somebody fall?"

"Yes."

"Where people were sitting, on that wall?"

"No, the other side. The water side."

Taylor takes a breath to find her patience. "That man out on the lake, riding around on that boat thing?"

"No," Turtle says. "The man that fell in the hole by the water."

Taylor can make no sense of this. "It wasn't on TV?"

"No!"

They're both quiet. They pass a casino where a giant illuminated billboard advertises the idea of cashing your paycheck and turning it into slot-machine tokens.

Turtle asks, "How will he get out?"

"Honey, I really don't know what you mean. You saw somebody fall down a hole by the dam. But not into the water?"

"Not the water. The big hole. He didn't cry."

Taylor realizes what she could mean, and rejects the possibility, but for the half second between those two thoughts her heart drops. There was a round spillway where the water could bypass the dam during floods. "You don't mean that spillway, do you? The big hole between the water and the parking lot?"

"Yes." Turtle's black eyes are luminous. "I don't think he can get out."

"There was a big high fence around that." Taylor has slowed to about fifteen miles an hour. She ignores the line of traffic behind her, although the drivers are making noise, impatient to get to Las Vegas and throw away their money.

"Turtle, are you telling me the absolute truth?"

Before she can manage an answer, Taylor U-turns the Dodge, furious at herself. She'll never ask Turtle that question again.

Angels

ANA CONSUELO MATIELLA

ANA CONSUELO MATIELLA, 43, was born in Nogales, Sonora, Mexico. She was raised on the Arizona-Sonora border by a clan of Mexicans and Spaniards and graduated without honors from Nogales High School in 1970. She received her BS from Northern Arizona University, and her MA from the University of Arizona. She is the author and editor of several books on multicultural education, and produces fotonovelas on various educational topics. She lives in Santa Fe with her husband of twenty-two years, their spunky eleven-year-old daughter, two dogs, a guinea pig, and sixteen chickens. "Angels," her first published fiction, is from Cuentos, Mitotes y Mentiras (Stories, Gossip, and Lies), *a collection of short stories in search of a publisher.*

YOU CAN FEEL THEIR presence sometimes. A brush of a soft wing, a light kiss on the eyelids while you sleep, but to actually see an angel is not good for your longevity.

My grandfather encountered several angels and lived to tell about them but that's why he died young. Nana said that he himself was on his way to becoming an angel and so had an ease of communication with celestial beings.

Although I love my angels, and sometimes leave little trinkets for them to play with or open books for them to read at night, I would much rather not come across them by sight, if you know what I mean.

It's the same with animals. Nana told me there was once a boy who lived in our old *barrio*. His name was Julio and he talked to his pigeons and they talked back and he died. Nana said he died because it's all right for you to talk to animals, but if they respond, it's too much for a human being.

Me, I don't mind talking to animals, especially dogs. They are the most dear to me, although I am somewhat infatuated by crows. But to tell you the truth, I am afraid of an audible response. So, when I ask an animal a question, I always stop and say, "Please don't answer that."

I have always feared crossing over to this world where animals talk back and angels make special appearances because I lack the courage to deal with them. But there are things that I know and stories I've heard that lead me to believe in angels and the conversational capabilities of certain animals.

TAKE WHAT happened to Heidi, for example. Heidi died in Magdalena, Sonora in a house facing the *acequia* that irrigated the dusty corn crops. She was eight years old.

I can still remember her face in the black-and-white photograph my mother brought back from the funeral I wasn't allowed to go to.

Heidi and I didn't meet until after she died when she smiled at me from her first communion photograph. She was kneeling down and looking up at the Sacred Heart of Jesus, a pearl rosary hanging from her two small hands.

"She looks like an angel," I told Nana, lightly touching the smooth surface of the photograph.

"She was an angel," my grandmother explained. "She was too good and God called her to help out someplace else. That's what happens. God takes the good ones and leaves the rotten ones for us to contend with."

I wondered how she died. Heidi would never have gone out to the slippery banks of the flooded irrigation ditch by herself, I reasoned. She sat by the old Philco every Saturday afternoon to listen to the Lone Ranger. Heidi embroidered little dish towels for her aunts and helped her mother in the kitchen. She never said, "I don't want to" to her mother or "That's not true."

Nana said she was so good, she had a star on her forehead. But one day, one of the only times she disobeyed her mother, she got up from the obligatory *siesta* in the height of a hot afternoon. She went to the backyard and peered inside the family well. In the reflection of the water below, she saw a pair of angel wings behind her, opalescent pink and white. Startled, she ran inside the house where she was immediately punished and given orange blossom tea to calm her nerves.

She died and no one every told me how. She died and I didn't get a chance to meet her until after the funeral when I held a black-and-white photograph of her in my hands. It was midday on a boring summer afternoon in Magdalena, Sonora. I was supposed to be sleeping and only the lizards were out hissing back at the noonday sun.

I OFTEN thought about Heidi and wondered how and why she died. I asked my grandmother, "Did she die because a child is not supposed to see the angels? Was it like Julio talking to his pigeons and the pigeons talking back?"

I repeatedly asked Nana about Heidi but Nana didn't want to talk. My grandfather had also just died and I think it was too soon for her to talk about angels.

On another occasion, feeling the emptiness my grandfather's death created in the house, I asked Nana, "Why did Tata have to die?"

She didn't look up. She said, "He died because he talked to the angels and the angels talked back. There are people who meet angels face to face every day and don't know it. But your Tata was different. He knew an angel when he saw one. He was too good for this world and he knew too much."

Then she told me about the time they were traveling to Ures, Sonora for the feast of the Epiphany.

WHEN MAMÁ and my Aunt Paqui were still little girls, about ten and thirteen years old, the family was on their way to Ures to see their maternal grandmother, Mamá Kina. It was January 5th, the eve before the Feast of the Epiphany.

Although the road from Nogales to Ures was already open, it hadn't been paved. When it rained, summer or winter, the soft desert earth turned into silt and slush. Cars would get stuck and would have to be retrieved by a team of mules.

During the holiday season, it was Tata's custom to collect old clothes, blankets, and used toys for some of the poor children who lived on the family ranch.

On this late evening, they packed the old black truck full of stuff and took off to Ures on their annual Christmas journey.

The children had hopes of waking up at the ranch to find little trinkets and candy left to them by the Three Kings. Nana and Tata were looking forward to a midnight dinner of Mamá Kina's tamales.

Tata drove a black Model T Ford truck. It was a cold and rainy night and they were slushing down the deserted road, loudly singing Mexican *rancheras* to pass the time away.

Out of nowhere, a man swinging a lantern walked across the road and stopped right in front of the truck. Tata slammed on his breaks and the overloaded truck fishtailed on the slippery road.

When the truck finally came to a stop, Tata was furious. The man with the lantern was standing by a mesquite tree, directly across from where grandfather brought the truck to a halt. It was odd because Tata had to swerve to miss him and it couldn't be explained how the man with the lantern had gotten across the road to the mesquite tree.

The stranger was quiet and reserved and was leaning against the tree waiting for Tata to get out of the truck. Nana was convinced it was Satan. Her flesh crawled with goose pimples and the children cried. They were ordered to stay in the truck and lock the doors. Nana prayed her rosary and all the children echoed their reply.

In those days, Tata always carried a pistol. He tapped his pistol to see if it was still there and got out of the truck. He walked over to the man with the lantern. In anger, Tata confronted the man and said, "Are you a madman or what?"

The man said, *"Buenas noches,* Pancho. Forgive that I startled you and your family but . . ."

Tata interrupted and said, "How do you know my name?"

The man shrugged and smiled and said, "I know many things that would surprise you, Pancho, but never mind. The left rear wheel of that old truck of yours is loose and it is dangerous on such a rainy night . . ."

Stunned and scared, Tata responded, "The wheels of the truck are fine, my friend. You are the one that has a loose wheel in that head of yours."

The man with the lantern was silent and merely pointed to the wheel. At the moment he pointed, the wheel fell right off the axle and the truck plunked down and hit the ground, lopsided.

My grandfather was shocked and turned immediately to the stranger, to thank him for his good deed, to ask him how he knew, to offer him one of his homemade *chorizos* and a shot of tequila. But when he looked up, the stranger was gone.

Tata felt the hairs of his back stand up; he broke into a cold sweat. Knees weak, he sat on a large rock by the mesquite tree, trying to keep his heart from racing and his hands from shaking. He sat there listening to the sounds of the light winter drizzle for a few moments before he attended to the fallen wheel.

After the family recuperated from the ordeal, they started on their way to

Ures again. Nana said that Tata got back in the driver's seat and took a shot of tequila, made the sign of the cross and closed his eyes. When he opened his eyes he said, "Concha, that was not a mortal man."

Silence set in and they drove for a few miles. Tata, sighing relief, looked out into the dark and rainy desert. He wasn't surprised at what he saw. He turned to Nana and the children and said, "Look, up there!"

Up on top of a distant hill, in the deep blue, they saw a lantern waving back and forth in the dark.

Leaving the Valley

MARY HOKANSON

MARY HOKANSON grew up in the Texas hill country in a small town just north of San Antonio. A seven-year drought and the rough chalky soil of her childhood, called caliche, taught her the preciousness of water and color. Summers spent with relatives in the Sangre de Cristo Mountains of New Mexico taught her the resiliency of pine boughs cut for mattresses, and of children. The scent of woodsmoke still clings to her memories. Although she currently lives in California, she has often driven to Texas. "Landscapes shape our inner lives," she says. "In the desert, I am drawn to essences. I imagine holding a human femur."

IT'S TWO DAYS BEFORE Thanksgiving, four years since Ellen was left behind in the Rio Grande Valley at her grandmother's citrus farm. She's become accustomed to heat and brown skins. Now ten, she's finally learning how to read. She's just set the oven to 350 degrees and crawled back on the tall stool to call out ingredients for cornbread to her grandmother.

She looks at a curling page in the cookbook and asks, "What does *jalepeño* begin with?"

"No peppers today," her grandmother says. "This cornbread is for dressing." She wears rouge on her high cheekbones and a silver and onyx brooch at the neck of a white shirt. Ellen once described her to a teacher as a straw wrapped around light and air like cigarette paper. Her grandmother is a heavy smoker. Her pale eyes are often squinted even when there's no extra-long filter-tip hanging from her lips. She sets canisters of flour, sugar, and cornmeal on the table for Ellen to measure.

Ellen picks up the nested silver measuring cups. Their neatness and exactness please her. Earlier she re-read aloud the litany of the conversion chart in the front of the cookbook, teaspoons to tablespoons to cups, all in sepia ink on aged paper. She levels off a one-cup measure of pale gritty meal with the edge of a table knife.

"Tell me again about how I fell in love with red," she says.

Her grandmother is pouring milk into a saucepan to scald. "That was back when you weren't saying much. When you first came here. You'd drag me to see everything red. The bougainvillaea on the side of the house. The salvia out front. My old chenille bathrobe in the closet. I could see you were bright."

"And the hot water bottle," Ellen says. "And the ketchup. I pointed to the ketchup, too, didn't I?"

"Even the comb on that nasty little rooster," her grandmother says.

"And anyone could see I was bright?" Ellen asks.

Her grandmother doesn't answer. She's dragging instead of lifting the saucepan from the glowing burner and her usually narrow eyes have widened. Her arms are trembling and Ellen smells first the musty clay odor of hot milk and then the muddy scorched scent of milk spilling over the burner. The empty pot clatters to the tiles and her grandmother pitches forward onto the stovetop.

Later Dr. Sturges will tell Ellen about a vein in her grandmother's brain bursting like an over-inflated balloon and Ellen will stare at ridiculous tassels dangling from his shiny loafers. But the damage she sees when she pulls her grandmother to the floor is the burn. There's an incomplete pattern of concentric circles pressed into the forehead and cheek. Ellen hates herself for imagining dotted lines connecting them. She hates herself for having believed in permanence.

She was six years old when she came to the Texas Valley where the land is clean and flat. No trees grow on it except those planted. The orderly groves of oranges, grapefruits, tangerines, and lemons suggested the possibilities for acts of will and self-determination. She'd sensed the heat of chemical reactions emanating from the black earth as sunlight bonded with lukewarm water pumped into the irrigation ditches and erupted green, row after row.

For almost half her life Ellen has lived in a landscape where the Rio Grande slithers south down the western flank of Texas, mandibles thrust wide at the edge of land, a slow brown river that thickens between McAllen and Brownsville and spills its guts to the Gulf of Mexico. The soil is dark bittersweet chocolate, friable, hot when she scoops up a handful. The thick air shimmers, magnifies like a lens specially ground to intensify green, orange, blue, and brown.

She stays on for two weeks with her grandmother's oldest friends, Nell and Walter Watkins, while they search for a nursing home for her grandmother. It's early December when the Watkinses drive Ellen into Raymondville to catch the bus to northern New Mexico. The air is soaked with the stench of vegetables rotting in fields where workers turned the cabbages, onions, and black-eyed peas ten days ago. Ellen will recall the smell each time she is afraid.

This morning she put on a short faded tomato-red skirt with a white blouse embroidered with doves and roses and a new pair of *huaraches*. It's not a suitable costume for northern New Mexico where a four-inch layer of snow whiter even than the sugar sand of Padre Island has already sifted over the landscape. But Nell Watkins did not ask Ellen if she'd forgotten the cold after living four years in the Valley and did not select warmer clothing for her.

"You're cosseting her craziness," Walter said to his wife. He considers Ellen stupid. Once she'd lied to him when he held up two shot glasses and asked her which one would hold more. Another time she'd asked him why wetbacks didn't get wet all over.

Ellen is labeled with a buff-colored tag. The cord cuts into her neck. The bus's engine fills the station with rasping exhaust, then shudders onto a street that will lead her away from her grandmother in the hospital in Harlingen and away from the colors and climate of a citrus-growing delta where life has been laced tight with safety and predictability.

She sits alone, not looking at the meatless arms of the bus driver wrestling the huge wheel or the port wine stain flowing down beneath his collar. She would never consider asking a man for help. Instead she focuses on the pale woman dressed in black across the aisle. Her wide-set eyes are like a Persian cat's, shrewd and implacable. She sits rich. Ellen pictures her house—long hallways of slate, white carpets, a black swimming pool, plenty of room for a girl if she liked her enough. Turn, look at me, like me. Ellen concentrates. But when the woman gazes at her, she feels words receding from her lips, leaving only numbness.

Ellen runs her palm over the disgusting plush and evaluates the meaning of sitting in the third seat. Three used to be her lucky number. She rode in the third seat of the school bus every day with Gloria Ozuna, a serene girl with a forward tongue thrust that would never be corrected.

She counts the windows in the bus, the seats, the telephone poles. The landscape slides by like a great bolt of fabric unwound by the clerk of a dry goods store. Once the geometric forms on the fields comforted Ellen. The precision of their squares and rectangles, the neat rows of beets, cotton, carrots, and tomatoes promised opportunities. The universe seemed to have a blueprint. Now she squints her eyes and the cultivated furrows riffle like shuffling cards. They no longer sustain her. Nothing can be planned.

She remembers chaos.

She recalls the smells of her family's trailer in the pines at the end of a chili-colored road: Chlorox, soaking diapers, sleep-scented blankets, scouring powder, grilled cheese sandwiches; the air heavy and warm like lumpy gravy; the television set never turned off. And the voices of the people never stopped: Matt, Chrissie, her mother.

Ellen pulls a flaccid three-by-five snapshot from her shopping bag and gazes at the image of her father. The powerful notion of a father alive somewhere in the world is diminished to wallet-size. She no longer remembers his features from his presence in her life. The black-and-white photo slides under her fingertips like cheap satin pajamas. He left right after Chrissie was born. When she was four.

Gradually his name wasn't mentioned. He faded away like the blue in a pair of jeans. She isn't even sure if there'd been a little gap between his front teeth although her grandmother told her there was and that there'd been no money for braces. She holds the picture closer. It was taken in front of a café where he worked as a cook one summer. His mouth is hidden. There is nothing of importance he could say anyway. Words are just cockscombs that grown-ups wear on their heads.

The speed of the bus never varies. The highway has no hills or curves. It is straight like a rattlesnake skin mounted on a board with its head pointed north toward New Mexico where her father no longer lives. Two hours into the trip the bus starts across the vast King Ranch, 250 miles without gas stations, doughnut shops, billboards, or vegetable stands. It's geography where color has been sopped up, leaving a brownish stain cordoned off with barbed wire under an aching blue sky.

"You know, there are people who've just disappeared here. Lots of them." The woman across the aisle is leaning toward her. There's a copper bracelet on her left wrist. Ellen notices hairs sprouting over her upper lip like the fine whiskers on a pod of okra. Ellen was wrong about her eyes. They are not shrewd, only sharpened by determination. Probably she is one of those cancer patients who travel across the border for strange treatments in Mexican clinics.

Ellen turns back to the window. There are no hiding places out there, just shallow gullies where mounted *braceros* with expressionless eyes and shotguns could easily see you hunkered down. She looks out and learns about duplicity, the layered potentiality of human beings, and the limits of loyalty. She doesn't care. She has no interest in ambiguity. She wonders if another baby is growing inside her mother, if her lungs can live on air not tinted with the scent of oranges, whether the school cafeteria will serve tacos on Friday.

The bus station in the New Mexico town is peeling adobe, doll-flesh pink. The Greyhound's engine deepens as it swings into the drive-through and Ellen remembers a bony gray cat coughing up black bile in a classmate's yard. When her right foot reaches the steep bottom step, all the faces of people meeting the bus look like a too-white flock of gulls.

Her family stands in a messy knot. Her mother's broad shoulders in Pendelton plaid are still half-turned toward Chrissie. She has just wiped the girl's reddened nose with a Kleenex. Ellen recognizes the blue car coat she is wearing. Chrissie started first grade this year. Matt slouches to one side in a stained maroon parka staring at her. Brown eyes, dark coarse hair. Like her own. They all look at her now. No one waves.

Three weeks later a social worker comes to visit. She's six feet tall and stoops when she enters the trailer. Her blue eyes are pink-rimmed and her limbs seem carelessly attached. Ellen wonders if she is double-jointed. There's a permanent onion taint to the air in the trailer, reminding Ellen of the deep black Dutch oven her grandmother made chili in.

"Have you made a snowman yet?" the woman asks her. When she smiles, her upper lip rises, exposing healthy pink gums.

"No," Ellen says. This woman is stupid. Doesn't she know about hard-packed snowballs laced with gravel? How has this woman made it this far?

As she walks back to the tiny cubicle she shares with Chrissie, she barely hears the woman tell her mother, "I want you to get her enrolled in school tomorrow."

Numbers are clicking through Ellen's mind with the persistence of a metronome. Twenty-two steps from the living room to the bedroom.

Through some bureaucratic fluke two Christmas baskets arrive at the trailer. One from the Rotary Club and one from the Methodist Church. Ellen watches her mother unload them: two frozen turkeys, canned sweet potatoes, pie shells, brown-and-serve rolls, a couple of dolls, a baseball bat, a box of Pampers. Ellen stares at the bumps on the skin of a turkey. How many feathers were attached to that skin? She feels her own flesh contract.

"What the hell am I supposed to do with these?" her mother asks, holding up the box of Pampers. She trades the diapers and one of the turkeys for three cartons of cigarettes from a neighbor. Ellen feels relieved. Her mother must not be going to have a baby. Why would anyone want to duplicate themselves anyway?

For the first few weeks after her arrival, Ellen watches the weather reports on television every day just as she had with her grandmother in Texas. Sometimes she was awakened there in the night, not by noise or light, but by the rubbery stench of tires burning in the orchards to spread a blanket of black smoke between the treetops and the freezing air. She saw yellow blooms of flames scattered through the orchard as if the insistent, volatile odor of the orange blossoms had ignited spontaneously, plucking hope from her mind out into the open.

But here in New Mexico cold is a constant. A weatherman with a foolish-looking Adam's apple and a pointer predicts disastrous temperatures every day. Ellen stops watching. Nothing she has learned has prepared her for life here. She would not be surprised if the stars dropped from the sky some night like corroded washers.

Once back in Texas she and Gloria spent the night with Gloria's married sister who lived in a beat-up duplex in Raymondville with a deeply fissured driveway. At the end of the street was the cotton gin. For two weeks puffs of white fuzz drifted through yards and vacant lots, a blizzard swirling on an otherwise imperceptible updraft, catching on bushes and tall weeds, clinging to the windshields of parked cars, adhering to the stiff fibers of welcome mats, silting in layers along the bottoms of window screens. The two girls spun across the lawn with outstretched palms, bits of fluff stuck to their tee shirts, hair and eyelashes. They called it snow. But it was dry and they were barefoot. It was nothing like the real thing. Ellen wonders how she could have been so mistaken.

You could say a word like *snow*, but it didn't mean anything. Often in summer Ellen's grandmother had run her hand along Ellen's tanned skin and said, "Brown as a berry." Not any berry that Ellen knew of. But she didn't ask which berry. Grown-ups said strange things. They lacked precision in their language as if they'd looked at something years ago and continued describing it without looking again. Ellen no longer paid attention. Her first grade teacher had jotted "poor listener" on her progress report. Ellen hadn't cared. She knew eyes and hands told more truth than words.

There are twenty-four windows on the school bus and eight in Mrs. Pitstick's fourth grade classroom. Ellen bends and crooks her left arm around her tablet to write. She wants to be a toadstool that barely pokes above ground, but she gets in trouble right away. For not flushing the toilet in the restroom.

The gurgle of water filling the bowl roars so loudly in her ears that it seems safer just to slip quietly out of the stall leaving the telltale bubble of lemon in the bowl. But when she returns to the classroom she sees a tall blond-haired girl whispering in Mrs. Pitstick's ear.

There's no one at home to call out Ellen's spelling words. Her mother is cutting up a chicken. Ellen stares at the flour mounded on a plate. There are specks of pepper in it that could be weevils. Please, God, don't make me get a drumstick. She walks around the breakfast bar to the living room. Eight regular steps.

Matt is watching television. He has a lazy eye and sometimes Ellen sees his left eye looking at the front door instead of the television. He's supposed to wear a patch over his right eye three hours a day, but he won't. He accepts the spelling list, but he calls out the words wrong. Ellen grabs the paper from him and hears it tear. There's no scotch tape in the drawer. She'll get another zero.

Sometimes at school the purple numbers on the mimeographed arithmetic sheets won't stay still. The fours have bent scratchy legs like a June bug's. Ellen can't understand why people hate roaches so much when there are insects in the world like June bugs that blur around yellow lights and crunch underfoot. How could God make something like that?

It is early March. "Tell me what a home is like," Mrs. Pitstick is asking her. They are alone in an empty sixth-grade classroom. Ellen hopes the sixth grader whose desk she sits at won't be able to tell that she's been there. She tucks her hands away from the red pencil lying in the trough in the desk.

"A wire," she answers. Mrs. Pitstick closes the manila folder before her and says nothing. All the way up the hall Ellen imagines electricity coiled up in the wire strung along the south side of the playground. "Snug" she had been going to say when Mrs. Pitstick asked her to describe the house.

Ellen's mother is called for a conference. Mrs. Pitstick and the principal are in the office. They ask Ellen's mother when Ellen learned to sit up, crawl, walk, talk. "She learned to crawl backwards," her mother says. Ellen gazes out the window. The sky is the same color as the muddied snow and the black telephone wires look emphatic against it. Ellen wishes she could call someone. Maybe she would tell Gloria the truth about snow. The adults decide to move Ellen back to the third grade.

At night she dreams of heat, numbers, and colors. Blazing orange sixes, smoldering lime green nines, hot burgundy twos. She wakes sucking her thumb, remembering the Popsicles in her grandmother's freezer and her grandmother telling her to close the lid. Would the escaping cold hurt the orange trees somehow?

Last summer she'd spilled sugar on the counter and slopped Koolaid on the breakfast table as she filled containers for the freezer. She experimented with shapes—juice cans, muffin tins, a thimble, a doll's tea set—and bent aluminum foil and wires and plastic wrap to form molds. She no longer ate the Popsicles. Layers of grape, orange, and cherry shapes accumulated in the huge white freezer. Were they still there? Unchanged and frozen?

Heat and cold have become issues too complex for Ellen to understand. She's no longer sure what is safe. She remembers carrying water out to the pickers in the orange groves. Together she and her grandmother lifted two empty milk cans into the bed of the pickup while Tippy, the crazy car-chasing collie, barked. They filled the cans with water from the heat-softened garden hose and added ice cubes that dinged against the metal sides and then melted. Two men with skin the color of golden raisins lifted down the heavy containers.

One evening she asks Chrissie, "Do I have a mole in the middle of my back?" Ellen has grabbed her shirt at the shoulder seams and lifted the fabric like a jerky theater curtain.

"You're a retard," Chrissie says. Her eyes are the color of pencil lead.

Later Ellen balances on the edge of the sink in the bathroom, her mother's hand mirror wavering before her face. Every night for a week she's prayed, but she cannot find a third mole. There's one on her right arm above the wrist and the special one just below her left nipple that is just like her father's. She glimpses the back of her head and patches of skin in the mirror, but she can't focus on the space between her shoulder blades where she's sure the sign, the third mole, has appeared.

The doors in the house trailer don't even have knobs. Matt and Chrissie are trudging up the red dirt road toward the hardtop to meet the bus. Ellen slips her fingers into a metal groove and slides open the door to Matt's room. The smell of him—crayons, kerosene, burnt matches—curls up from snarled sheets the color of cauliflower. She scans the room, then worms two fingers along the edge of the foam mattress and bumps into two cigarettes laid end to end.

Ellen smooths a patch of sheet and then breaks each papered cylinder in half. As she crumbs the tobacco, tawny shreds drift down. She remembers the way her grandmother breathed at night, a crescendo of sighs. Does she breathe like that in the nursing home? Has someone fixed her hand so she can still plait her hair in one loose braid before bed? All day at school Ellen's fingertips remember tobacco.

Ellen walks toward the mail boxes mounted on posts at the entrance of the trailer park. The tidy apertures remind her of the gray papery wasps' nest she and her grandmother had burned out from under the eaves with a torch of newspaper and sweet-smelling gasoline. The flag on the side of the box is up like a little red hatchet. She'd never known that she was one-eighth Cherokee until her grandmother told her. Ellen is glad her mother doesn't have any of the Cherokee blood.

There is no letter in the box for her, just a bill from the electric company and a flyer advertising a shoe sale at J C Penney's. Ellen has received only one postcard from her grandmother.

It came in February. The handwriting looked like bent fishhooks. Ellen couldn't read it. Someone else had printed the name and address. On the reverse side a vermilion sun bloodied coastal clouds and dark faceted water. That was probably what an X-ray of her grandmother's brain looked like now.

"How's your grandmother?" her mother had asked.

"Nuts," Ellen said.

In northern New Mexico there is so little sky. Insatiable pines gobble up the space and the light, shadowing the land with their shapes, littering the ground with dropped needles and cones. Ellen hates the gold resin leaking down their trunks like pus.

Everything is an icy muddy white for months as slush melts and refreezes, trapping debris. In the ditch along the road where she waits for the school bus, she sees a milk carton with its spout open, crushed beer cans, gray plastic bags stripped from newspapers. Each day she must work harder to hold on to the exact shade of the bougainvillaea spilling over her grandmother's roof.

The Mark of the Serpent

LINDA THERESA RACZEK

LINDA THERESA RACZEK, 41, was a "Navy brat" whose father bargained for a permanent transfer to Albuquerque, New Mexico, in 1966, in exchange for extended duty on Kauai, Hawaii. She lives in Cortez, Colorado, with her nine-year-old daughter, Autumn, a member of the Ute Mountain Ute tribe Linda adopted as a single parent. She earned science and law degrees before turning to freelance writing, and she now writes regularly for children. Her first children's book, The Night the Grandfathers Danced, *will be published by Northland Publishing in 1995. "The Mark of the Serpent" is the first adult fiction Linda has ever written, and she says, "I realized after writing it that I'm still trying to reconcile my many childhood lives with the real home my parents finally gave me in the Southwest."*

I HAVE ALWAYS BEEN a dreamer of exquisite and terrifying dreams. I was only three when I first woke in the night, wailing that a snake had bitten me. The serpents of my dreams had ivory razor fangs and eyes as dull and cold as gray meteors. They struck so deftly—in the forehead, behind the ear, in the throat—that I felt blinded by their very swiftness. The snakes first came for me the year my mother died.

When my father returned from the Cuban blockade in 1962, I was ten years old. He came back a changed and troubled man. He asked the Navy to send him and his two young daughters as far away as possible from the urban nuclear targets and backyard bomb shelters of the East. Ironically, by year's end, we were riding a marine transport ship toward Hawaii, the only American soil ever bombed by a foreign power. On board ship, I was befriended by a young soldier bound for a place I'd never heard of: Vietnam.

For me, so long plagued by nightmares of snakes and rabies, Hawaii was a godsend. I now lived, unbelievably, in a paradise that had not yet fallen from grace—no snakes, no rabies. Isolated on a rural island, my frail younger sister Jade and I grew close. I protected and mothered her. We bought our first Elvis album together, played ongoing episodes of Barbie-goes-to-the-beach, adored JFK and Jackie, and secretly watched "The Fugitive" on a grainy black-and-white screen from the hall after our bedtime. Sometimes we pretended that the handsome and kind Dr. Richard Kimble was hiding in our own garage, and felt a heady yearning for justice we'd never experienced before.

On the day President Kennedy was murdered, my father's shoulders shook as he cried. His tears robbed me of my own. I was twelve then, and felt a dry, cutting grief in my heart—for my poor widower father who had no one to hold him, and for the world. In that moment, my life became unanchored from childhood and sentiment and the fabric of belief.

That night I dreamt of the snake again, for the first time in almost a year. I felt a hardness where the hot venom sliced into my throat.

So it must have been for my father as well. Not long afterwards he resigned his commission in the Navy. My last memory of Hawaii is of my father braking the car in sight of an American flag at half-mast, stepping out at attention in his brilliant white uniform, and saluting smartly. In the background, one lone palm tree moved in slow motion.

Inside the car again, my father's blue eyes misted over. "Avery, Jade," he said, clearing his throat. "We're going home now." He meant to the place of his dreams. New Mexico.

ALBUQUERQUE WAS a spectacle of sparsity for two children grown in lusher climes. It was a vision in the negative. Where once tropical greens and stunning pinks ruled the day, here the eyes rested on earth as brown and dusty-backed as a rattlesnake. Instead of cool blue water and surf, heat shimmered off the dry, buzzing mesas. An overexposed landscape, spotlighted in a white ethereal light that made my brains boil as I pedaled my bicycle along the soft asphalt streets. And the name itself: Albuquerque. Jade despaired of ever spelling it right by the time she started fifth grade in the fall.

We lived, as my father said, "at the end of the road." To the west, the city spread evenly over an endless panoramic bowl, the sun glinting off millions of windows and side-view mirrors and the cool, muddy Rio Grande, a backbone of life-giving *agua*. But behind us, to the east, only houses away, were the brown foothills, hissing with cicadas in the bright sunshine.

Flying into Albuquerque the first time, I knew, among other things, that we were now in the very cradle of the atomic bomb. I had turned knowledgeably to my father, now in civilian clothes, and pointed to what I believed were tailings piles. Dad smiled, obviously amused at my usual drama. He shook his head.

"Mountains, sweetheart," he said. "Those are the Sandia Mountains—the watermelon mountains to us gringos."

That was the first hypnotic suggestion tying me to this strange place. I waited patiently those first afternoons for the sweet pink of watermelon that my father had said would color those plain piles of rubble he called mountains. But as long as the hibiscus remained fixed as my reference point, I couldn't see it.

In late July, the foothills were sometimes gray with the brush strokes of tattered rain clouds. Almost overnight, the land was alive with pastel-colored grasses and minute, conservative flowers, well-spaced in deference to others. The way of the desert.

It was time to explore. I lowered our bicycles gingerly over the cinder-block wall that surrounded our backyard. Jade squinted up at me through pink-rimmed glasses and almost white, fine hair.

"I'm getting stickers," she said, brushing at her socks in a panic, as though they were red ants. And then, "Avery, why can't it just be us?"

"Shh. No more talk like that, Jade."

Just then we saw Albuquerque's answer to Twiggy mounting the wall three houses down and dropping ungracefully to the ground.

"Damn!" she muttered, extricating herself and her bike from dried tumbleweeds piled against the wall.

It was Diedre, our new friend, and my new source of information on being thirteen. Jade and I gawked at her as she stomped over, admiring her teased brown hair and the clear outline of a bra showing through her tight polyester blouse.

"Hi, Diedre," I said, smiling.

"Oh, I hate that name," she shot back. "Try to remember to call me Dede, okay?"

I had never been big on double names like Dede or Mimi. My nickname as a baby had been "Rivi"—which supposedly had been my own utterance for Avery. I had a hard time accepting that I hadn't been more precocious as a baby. But then, for all I knew, I was really saying "TV" or "gravy."

"This way," Diedre snipped impatiently when Jade straddled her bike and started down Candelaria. We headed uphill. The grade was steep, and we ended up trudging on foot in a morose procession toward the foothills. Heat was already radiating off the blacktop like a Teflon grill.

Diedre finally seemed to shake off her troubled mood and smiled back congenially. "Don't ever do this when it's raining, you know. The arroyos fill up fast and, you know, you don't want to be caught in a flash flood. I've even seen rattlesnakes washing down the gutters after a storm."

"I don't believe it," Jade said flatly. I shot an angry look her way and smiled conspiratorially with Diedre. She was surprisingly generous.

"You'll see," she said.

I was holding a pain in my side when we stopped to rest at the end of the pavement. A long dirt road with no end in sight, either way, intersected out path. The brand-new street sign read, "Tramway."

"It's in English," Jade said.

"No shit," Diedre said, wrinkling her face scornfully.

I ignored them and pulled our two walkie-talkies out of my saddle bag.

"Here, Dede. Jade and I can share."

Jade's thin arm struck out without warning and grabbed the walkie-talkie from Diedre's hand. Clutching the radio to her chest, she stood there a moment, too upset to speak. Then the energy of her anger seemed to propel her onto her bike and on toward the mountains.

"We're going to the Whitewash!" Diedre yelled after her. "That big, smooth rocky area. See it?" She looked at me and shrugged. "I hope she heard me."

"Don't mind her," I said.

"Avery, I hate to say it, but your sister's kind of a reject, isn't she?"

I stared at her, noncommitally at first, feeling guilty that the words had been said at all, feeling that I had said them myself. They hung there in the air alone, without contest. I was glad she hadn't said them about me.

The ascending mesa was riddled with smooth, worn trails, gutted out by dirt bikes, bicycles, and rain, then baked hard as stone. The skinny tires of our three-speeds occasionally bogged down in sand or slid on gravel. As we gained on the steep incline of the mountains, breathing hard and overheated, Diedre and I decided to ditch our bikes and hike. Apparently, Jade was keeping an eye on us, for we soon saw her lay her bike down, too, and begin rock-hopping up the side of the mountain.

I cupped my hands around my mouth and yelled as loud as I could. "Jade! Come back!" If she heard me, she didn't let on. I switched on my walkie-talkie and pressed the speaker button; no answer.

We clambered over rocks and up a steep incline studded with wiry shrubs. When we reached a false summit and dropped into a cooler draw, Diedre pointed out our destination: the Whitewash, a rock formation at least three stories high, smooth and cascading, whitish-gray as though multi-gallons of paint had been spilled down the mountainside.

"It's where all the kids go," Diedre said, puffing up. "There's all kinds of cool stuff—last time there were some guys up here on their dirt bikes, with music, beer, everything." What "everything" was I couldn't begin to guess, but at the moment I was preoccupied with a ringing in my head that was more than the beating sun and chorus of insects around us. Jade was nowhere to be seen.

Diedre knew what I was thinking. "I bet she headed up the draw instead of crossing over to the Whitewash."

"Jade!" I started up the draw, kicking a rock loose here and there.

"She wants you to come after her, you know," Diedre said, disgusted. "She just wants her way."

"No, you don't understand her . . ."

"Wait, Avery, I've got an idea." She smiled, excited. "Can you get her to tune in to you on that thing?" She pointed to the walkie-talkie clipped to my belt.

"Well, we do have an emergency signal my dad taught us, but . . ."

"Do it!"

Slowly I beeped out the attention signal: Dot-dot-dot; dash, dash, dash; dot-dot-dot. SOS in Morse code, the legacy of our father's naval career transplanted to the desert foothills of his dream place.

The radio crackled. "What is it?" Jade's voice sounded worried. "Avery, are you all right?"

Diedre snatched the walkie-talkie away and pressed the speaker button. "Jade, come quick! Your sister's been bit by a rattler!"

I shook my head furiously and struggled for the radio.

"Make sounds like you've been bit," Diedre shrieked, pushing me away. "Listen, I'm not wasting time going after that little brat. Come on, do it!" Suddenly she regained her poise and said, almost sweetly, "Besides, it'll be fun."

Our eyes met. I felt a surprising thrill in the pit of my stomach. A painful moan pushed its way through my lips. "Jade, come quick—I need you. Please!"

A dull, sick feeling radiated out from my heart, as Diedre lay me down on the ground, while my mind sent out excuses in Morse code: It's a game. It's not wrong. She'll forgive me. But the evil set in motion, the guilt-venom already dispersing, I rode the thrill wave with my new friend Dede.

We heard the clatter of rocks echoing against the canyon walls. Two small brown birds fluttered up from the underbrush as Jade's spindly legs carried her to the place where Dede crouched over me. The anguish in her face was almost palpable. I wished with all my heart in that moment that the lie could be made true, so that love would not be betrayed.

But I had already fallen from grace. Jade froze, her arms held rigid at her sides, her hands clenched in tight little fists. Across the chasm that stretched between us, surrounded by a stranger's hideous laughter, I saw the serpent strike my true Jade in the forehead. On her face, the mark of betrayal, of suffering, the knowledge of evil.

Jade turned and ran. Diedre was on the ground, laughing, catching her breath, slapping at me but hitting air.

"Did you see her face? Now that was a piece of work!"

I ran for Jade. Not far away she let me find her, sitting on a rock, a thin rivulet of blood trickling from a cut in her knee.

"I did it when I was coming for you," she said, her voice catching in sobs. "I thought you were really hurt."

I started to cry. "I know you did, Jade."

I reached for her, to somehow make it right, but she pushed me away. She withdrew warily against the rough canyon wall.

"I'm sorry, I'm sorry!" I pleaded.

"Why did you do that to me?" she cried.

I had no answer for her. I wanted to say, "I'll never hurt you again," but such promises were not even made for paradise. "You're all I had, Avery," she whimpered.

"I know."

Her body heaved in the aftermath of crying. She didn't move away when I slid closer and touched her shoulder, lightly at first, then rested my hand there. A shudder ran through her.

"I am so sorry, Jade."

She nodded slightly. "I'm sorry too, Avery. I was so jealous of you and Dede."

We sat there for a long time, fixtures in the landscape. Then, somehow, we made our way home together, retrieving our toppled bicycles and riding through lengthening shadows, the white desert light congealed gold in the west. I gripped my gilded chrome handlebar like a divining rod as it pitched and jounced over what seemed barren land.

We climbed onto the wall behind our house, and when I turned for one last look at the mountains, I saw that afternoon clouds had crept in stealthily from beyond the Sandias, spilling over the flat-topped crest like surf on a reef—but on the gargantuan scale that was New Mexico. Suddenly, the Sandias were awash with a pink so subtle and tender it made my heart ache, and I cried. It was like the past had winked at me and said goodbye.

Neutral Zone

ANN CUMMINS

ANN CUMMINS, 40, was born in Durango, Colorado, but she spent much of her child-hood on the Navajo Reservation where her father worked in a uranium mill. She began writing fiction in her late twenties, and attended Johns Hopkins University, where she received an MA in writing seminars, and the University of Arizona, where she received an MFA in fiction. Recipient of 1990 and 1993 Arizona Commission on the Arts creative writing fellowships, her work has appeared in publications such as The New Yorker, Antioch Review, Quarterly West, *and* Sonora Review, *and has been anthologized in* Best of the West *and* Best American Short Stories. *She currently lives in Flagstaff, Arizona, where she is an assistant professor at Northern Arizona University.*

FINALLY, PURPLE GOT SO big she had to quit the team or get kicked off. The girls said she was showing off by staying on so long, but I don't know. Sometimes I thought she may have been trying to shake that baby out of there. Once, this was toward the end, just before she had her visit with Mrs. Adams, just before she dropped out of school for good, I saw Purple practicing alone in the gym, and it wasn't like usual. I agree, Purple was a show-off back then. I remember in practice she'd throw herself into a round-off or back handspring with a force that landed her feet smacking against the mat; then she'd shimmy around holding a backbend and doing a little upside-down duck walk until Mrs. Adams got exasperated. But that day it was . . . I don't know. Call it serious; call it mean. I don't think she wanted to be pregnant, that's what struck me watching her.

She'd been at the far end of the mats away from the mirrors. It was late afternoon, almost dusk and the lights weren't on. In the shadows, she looked thin and small like a little girl playing at acrobatics—except for the belly. The belly on that tiny body seemed a bad joke. I watched her take a short run, then do six front hand-springs across to the opposite corner. No pause, she sprang back, six flips, then forward, cartwheels, round-offs, forward rolls. It was crazy the way she threw herself around—no precision, you know, just flopping from corner to corner. It couldn't have been good for the baby, and it made me dizzy just to watch. She reminded me of a fish flipping on sand with the gills slowly clogging up until—you could see it—she wore herself out. Kind of lost direction and ended up tumbling off the edge of the mat where she stopped dead. She knelt there on the polished wooden floor, her shoulders slumped forward, chin jutting out and down. Strands of wiry black hair were plastered across her sweaty face, and on the face . . . Purple looked doped. Eyes glazed, mouth half open, brows arched up, she was puzzling at something. She stared with peculiar intentness at the floor as if wondering how she got there. As if trying to remember something.

WE CALLED her Purple because of the great purple sweater she wore through grade school; the sweater grew as she did—she'd tug at the knit stretching it from year to year until, when I first saw her in fourth grade, it covered her arms and hips respectably but left holes where the yarn had pulled loose at the shoulders and collar. That first time, I met her behind the band building. Purple was waiting to punch me out. I used the short-cut behind the band building on my way home from school until Purple and her cousins taught me the ropes. The cousins were fat-cheeked girls who never took their government-issued coats off, winter, summer, indoors, out; they flocked around her like little warriors with grim, serious looks on their faces, but Purple was the heavy—has always been the heavy—and she gave me a remarkable fact: Indian girls would hit you.

I remember being very impressed by this fact, so much that as I sat cleaning dirt out of my mouth I considered telling my mother, who knew better than I how to handle big truths. Mom tallied facts in those years, hoping to collect enough to justify marching us off the Reservation ("You're a smart man, you can get other jobs," she'd plead nightly to my father that first year after his company transferred him to the new vanadium mill in Shiprock, New Mexico), back to civilization and Catholic schools. It was a pitiful and inexcusable fact, for example, that we'd given up paradise for a wasteland in moving to the desert from Colorado. "Nothing but empty, ruined landscape." My mother would shake her head at the disgrace of it as we drove back and forth across the desert. (If you live on the Navajo Indian Reservation, you drive. And drive. You think nothing of a hundred-mile jaunt into Gallup to see a movie, or a hundred-and-fifty-mile ride over the Lukachukais to check out the new paved road.) She spoke with such finality it never occurred to me to question this truth; nor did I ever puzzle over the contradiction that I loved to ride shotgun through the emptiness with my forehead pressed to glass or, in the summer, with the window open and the hot, dry air rushing me with a force that took my breath away. Ride through the emptiness dreaming of Nancy Drew, whom I liked to imagine riding beside me in her spiffy red convertible. She'd bump along right next to me with a white scarf knotted at her throat and an exultant laugh on her face; she would not notice the sagebrush she crushed, or the arroyos she sailed over. She'd dip in and out of dry washes, leap over wicked prickly pears, dodge hogans and sheep dogs and telephone poles. . . . Sometimes, I'd imagine that my bicycle was hooked to the back of her car and she'd whiz me along with her. I had fat bicycle tires that could easily handle the heat and sand, and I'd roll over the heads of rattlesnakes and zip up utility poles to follow along the electric wires. I suppose it was a long rope that connected me to her car, and I held it like a water skier carried almost too fast—too fast, certainly, for the electricity in the wires to catch up to me (I never got electrocuted)—but not too fast to hold on. Once up there, though, I could never help thinking about birds. They aren't little sparrows along the Reservation roads, but big black birds—magpies, ravens, crows—that pick at the pinkish gray flesh spattered along the blacktop, then fly to the tops of telephone poles when they see my mother's car approach, fly up just in time for a head-on with my blue bike; I never imagined that I had a baseball bat to knock them out just in time.

I don't remember fantasizing about the Indians in their hogans—I didn't know any then. The Indians I knew saved me swings on the playground. I don't remember fantasizing about the healing rituals held in canyons between landmark mesas we passed, ceremonies where medicine men drew intricate and powerful pictures with sand; I didn't know about these secrets yet. Dumb bike fantasies without beginning or end. I rode thousands of miles over dry desert terrain, figure-eighted it, coasted over piñons, until by sixth grade, two short but active years, I'd touched it all. It's hard, when grains of sand hang between the rubber treads of your blue racer; when fat birds on telephone poles make you thrill at the danger of impact; when you've vaulted crags and zigzagged through canyons; when the pupil of your eye shoots a thin but sturdy connecting line to that other line where brown earth meets blue sky, and you ride to the junction of the two and pop a wheelie; when the feeling you remember passing Tohatchi or Newcomb or Sheep Springs is a feeling of what it's like to move almost too fast, it's hard then to remember the fact that the desert is empty.

This had nothing to do, by the way, with what Purple was trying to tell me that day behind the band building. "What would you do if I socked you in the stomach?" I can still see her as she says this, and it's not what you would expect; her face is not gray and sullen, her lip doesn't curl in disgust. It isn't a "Who the fuck do you think you are" or a "Don't kid yourself." The girl who sent me flying to the shady side of the band building was delighted. A taunt, a laugh, a fierce, excited tone that said, you indeed, I do dare punch a hole through this scared little white girl in her corduroy coveralls and saddle shoes and pin-curled hair. Yes, I'd be pleased to roll this little puff of kitten fur in the dirt. A challenge, and it thrilled me and filled me with dread, a tone that left me hiccuping with wonder. A tone that said—and this, I think, was what Purple was trying to get across—I notice you. And a fist to confirm it. Purple was the first Navajo I ever remember touching me and the only one who ever went so deep (from the rim of my belly button through to the mole on my spine). That's how Purple was. She noticed things in a deep way.

I did not forgive her for noticing. Being the fourth of six children and neither loud enough to outshout my older brothers and sisters nor young enough to outcry the little ones, I had managed to escape notice for the first nine years of my life and had fully intended to go on doing the same. ("Our little pill has to raise her hand if she wants to get a word in edgewise," my mother would say affectionately every time I opened my mouth. "Quiet everybody, the little pill wants to speak.")

I lived the first nine years of my life in a huge Victorian house in Durango, Colorado, and in this house was a staircase where I grew up. It was a windowless place walled with plaster, tan I think, although the dimness made it difficult to see the color, with a door at the bottom separating it from the kitchen and a little brown fence at the top for baby safety. Light would filter down from the bedrooms above where my brothers would be parachuting each others' underwear out the window. Below, my mother would be clanging lids together to remind us how much she hated to cook. I liked sitting there on the middle step between levels, watching the right angle where the roof sloped down to the door and thinking about trapezes.

Not trapeze artists. I never saw myself swinging in a domed tent with a hushed crowd below. I saw only the trapeze and me on it, holding the bar in the crook of a knee or the arch of a foot. A long-roped trapeze, thousands of feet long with no floor below nor ceiling above. It would swing me lazily and gracefully—I loved the feel—through vast black space, and I would stretch luxuriously. I knew how to stay in sync with the moving rope, making my muscles reach their maximum stretch at the very point the trapeze slowed to its apex, and I would flip off at the last possible moment—drift off, really, off and up, drawing my limbs slowly around me in a roll. I could roll twenty times in twenty perfect somersaults before it was time to catch the next trapeze that was floating lazily up to me.

To sit between levels and flip with grace to the cadence of clanging pots—it was a lovely way to live, but Purple spoiled that. Purple took notice, and for the first time I started thinking about sand in my mouth. Or fists in my stomach, or shady spots in the short-cut home. For the first time I started thinking about the floor. Of course, the floor part didn't happen until the ninth grade. Actually, the sand and shade didn't do much damage to my perfect roll. Purple was sent off to a Mormon boarding school in Utah in fifth grade (her father, they said, got drunk one night and went out and killed twenty sheep belonging to his neighbor, a man with whom he was feuding; he was promptly put in jail, the unnecessary slaughter of animals being among the worst of sins on the Reservation, and Purple was sent to Utah). Without her actual presence to reinforce my memory about the band building, Purple's fist shrank in importance. It was merely an incident, something that happened to me in fourth grade.

But Purple came back. She came back in a big way. Purple and I were not the same size, I don't care that the scales read ninety-three pounds for both of us and that the metal measuring stick resting on the tops of our heads showed our heights to be fifty-eight inches exactly. She was not my size. Stand us next to each other in our blue cotton uniforms—they were one-piece, button-down gismos, short sleeves and a metal Wonder Girl belt at the waist, with folds of blue cotton ballooning out and then gathering in tight elastic that would leave lines of pink dashes imprinted on our legs (the elastic was supposed to circle the tops of the thighs with the bloomers fluffing out dresslike, girllike, but we'd tug them down toward the kneecaps, then worry the elastic limp so it wouldn't hold when Mrs. Adams, who had no shame, told us to blouse the bloomers)—stand us next to each other out on the football field in the three o'clock sun and Purple would cast the larger shadow. I swear it. That first week when Mrs. Adams made it clear that Purple and I would spot each other throughout the entire gymnastics season, I wanted to demand that we take a measurement of shadows out on the football field. Take her out on the field where I knew her malice would manifest itself in her shadow, a yeasty shadow that would spread ominously, slowly, malignantly over every inch of turf and beyond. Somewhere between goal posts it would lose its girl form, transforming clearly into giant bony knuckles. Just to think about the football field during my ninth-grade year left me winded.

Once I had Purple staked out below the parallel bars (I settled for the parallels since there were no trapezes in the gymnastics equipment) waiting to not catch me should I fall, I thought a good deal about the floor. Of course, she wouldn't catch me; Purple made that clear.

"Now girls, don't be shy." We were in the locker room, this must've been the day after spotters were assigned, and Purple was mimicking Mrs. Adams in that high sassy voice she got sometimes that made the cousins smile secretly at each other. "Hesitate, and somebody'll get hurt."

They were ratting their hair in front of the mirrors, Purple and the cousins. "She won't break," cousin number one said, nodding her head vigorously at her reflection.

"She might break," Purple responded, and she watched me in the mirror with this evil grin. Then she wiped the grin off, but she still watched me with a concerned look like Mrs. Adams got when she talked about the gravity of the spotter's responsibility. "Remember," Purple said solemnly, "a spotter breaks the fall, not the back."

Something in the way she said this made me think about hands. I couldn't help seeing myself boomerang up from the low bar, reach back for an eagle grasp of the high, and feel my fingers cramp, unable to curl around the steel; I'd watch nonchalantly, almost an afterthought, while I drifted down toward the chalky glazed paws of the beast, paws that would suddenly disappear at a crucial moment, and we'd both listen for the splat. Or they'd catch me, catch me on the spine, jerk up quickly; then we'd listen for the snap (". . . breaks the fall, not the back," Mrs. Adams chants in the background). I don't know that Purple had it in for me personally. It was a gleeful grin she'd give me, just like behind the band building, not that she *wanted* to cripple me, but that it might be fun. Maybe just an anxiousness in her muscles—like when you hold something very fragile, a bony kitten, that urge to crush it just to hear the bones crunch. I suspect Purple felt that urge when she held something very white. Just a curiosity about how the bones would sound when they snapped.

IT WAS the year I considered Skinwalkers. This is the English word for Navajo witches, but if I were thinking about the sect that wears coyote or wolf skins and feeds human flesh to their victims it was only in the abstract. Mostly, I was thinking of Purple and how she made me feel like she walked on my skin. With her eyes; with her concentration; with her bored, smug smiles. It was the year I forgot how it felt to float obliviously through a routine. It was the year I started thinking about the crowd. "You have to know how to make eyes follow you and make them grateful for the privilege." I read this in the *Albuquerque Journal*, and it was an article on dancers. On women who dance in cages. The journalist asked one of the dancers if she got embarrassed with all those men watching and she said, "What would be the point if they didn't watch?"

I could think of some points. A decent lunge, maybe, or a dismount where the feet landed first. With Purple watching, I didn't spring to the bar, I assaulted it. I didn't glide, I clambered. I never posed, I perched. "Just ignore them," Mrs. Adams would say, referring to the crowd in the bleachers at meets and not suspecting that the eyes that turned my limbs to silly putty were stationed not a foot away on the mat below. I felt most sorry for Mrs. Adams, who would watch me, the girl she'd "honed to perfection," as she said, with a certain desperation that year as she saw how temporal that honing was.

Anyway, ignore is a word I didn't understand. Pretend, I got. You could pretend nobody was watching, wink at yourself and watch the wall. But it was clear what was going on in Purple's head. I knew she hadn't forgotten the band building; I could see she was biding her time, waiting for me to slip up; rather, to slip, period. Knowing that, I could pretend that Purple didn't want to pounce on me, but I couldn't ignore it because it was true.

I had always thought that caged dancers pretended they were somewhere else, and that's how they could dance; that's what surprised me in that article. They had a picture of one of the women, a striking woman who slouched in her chair with one arm thrown over the back and the ankle of one foot resting on the knee of another.

This was the woman who said, "make them grateful for the privilege," and in her face you could tell she did. Her hair was curly and short, the face shapely, thin, unblemished skin, and a certain languid boredom in her eyes. An indifference and an interest at once. She was one hundred percent there, that was obvious; not only did she not pretend she was somewhere else, she didn't seem the least embarrassed about what the men thought of her. You got the feeling she didn't care what went on in their heads because it wasn't important. No. You got the feeling that what went on in *her* head while she danced was what was important. That if she danced and looked at you with those frank and interested eyes, you wouldn't see just the body, but the face telling you how to see the body. This may all be nonsense, and maybe you'd have to ask the dancers to know for sure, but I got the feeling, looking at her picture, that when she danced the crowd thought what *she* thought—and that was performance.

Purple understood about performance. It didn't matter that she was a lousy tumbler, unable to get the height on her stag leaps or get the timing down on a forward dive. That wasn't important. Purple knew about making eyes follow her and about making them grateful for the privilege. She was always calling attention to herself, and if you tried calling her a show-off she'd stare you down until you saw it like she did: that her point of view was absolutely correct and worth hearing. Like, she'd interrupt Mrs. Adams lecturing on the proper way to do an arabesque turn.

"Arch the arch, isn't that right," Purple'd coach. We'd all be standing around the mat, and Mrs. Adams would have her knee crooked to show us the proper angle, but Purple would notice the foot.

"That's right, Evangeline" (that was Purple's real name), Mrs. Adams would say. She was always harping on how we had to develop our foot muscles and cultivate a perfect curve.

"Round like a taut bow, isn't it."

"Yes, dear." Mrs. Adams could be very patient. You could hear patience in her voice, that kind of concentrated patience that tells you she's an inch away from being fed up.

"And if you spread your toes, you look like a duck, huh."

"Evangeline, do you want to teach this class?"

"Yes, I do." And Purple would grin a grin at us as she made her way to the bench that said clearly she would make the better teacher.

That's what started me thinking of Skinwalkers. Purple watched me, and she watched like she *knew*; in my worst moments I had no choice but to see the whole thing like she did, and it was my responsibility to tumble off the bars into her arms. A girl I knew got killed by a Navajo witch the year I was in ninth grade, at least this was the story that went around. She was a cheerleader. Some said she was Apple (red on the outside, white on the inside). They found her dead in her bed with no clue about what killed her, not even after the autopsy. But they found bone dust under the bed. A Navajo witch will blow the dust of a dead person's bones in your face and it'll go straight to the heart. But that's not what kills you. Some say it's just knowing that the dust is there, that there's something foreign in your body, that drives you crazy: a fatal itch out of reach, or a frenzy that comes from listening to your own voice and the voice of a dead person talking at once. That's how Purple made me feel, that she'd gotten inside somehow; her laughter slipping through the advice of my own brain threatened to break my concentration and promised, someday, to break my neck.

I was raised to believe that a devil couldn't touch a true Christian and a Navajo couldn't witch a white. And I believe this. Some part of me believes this, and the only reason I started working Purple backwards was kind of a playful precaution. I didn't really think she could hex me, and I worked her like we used to as kids (you unknot the hex by imagining or practicing its opposite) just for fun. I'd go home after practice and I'd be tight, so very tight from concentrating on not falling, that I'd have to soak in the tub for hours to relax. I'd lie in the tub sliding a bar of Ivory from the ridge between my breasts down the slope to a skidding stop at my belly and I'd focus on the hands. I'd think of my Aunt Mary's hands, which were rheumatoid, practically doubled over they were so crippled, but they crocheted intricate lace doilies until they died. Or cuticles. I'd think about a picture of the fine fleshy hands that I saw in a book once; the nails were perfectly tailored and cuticleless. The owner of those hands, according to the caption below the picture, never ate sugar and that's why you'd never find a white spot on the nails. Busy hands. Clean hands. Neutral hands. I'd lie there in the tub until my skin started flaking and the water turned tepid, sliding the soap from breast to belly, and by the time I got out, toweled myself off, slipped into my flannel nightgown and under the sheets, there would be no hands but friendly hands. I would put myself to sleep imagining Purple, no longer with paws, but dancing fingers, long, brown, and strong, that were a part of my routine: There was a mount, a straddle, a twist, a hurdle, Purple's hands, and the hands would make tiny tucks, just minor adjustments that would flip me, a perfect roll over the high bar, tucks that would propel me upwards to maximum height and then ease me back down, maximum control, and I'd be asleep before it was time to dismount.

Or on the bars. I'd do a glide kip on the low bar, then catch the high, swinging my legs over to straddle the low, and instead of imagining my knees catching the bar, shattering and sending bone shards glittering toward the skylights as I had all season, I began to imagine things the Purple of the graceful hands might think: "She looks good. This white girl knows her stuff." Toward the end of the season, I began to see that my fantasies weren't far off. Wasn't that a benign glint in Purple's eyes? Perhaps I started to believe this a little . . . but you can't tell what's really in another person's head. I learned this.

It was at the Window Rock Invitational. Purple had just done a fair routine and she rounded off the end with what looked to me like a benign glint in her eyes. On impulse I ran up to her—make her my friend, she's willing; that may have been what I was thinking. I ran up to her and she was walking—strutting, really, in that cock-sure way she had after the boarding school—toward the water fountain, and I said, "Great routine. Keep that up and you'll be the best thing on the Reservation." This is what I think I said, although now I can't be sure. Often, I think too fast and I may mean to say one thing but there's already a new word in my mind that jumps into the talk out of context. This may have been what happened. I may have said something I didn't mean; that's the only way I can account for her reaction.

Purple stopped dead. Her head was lowered like an animal ready to butt and she had to roll her eyes to look at me. She looked at me from under her brows. That was not murder in those eyes. There wasn't a taunt or a come-on. There wasn't even hurt or tears. She looked at me like I'd just put knuckles through her stomach and she couldn't quite catch her breath. And yet it was a neutral look—like she didn't much care. She said a Navajo word in flat, tired voice: "*Neeshla.*"

I KNOW what it means: same to you. But I don't know what *she* meant. I don't know. And I don't know why, that day when I fell for the first time that season, from the high bar just as I'd imagined it, head first over the bar, cracking my kneecap before floating in a dive, the float was interminable from that steel bar to those blank brown eyes, that placid, secretive face, belly-first toward the gray mat, I still don't know why she caught me. She didn't catch me with fingers, but with the insides of her arms that gave just enough to break the fall but not the back.

I don't know why she caught me, and I don't know why she went and got herself pregnant that next summer.

I don't know why we ever had to move to the Reservation.

I don't know why I can't get her out of my head. Sometimes, just before I go to sleep at night, I think of her. I'm at a right angle on the high bar and I'm boomeranging around and around, my muscles perfectly tight, my head perfectly clear, arms spreadeagled. I'm not disoriented when I slip off; I just want to feel the float. Sometimes it's her long graceful fingers I float into; sometimes it's the backs of her arms. Sometimes it's something smooth and round, solid yet soft; I'm tumbling up against that belly, that great belly on that tiny body, and I curl around it, but just for a moment; I know she will roll me off, resisting the closeness. And I let her. She rolls me firmly and slowly in a perfect roll onto the gray mat.

That Horse

—

LINDA HOGAN

LINDA HOGAN, 47, was born in Denver but has maintained a strong connection to her family, her Chickasaw tribe, and their land in Oklahoma. Her views about relationships between humans, the land, and its other inhabitants, "a 'sacred covenant' that's been broken and needs amending to keep the agreement intact," are reflected in much of her recent work. A collection of essays, People of the Land *(Norton), will be out in 1995, as will a novel,* Solar Storms. *Her other publications include* Mean Spirit, Red Clay, Savings, *and* Seeing through the Sun. *Linda lives in Idledale, Colorado, near her daughter and four-month-old granddaughter, and teaches at the University of Colorado, Boulder.*

THE DREAM MEN WORE black and they were invisible except for the outlines of their bodies in the moonlight and the guns at their sides. Will walked slowly behind them until their horses turned and began to pursue him. He could not run and they had no faces in the dark.

It was early morning and his heart was pounding like the horses' hooves. The crickets were singing but there were no birds. Will pulled on his jeans and boots. Outside, mist was snaking over the land between trees and around the barn. It absorbed the sounds of morning. The rooster crowed as if from the distance.

The horse trader stood beside his wagon talking to old man Johns. He had arrived in Will's dreamtime with his horses of flesh tied behind the wagon: an older paint, a white stocky work horse, two worn-out mules, a drowsing bay, and the black colt. Will eyed them while he walked to the barn.

Will's father stood leaning against the rake as if he'd been caught hard at work. It was clear by the way he stood that he didn't want to trade.

"I been to Texas and all over." The trader removed his hat and wiped his fore-head with a rag, though there was a chill in the early morning air and ghosts were flying from the breathing mouths of horses.

"Picked up that bay over there in Tishomingo."

Will stood just inside the barn, watching the men and listening.

"How's the Missus?" the trader asked as he pulled back the lips of the bay to show Mr. Johns that her teeth were not worn down.

"Just fine."

"The boys?"

Mr. Johns was not interested in the bay but he put aside the rake and helped the trader through the steps of his work, lifting her leg to examine the hoof. The horse pulled away and twitched the men's touch off her back. She knew what Will had begun to think, that a danger lies in men's hands, that whatever they touch is destroyed. She shook their bitter taste from her lips.

After the men went indoors, Will looked over the horses. He was curious about the contents of the wagon, the leather pouch alongside ropes and horse blankets, the extra saddle and burlap bag bulging with trade goods.

In the kitchen, Josie served the men thick slabs of bacon and corn bread with eggs. Will sat quietly. His brothers had gone to put up a fence at Uncle Ray's so it was a silent morning without their loud boots hitting the floor, without the young men's disordered conversation.

"I got this black colt too young to travel. Comes from real good stock."

"I got no need for a colt. It don't look too young to travel."

"You can give me that work horse out there—it's nearly broke down anyway, see the sway of its back? And give me five dollars to boot, I'll give you that colt. An Indian around here has need of a black horse."

Steam boiled from the kettle. Josie held her hands in the heat of it.

The trader continued. "Picked up that colt from that new white sheriff over in Nebo county."

"That so? Haines?"

"That's the fellow. The colt's too young to travel."

"Haven't got five dollars anyway." Will's father rubbed his chin. "All I got is dried meat."

"That'll do."

WILL DIDN'T know where the riders came from or where they were going. All that year, his father rose from his bed at night and went outdoors, his pistol concealed at his side. He exchanged words with the men who rode out of the darkness, or he fed them or gave them money, or offered them fresh horses for their journey.

Sometimes they sat around the table like bandits, all of them dressed in black, their dark horses hidden in the trees. Or they sat on the front porch where they would not disturb Josie and the boys, or Will, who was supposed to be studying arithmetic.

The men sat with their boots up on the rail, their chairs tilted back on two legs. Will heard the words again about the sheriff, oil accidents, manhunts. Heard the whiskey bottle hit against a glass and return to the table.

About this time, a Choctaw family named Hastings who lived nearby had all disappeared except for the grandmother who was declared mentally defective. She was taken away, protesting in Indian that the sheriff and deputy had murdered her sons and daughters, and that the government officials wanted her land and the mineral rights. The sheriff who hauled her off did not understand the language she spoke. He said she was crazy as an old bear because her family had gone off to Missouri after work and jobs and left the old woman behind. The grief of it was about to kill her, he said, and she'd be better off in the hospital up in the city. But James Johns and old man Cade, a full-blood, heard the woman's words and understood. They knew she never lied and she was sane as a tree that had watched everything pass by it.

"She's crazy, all right," lied Cade to the sheriff. "Says there's ghosts on the place."

Afterwards, when they went to the hospital to talk to her, she agreed to stay there until it was safe to return to her allotment land. They didn't tell her that the land was already torn up and that it spit blue flames into the night from the oil works and that the small pond she had loved was filled in with earth.

In the hills there were bodies of Indians, most of them wrapped in blankets, the smell of whiskey on the clothing of even those who were known teetotalers and Baptists.

Mr. Johns' face hardened, but he set to work. His routine included brushing the horse, Shorty, until the black fur was like water reflecting the sun. He kept him separate from the other horses as if they would give the men's secrets away to that one who had been owned by Sheriff Haines. The horse heard only the voice of James

Johns. As it grew, it was enchanted by the man's voice and tales. Mr. Johns allowed no one else near the black horse.

He grew muscular, that horse, and his stamping hooves shook the ground.

ONE DAY the Indian agent arrived at the door. Mr. Johns said to Will, "Don't you ever forget that the only goal of white men is to make money." And he went out like he had nothing but time and stood on the front porch and looked squarely into the agent's face.

The young man was fair-haired, like cornsilk, and had flushed cheekbones. He gave a paper to Mr. Johns. "You are good honest people and you have been wronged. If you sign this you will be repaid for your damages over there by the Washita."

Will thought the young man looked sincere enough.

"I don't sign government papers," said Mr. Johns.

"Uncle Sam's been real good to you, hasn't he? Just your 'John Henry' is all you need."

A week later, Mr. Johns returned a check the agent mailed to him, knowing that to cash it would legally turn his land over to the oil men.

THE RIDERS on their shadowy horses arrived like the wind. Will heard the horses out in the trees and wondered if the agents were stalking the house around the boundaries.

There were more men than usual. There were even a few older gray-haired men, those who wanted to go back to the old ways. They were talking about dangers and people missing from their lands and homes. They sat at the table with an open map of Indian lands, and when the door crashed open one of them hurriedly tried to fold it away.

Will went pale with that crashing and there were demons of terror in him when Betty Colbert rushed in. She was in a terrible state. Josie, about to offer her some coffee, backed off when she saw how Betty's face had darkened, how her hair was wild and her eyes furious.

Betty was breathing like a runner. "You men tell us we're in danger and don't tell us anything else that's going on and then you go off at night leaving us alone with just a gun. To shoot who, I want to know?"

Will was already in the room. He was drawn in by the angry power of this woman whose voice came from the house of wind up in the hills.

Mr. Johns said, "Your house is protected, Miss Colbert. My older boys probably followed you here to make certain you are safe."

And though he was carried into it, Will had a feeling beneath his heart that he wanted to cry. His brothers were not helping uncles after all but were out there at the edge of the clearing, watchers in the dark, hidden from the thin lights of houses.

"This didn't used to be such a hard country," Betty Colbert said. She sat down, almost in tears. "Then they go and cut down all the timber and the young people disappear when they get old enough to sign over their land, like Mr. Clair's son showing up in England with those oil men. Kidnapped all the way to England. Then the best land is turned to oil so we can't even feed the animals or us."

So the women went to work too and Josie sat up alternate nights with Will out on the porch, hiding the pistol in the folds of her skirt while James was riding patrol. But here and there a body would turn up, in the lake or hidden beneath leaves the wind blew away.

IN THE white fire of noon, the air slowed. It was a beautiful summer day and in the light there were no hints of any danger.

Will's brothers had gone to the rodeo where they rode bareback broncs and roped cattle to earn extra cash. Last year Dwight paid a two-dollar entry fee and won the $40 bullriding purse. Ben lost more money than he made gambling on the horse races and he accused the horses of being cursed and went to pick up the dirt from their tracks, while the white men called him a "Crazy Indian." But he had known all the horses and each one's flair for speed and sure enough in the shadows of the horses, he found lizards with new green tails. He threw back his shoulders: "You whites are all fixers."

Will thought of this as he stood beside Shorty, the black horse. He thought how Shorty was like silver and not a skittish bone in his body. He'd ride that beautiful black horse to the rodeo and sit straight like his father and be proud of the way his shirt sleeves billowed in the wind. He'd keep the mighty energy of the horse reined in just enough to pull back the wide strong neck like a show horse.

He put the bit in its mouth, a red wool blanket on the back of the horse, and led him outside the fence. The horse was quiet and passive even after Will's weight was on him. "Gittup!" Will hit him with his heels and tightened his knees.

The black horse stood there a moment, then he was like a fire going through straw, burning and moving all at once. He turned in circles while Will leaned forward to hold on, his legs without stirrups unable to hold the horse's body.

It was a delirious sparring match for the black horse, raised to be invisible in the dark, trained to James Johns' body, hypnotized by words to know all the stories of humans, even those of a boy's pride and vanity.

Will tried to run Shorty into the trees to slow him down but the black horse cut a tight corner and veered off again before Will could leap down or grab a branch. The branches slapped at Will until he was forced to bury his face deep into the black mane and wait for the horse to tire, but Lord, the entire earth would be threadbare before one muscle on that animal wore out, and Will tasted blood on his lips. The horse was the wind or a river and Will was only a leaf on its current.

Will didn't know how long his father had watched before riding up alongside Shorty and stopping the wild horse from his dance of fire. Shorty's fur was damp and smelling like hay and Will and the red blanket slid down.

"I told you, stay away from that horse," said Mr. Johns and he whipped a leather strap against Will's leg while Shorty snorted and whinnied and stamped the ground like he was laughing.

Later, the rodeo still going, Will sat over his schoolbook and thought what his act might have cost. He hadn't known his father was guarding their house in the daylight or that the Willis house had been dynamited the night before.

IT WAS not so much that Will was down at the heels about missing the rodeo or being humiliated by that horse as that he was learning too young about fear and hatred. The Indians thereabouts had just begun to learn not to trust the agents. They were slow to understand that white people spoke words they don't mean when they want land or money, that when they said life, what they meant is death. The more Indians that began to understand this, the more deaths there were. The gods had lost their ways and all Will knew was that the midnight cries of birds terrified him and he woke sweating in the night when the riders passed by.

It was an unseasonably cool year and the pasture was not rich and green, so one morning Mr. Johns woke the boys early to drive their uncle's cattle and their own few head to a better pasture.

They'd been under surveillance by the Uncle Sam officers, especially now that Dwight was about to turn the age when he could sign over the lands the oil company already held down by the river valley, so Ben and Josie remained at the place with an uncle while Will rode along with the heavy plodding cattle.

Will looked tired with dark circles under his eyes. In the saddle he was slumped as if he were sleeping in the few warm rays of sun. They rode past the Hastings place and he thought about the old woman sitting in the hospital wrapped in a shawl of hope.

All the deaths had taken their toll on everyone. Mr. Johns had been thinking of moving the family out and letting the agents and crooks and leasers have all the allotment land, but each night when darkness fell, after he vowed to himself that they would leave, he found himself again saddling Shorty or sitting at the door listening for strangers. And Josie said she wouldn't leave any place again and what would become of the boys moving on all the time to escape the Uncle Sam agents.

James Johns rode up alongside Will and touched the side of the boy's knee. He felt amazed at the life and warmth of him. Will felt a promise in the heavy hand.

"Son, I was just wondering if you'd like to ride Shorty." That damn horse laughed. Will saw it. That horse laughed, and the cattle moved a little quicker toward the pasture and the clouds brightened and there were flowers in the fields.

Acts of God and Mortal Men

LISA LENARD

LISA LENARD, 42, was born in Buffalo, New York, but has lived in the Southwest for twenty years. Of Spanish, Italian, and Russian Jewish descent, she finds in the Southwest a multicultural heritage that mirrors her own. Her fiction and poetry have appeared in a variety of journals; her lyrics are on the album Mancos Blues; *and her MFA in creative writing–fiction is from Vermont College. Stories, she says, "should not affirm our beliefs but shake them up." She teaches writing courses at Fort Lewis College and at Pueblo Community College in southwestern Colorado, where she and fifteen-year-old daughter Kaitlin Kushner, long-time partner Bob Cook, three dogs, and two cats share sixteen-plus acres near the foot of Mesa Verde.*

THE PADRE, HE TOLD her it would be Jesús with whom she slept, it would be God. It was He who had spoken to the padre, who had said to the padre, I want my child of Angelina. So Angelina, who was she to question? Was it not the padre who, with twelve Hail Marys and twenty-four Our Fathers, plus a Novena published in the *New Mexican*, had absolved her of her sin with Lalo, that punk, that worthless scum, nowhere to be found now, their child Jesús already two years old?

It was the padre to whom she had come when she had left Rio Rojo and come to Santa Fe, a place where she could be one of many instead of the village *puta*. Eighth child of her mother's twelve, *prima* to the rest of the village, or *sobrina*, or *tia*, in Santa Fe she was nobody's *hija*, and nobody's fool. She had found work, stripping the beds of the Anglos, stretching taut the crisp white sheets and folding the corners so, and so. This was at the Super 8 Motel, on Cerrillos, not so far from where she lived at the El Rancho Apache Trailer Park, next to the Sunset Drive-In, whose sky-sized screen she could watch through her dust-grayed kitchen window: Robert Redford, and

Mel Gibson, and her favorite, the fiery William Hurt. She could not hear the words their mouths made, and so she made up the stories from the pictures, stories that were after all not so far from what she knew of other films and not so far from what she knew of life. Angelina understood that all that happened was because of sins against God, that people could not help but sin but must also repent their sins, a circle of sin and penitence over and over again: that was life.

And whose voice was it that had whispered in Lalo's ear, the whisper that Lalo repeated to Angelina: From love will grow life. Angelina fell in love with the words, with the music of the words, from love will grow life, and perhaps, too, she fell in love with Lalo, with he who whispered the words into her ear, who whispered her name, Angelina, as if it were a prayer, Angelina, *angel mio*.

And if Lalo were to find her now (and who knew, after all? Was it not possible that he looked for her?), would he not be surprised? She had now her certificate, her GED, to show she had finished all the work required of high school. She had now Jesús, so happy and fat, the face of his father and the disposition of his mother. Jesús spent the days with Mrs. Romero, two trailers down, who had a white picket fence around her yard of dirt and gravel, upside-down Tonka trucks and abandoned blocks: A or M or W fading in the sun. Mrs. Romero too had a certificate; hers said she was a Certified Day Care Provider, and it hung next to the crucifix just inside the door of her trailer. Jesús called Mrs. Romero *abuelita* and she called him *niño mio*, and Angelina did not worry to leave him with her each day.

And on Saturday evenings, she took Jesús by the hand and they went together to the Church of the Immaculate Conception so that she could attend the Mass and make her confession to the padre. Because the bus was often late, she did not always arrive in time for the Mass, and sometimes all had gone by the time she came and her confession then would echo off the high ceilings that yearned towards God. These times, the padre would meet her coming out of the booth, would sometimes say, Have you eaten, Angelina? No? Will you have supper with me, then? And Angelina would walk with the padre—Jesús between them, clutching each of their hands—down to the Plaza, where the padre would order *carne adovada* for each of them and *uno burrito con frijoles por el niño,* and the waitress would smile and bring extra *sopapillas,* quickly, so that Jesús would not begin to fuss, and then, while Jesús squeezed the honey into the puff, the padre would tell Angelina of his life.

The padre was not so very old. He was older than Angelina, yes, but he was younger than Robert Redford. It was William Hurt whom he most resembled, his fine tawny hair that he pushed back with his hand only to have it fall once more over his forehead, his most thoughtful eyes that were never still, his long-fingered hands that drew the words as he spoke them. The padre's name was Winston Salem ("It's not a joke," he said. "It's where I'm from."), and he was the youngest of five sons of a Carolina farmer, a man who grew many miles of tobacco, and a mother who had died bearing him. The padre's voice was soft and warm, with syllables that wove into each other so that one could rest in his words, in his sentences; one could feel in his words the gentle breezes of his home.

He had been first in Madison, Wisconsin, a place that had been very cold, and then in Waco, Texas, where it had been too hot. Santa Fe, the padre said, was just right, like the fairy tale, he said; did she know it? No, she did not, and so he told her and he told Jesús as well, and when he came to the ending and the Little Bear said, Someone's been sleeping my bed and *There she is*, in a voice that was not Winston Salem at all but entirely the Little Bear, Jesús had squealed and thrown his chubby arms around the padre's neck and the padre had hugged him back and Angelina had thought, This man would be a good father for my Jesús, then at once crossed herself: He was the padre, after all.

The padre called her Angie, the Anglo G of German, of George. Her supervisor at the Super 8 Motel, too, called her Angie, and she came to think that the Angelina who had first come to Santa Fe was now Angie, a different woman: older, wiser. Angie, the padre said, I am glad you are my friend. And Angelina too was glad, and happy to see the light that she made in the padre's most deep-thinking eyes.

At the hearing, it would be said that Angelina took advantage of the padre's weakness as a man, that Angelina did things in such a way that the padre could not control himself. Angelina thought, Perhaps I have done this, and then she thought, No. I have not. She had sinned, perhaps, in thinking that the padre would be a good father for her Jesús, but had she not confessed this sin to the padre himself, had she not said twenty Hail Marys as penance?

The padre, at this hearing, would not look at Angelina, which was very sad. His hands moved about in his lap, as if they were not his, as if they were something that he could not control. Angelina remembered the feel of those hands, so soft and cool against her skin. She remembered the night she had lain with him; it had begun to snow, when they came out from the *cantina*, and the snow was like dust that moved beneath their feet. The streets were silent with the absence of the cars, and the padre said, Perhaps you should come back with me. It doesn't seem that the buses are running. The padre carried Jesús over his shoulder, the child's eyes nearly closed with sleep, and the padre said, Jesús can nap there until the snow stops; you should not have to wait for a bus that may never come in a snowfall such as this.

And so at the padre's little adobe house, which sat in the courtyard behind the Church of the Immaculate Conception, Angelina laid Jesús down upon the padre's sofa. The padre brought out a blue woolen blanket with which to cover the child and then he said, Would you like some tea?

Angelina said that would be very nice, and she followed the padre into the kitchen, watched while he set the water on to boil, measured the tea into the white pot, took down two white cups from the cupboard, poured milk into a little white pitcher and set the white sugar bowl and a spoon onto the tray, just so. The padre's hands moved precisely in all he did, and when the tea was brewed, he lifted the tray and carried it back into the parlor, where Jesús slept upon the sofa, and then he laughed and said, Oh, there is nowhere for us to sit, which was quite true: Jesús slept the length of the sofa, and there were no other chairs.

Come, said the padre, we can sit on my bed. It will be like a picnic. And so they did, the padre measuring the sugar into each cup and then pouring the tea. Milk? he asked. *Bueno,* said Angelina, and he poured a bit into her tea, the white weaving into the brown, and then the padre stirred it to the color of dust and handed her the cup.

They drank their tea and watched the snow fall in the light that went out through the bedroom window. In Carolina, it seldom snows, the padre said, so Angelina told him about the snow in Rio Rojo, the way it seemed to gather in the narrow canyon, to make the canyon both smaller and larger. She told him how, on the mornings after a new snow, she would go with her brothers and sisters and make angels, moving their arms and legs up and down as they floated atop the new blanket of white. She stood to show him the movements they made, and the padre had suddenly set down his tea cup and risen as well, come and put his hands onto her shoulders and looked far into her with his deep-thinking eyes and said, Ah Angelina, you are so lovely; you are indeed an angel, sent from God.

But how could she tell this to these people, these strangers, at this hearing? The state had assigned a woman to represent her, a woman named Carol Blythe, most mannish in her tailored suit and her hair that was cut so that it did not even touch her ears. Carol Blythe had told Angelina that what the padre had done was unforgivable, that he had taken advantage of her, of his position, that the padre must be punished. Carol Blythe said the Church would say things about Angelina, about the way she dressed to show her breasts and her buttocks, about the way her hips moved when she walked, that she had tempted the padre in such a way that he could not be other than a man, priest or no.

But no, Angelina said, that is not the way it was, and Carol Blythe had interrupted her, had said, I *know* that, Angie, and that's why we're here, that's why the state has brought this suit. We must make an example of this priest, to show that priests too must pay when they do these things to women. It's good that your neighbor told us.

Mrs. Romero should not have told them, or perhaps Angelina should not have told Mrs. Romero. She had thought the older woman would be pleased for her, that she had found love in the Church, that she was once again with child, from the padre. But Mrs. Romero said, that son of a bitch, that whoring coward, and she said if Angelina did not come forward she most certainly would.

The hearing was on the television news, and that was how Lalo found out about it. He told her this the day he appeared in the courtroom, looking very handsome in his black suit and pale blue tie. Lalo said he now lived in Albuquerque, and that he had a very good paying job with a construction company, for whom he drove a grader. I am paid twenty dollars an hour, Lalo said, more than enough to support you and our son.

And the other child? Angelina asked him, watching his eyes move to her still-flat belly. When they moved back up to her face, they had changed. Oh Angelina, Lalo said. Oh Angelina. He left her standing there by the low gate and went to sit in the back of the courtroom, lowering his head into his hands and then shaking it back and forth, as if it were a melon he were testing for ripeness. Angelina looked over to where the padre sat, and then she looked again at Lalo, and she could not remember why she had ever loved him.

Carol Blythe came through the courtroom doors, briefcase at her side, all quick motion, contained wholly within herself. She set the briefcase on the table and then turned to Angelina, still standing by the gate. They want to cop a plea, she said. Public apology with no admission of guilt, though an apology as good as does admit it.

I do not want the padre to be punished, said Angelina, and Carol Blythe paused in her removal of papers from the briefcase and looked at her.

You want to accept their offer, she said, flatly, not as a question.

Who would make this apology? Angelina asked. She did not want the padre to be the one standing there before the many cameras and faces, his hands kneading each other, all the world looking into his deep-thinking eyes.

The Archbishop, I imagine, said Carol Blythe. That's how they do it, save face, cover their asses.

All right then, said Angelina. This seems the thing to do.

Carol Blythe crossed the aisle to the other table and talked to the lawyer who sat next to the padre. The lawyer looked at her and smiled, a smile with nothing in it, and then turned and leaned over to talk with the padre. The padre nodded, then lifted his head to meet Angelina's eyes, but his eyes could not stay and he looked down again to where his hands lay quietly folded on the table.

Lalo was waiting for her outside the courthouse. Could we go for coffee? he asked. Perhaps we can talk.

Angelina studied Lalo's face, the face of a boy—no lines, no creases. His eyes were dark like her own, the color of the river's bottom, but they were not deep-thinking and she could not love them.

I am late for work, she said, moving past him to the street.

Lalo said after her: Can I call you? but Angelina did not turn. She only said, I do not have a phone. And then a bus pulled in front of her and she got on.

MANY MONTHS after the padre had been transferred, when the baby had grown so big in Angelina that she knew it would soon be time, a letter came from Ukiah, California. It was addressed to her at El Rancho Apache Trailer Park, and Mrs. Romero had written across the front: Forward to Rio Rojo, NM.

Angelina took the letter out onto the back step and sat down to read it. I cannot stop thinking of you, the letter said. I have enclosed one hundred dollars. If you come, I will leave the priesthood, and I will marry you.

Jesús was playing with his cousins in the woodpile. Jesús was at the top, and the others scrambled over the logs, trying to touch him, but Jesús leaped to and fro like a flea, and all the children laughed but could not touch him. This had always been his way, thought Angelina. This is not a way I made him, but a way that he is. And Angelina, too, was the way that she was, which was her own way and one that had nothing to do with Jesús, or the padre, or even the child who had not yet been born.

Jesús, Angelina said that night as she covered him, the padre would like us to come and live with him, in a place called Ukiah. It is in California. Do you remember the padre?

No, said Jesús, and why would we want to leave here? Here we have *primos* and *tios* and *tias*. Here is my *abuelita*, and my *perrito*, my Pepe.

Pepe could go with us, Angelina said, but the little boy had already squeezed his eyes tightly closed, as if shutting them would keep out the words. So Angelina said, *Buenas noches, niño mio*, kissed his forehead, and left the room.

Angelina packed a small suitcase and put the hundred dollars into the pocket of her dress and left without saying goodbye to anyone. She walked out to the road, then down the road to the front of the *cantina*, where she set her suitcase down and then waited for the bus that passed through Rio Rojo each night on its way to Santa Fe from Denver.

And when the bus got to Santa Fe, Angelina got off: She did not wish to go any further. But the padre would know where to find her, if that was what he truly wanted. And if he did not, Angelina understood it would be because of the way that he was, and not because of her.

Taking Baby Home

LISA SHOOK BEGAYE

LISA SHOOK BEGAYE, 37, grew up in Indiana, but she has spent much time in the Southwest, particularly on the Navajo Reservation where she learned the quiet spirituality of the Diné, the Navajo people, and respect for Mother Earth, herself, and others. In addition to being a writer, she is an actress, a stage director, a teacher, a painter, and a mother of three. Her first children's book, Building a Bridge, was published by Northland Publishing in 1993. She currently lives in Richmond, Indiana, where she teaches writing at Indiana University East Continuing Studies, and works entertainment security in Indianapolis.

SHE TOOK THE BABY home. They tried to talk her out of it, but she took him home anyway.

He looked just like his father. Brown hair, black eyes, Navajo nose. Just like his father. He was all she had left of the love they had shared. She took the baby home.

People stared—a lot. Rudely. The Midwest just wasn't prepared for him. John Wayne movies and *Dances with Wolves* were the closest to "real live Indians" that any of them had ever been. Having the living proof that Indians were alive and well seemed somehow a slap in the face to them.

She put him in his car seat and took him to Wal-Mart. People stared. She strapped him to her in his Snuggly and walked to the Dairy Queen. People stared. She pushed him to the library in his stroller. People stared.

She took him home and snuggled with him. She cried. She sang him to sleep, not "Rock-a-Bye-Baby" but "Today an Indian Boy Has Been Born." She tried chanting to him, but she couldn't do it near as well as his father could have. They slept.

Morning sun shone through their window and cast a brightness on her blonde hair. During the night, he had clutched a handful of it in his hand. It looked almost white against his dark little fist. She lay quietly. She remembered mornings of a larger dark hand in her hair, brushing it from her eyes, caressing her cheek, her shoulder. She remembered the softness of kisses on her neck that lingered as the sun rose higher. She remembered mornings of love so strong, so real, that her heart wanted to burst with the pain of her loss . . . and her gain.

Her son began crying. His diaper leaked onto her sheets. She cried with him.

Time passed. Day after day, she sank deeper into the pain and ache. She placed her son to her breast. Not even the comfort of his feeding could ease the growing restlessness in her soul.

On Friday, she went to the grocery store. People stared. She noticed less. Her mind was on the sunset behind Gray Mountain. On Saturday, they went to the park. People stared. But she was sitting on the mesa, looking for a hawk. On Sunday, they strolled through the gorge. People stared. She didn't see. She was sitting in a road-side stand selling her husband's artwork.

She lay down that night, her son next to her. Dark lashes cast shadows on his cheeks. His umbilical cord had fallen on the blanket. She picked it up and placed it, dry and crusty, on her nightstand. She stared at it for hours. She was standing on the Rez, smiling into her husband's camera. She felt the magic of Monument Valley. She saw her husband's hair blowing around his face. She felt his hand pulling her onto the mesa. She tasted the bitterness of the sage as he placed it in her mouth. He softened the bitterness with the sweetness of his kisses . . . his kisses. She drifted toward sleep, feeling the warm memory of his hand on her breast.

Monday brought a Male Rain, as hard as any she had seen in awhile. It didn't even register to her that she thought in terms of the *Diné*—the white world no longer existed for her. It was time to go home. So, she took the baby home. They tried to talk her out of it, but she took him home anyway.

Across the Illinois line. Across the Missouri line. The Oklahoma line. The Texas line. The New Mexico line . . . ever closer, ever stronger, pulling her forward across miles of U.S. 40.

When she crossed the Arizona line, she stopped, knelt on the earth, and listened. When she saw the Navajo Nation sign, she cried. She turned the radio to KTNN.

She glanced at her sleeping son. She didn't stop again until she arrived in Cameron.

She went to the bathroom. She bought some bottled water. She adjusted her son in his car seat. She turned toward the canyon and when she reached their mountain, the mountain where they had dreamed, she drove off the main road. She parked her car by the old hogan.

Unstrapping her son and taking him in her arms, she walked. Tears streamed down her face. Her son slept. The jostling of her steps did not disturb him. He slept. He was content.

She reached the spot. She lay her son on Mother Earth. She removed the dark velvet bag from around her neck. She dropped her son's umbilical cord into her hand. She dug a small hole. She buried the cord. She held her son to the sky and prayed. She cried. She missed her husband. She was *bilagáana*, but her son was *Diné*. She asked Mother Earth and Father Sky to forgive her if she didn't do all of it just right.

She ended her prayer. A screech pulled her eyes skyward again. A bald eagle circled overhead. She thought if she reached up, she could touch him. It was her husband. She was sure. She had brought their son home. He would grow here. The *Diné* way. His family would teach what needed to be taught.

She wrapped him up and headed toward a hogan where she knew harmony would be restored. She took the baby home. She didn't know where she would fit in, but she took him home anyway.

Monsoons

LARAINE HERRING

LARAINE HERRING, 25, moved from a childhood in North Carolina to Arizona. She did not adapt well to the desert when she first arrived, missing the thick green trees, azaleas, and daily rains of the South, but, she says, "the Southwest has a mystery and a power that slowly works its way inside." Laraine has a BA degree in English literature and creative writing. She works as an art director for a cosmetics manufacturer by day and teaches writing workshops by night. Her fiction and poetry have appeared in Willow House Review *and* The Bohemian Chronicle. *She has had three plays produced in the Phoenix area, where she resides.*

SHE IS AS FAR away from the fire as she can go and still stay warm. She rubs her gloved hands together and crouches, waiting to feel his touch on her neck. Then she remembers. It was a split-second decision, really, and she wonders if it will even make the papers. Here, in the cold black of the desert, alone somewhere between Globe and Albuquerque, she wonders if they will find her. And if they do, will she be hero or villain? She sits now, feeling the jaggedness of the desert through her jeans. Things just don't happen, she thinks. Everything is for a reason. She lies back on a rock. The stars are hundreds, thousands more than she can see in the city. Thousands more than she ever saw from her tiny bedroom window. When she would lie with him, in much the same position as she lies now, she would wait for one to fall so she could make her wish. Always the same forever wish.

The silence is consuming, so completely powerful and encompassing that the night takes on a life of its own, its thick fingers closing around her neck, lingering, sticky, on her collarbone. The gunshot snap-crackling of the logs in the fire and her own slow, steady breathing . . . in-out, in-out . . . as if from a cave, the oxygen and carbon dioxide maneuvering through tunnels, around stalactites, finally exhumed in one long, exhausted sigh—these are the sounds of the desert at night.

She comes here often. Sometimes with him, but that was before. Now she would most certainly come alone. She sits up straight, looking for the moon. Out here, so far from the city, the moon blends with the stars, a brighter, larger orb surrounded by its sparkling children. She loves the moon and she thinks she remembers he did, too. But that was before. She finds the moon in the east and stares at it, mumbling a little prayer. The moon controls all things, she thinks, from the tides to her menses to her moods. Maybe it could find a way to set her free. The stars are moving now, swirling through her mind. She feels his hand on her shoulder again, she's sure of it, but when she spins around to look, she sees nothing. She feels it again—icicle fingers walking down her spine, fingers pinching her flesh and freezing her blood.

Why has no one come looking for her? How long does a grown woman have to disappear before someone starts to search? She plays tic-tac-toe in the hard red earth with a rock, then freezes, unsure if the rustling she hears is from the wind or a rattler. Snakes love desert evenings, she reminds herself, and tucks her jeans into her boots.

It was several years ago, she remembers, at least that, when she first met him. She'd seen his cockiness as confidence and his condescension as artistic brilliance. His smile was as transparent as his hairline and his eyes were brown and bubbling with good intentions. Women are conditioned to fall for that, she thinks. Unfortunately, the signposts to the perfect mate are hazy at best, like the Magic 8 Ball from grade school, "Outlook Hazy. Try Again."

A coyote howls from the nearby mountain, setting off a barrage of responses from neighboring canines. She isn't so far from civilization that she can't hear the private conversations of the house dogs sentenced to the backyard to enjoy the beautiful evening.

Slowly, during her life with him, she claimed less and less as her own. She would walk into her closet and notice that his suits, ties, button-down oxfords, and wingtips had moved in. Polyester is a stifling, repressive fabric. It behaves differently from the soft swish of her rayon skirts and silk blouses. It is stiff, erect, and always creased. When they made their inevitable decision to separate, a court of law determined that he would make a better custodial parent because she had chosen to love one of her own.

Sure, the decision is under appeal, but that could take years. Her daughter Toby might not need a custodial parent by that time.

At least Toby was with her grandma now. She would be safe until a plan be could figured out. The woman is starting to get frustrated. Why has no one come for her? Why did she feel it necessary to run?

It had been a natural progression of events. She witnessed initial action "A" and followed it with consequential action "B." Anyone would have done the same thing. The law has nothing to do with justice.

The moon is directly overhead now. She moves closer to the fire, stomping her feet to wake them up. The air is crisp as new money and she can sense the mountains and the canyons around her, as if rising slowly from the baked earth to surround and guard her. "None shall pass!" She thinks of the Monty Python skit and laughs softly, perhaps because she knows the irony of the words, "I will protect you." Perhaps because she knows she may be her own worst enemy. She remembers something she read once in a magazine, only she can't remember if it was intended to be humorous or factual. She read that the male brain is only capable of thinking of one thing at a time. That tidbit of information would go a long way towards explaining the random violence and extreme mood swings her ex-husband had experienced.

"I just see red," he had once said. "I don't know what I'm doing. Something snaps." Men accept that in each other. Much like underarm hair or 5:00 shadows. Nothing can ever snap in a woman, because, although perceived as weaker, the woman must continually be the strength. The balance of power is so shaky. She laughs again, wondering what it was that snapped in her and how long it has been gone.

She, too, had seen red. But it was different. The sun was setting and as so often happens in the Southwest, it pours through all the western exposures, washing the rooms in a blinding white-red light, silhouetting the people and objects in its path. She had seen him, an exquisite black outline, sleeping on the couch. That was how she had entered, as a silhouette, and that was how she crept through his house, on exaggerated tip-toe, like a Bugs Bunny cartoon.

She'd inched toward Toby's room. The suncatcher hanging from her bedroom ceiling spun around, tossing bright fairy-dust sunbeams across the room. She wished she had a camera. Her daughter's face brightened when she saw her mother, but she had calmly placed a hand over Toby's mouth. "Shhh. We don't want to wake up Daddy. Take this," she placed the marble cat statue she had given her last Christmas in her tiny, sleepy hands. Toby loved this new game and had followed her, noticeably silent, clutching the statue, through the reddening house.

She had parked her green Dodge Dart a few blocks away so the engine noise wouldn't attract attention. Toby skipped ahead an extra few steps while she, head wrapped in an enormous brightly colored Jamaican scarf, kept looking over her shoulder and in the bushes. Once they were driving away, she relaxed a little, allowing Toby the anticipation of McDonald's cheeseburgers for dinner. She felt at complete peace for the first time since the hearing. Suddenly, a frozen panic clawed her throat. She had no course of action, no plan of attack. Mom. She would drive to her mother's house, leave Toby for a while, telling her she's going on a great adventure, like the movie *The Incredible Journey*. That would give her enough time to think. The panic slid from her throat and settled into her stomach. She drove the eight and a half miles to her mother's house, cool and collected, both hands on the wheel, radio loud, but not too loud, with all her mirrors in proper alignment. Her mother had been surprised, then concerned, when she opened the door to her bitter divorced daughter and smiling grandchild, clutching a marble cat. She had, of course, ushered them in, asking few questions, the exception, "Where's her father?" to which she got no reply. After that, all conversation that might matter dissolved into routine actions.

She knew her mother would protect Toby. Soon he would realize his daughter was gone, and, always a man of reaction rather than action, would immediately drive to his ex-mother-in-law's, banging on the screen door like the Secret Police.

She hears a low rumble and the top layer of earth shifts slightly in the breeze. The flames leap high, each flame trying to best the other before returning to the A-frame to try again. She hears a loud POP! and a lone spark spirals down with the grace of a feather. She sits cross-legged, facing the fire. The stale, catacomb-thick air changes to a volatile, hot organism blowing and spewing its waste in her face. Her long hair slaps against her cheeks like flyswatters, the wind belching like an alcoholic lover. The low rumble peaks, and pale sheet lightning electrifies the mountains. It will happen soon, she thinks, but she does not move. She stands, touches her toes to stretch her back, and waits.

The next burst of thunder growls so loudly she feels a firm tugging at the base of her heart. It is here. The first cold, fat drop lands in her eye, leaking over her lashes. The second one hits her nose and soon there are too many. Her eyes close and the diagonal spurts of water pelt her face like tennis balls. The angry fire hisses and spits sparks like bullets into the storm. It is not enough. Like a condemned animal, the fire whimpers and dies, its spirit rising with the gray-blue smoke. She leans against a rock, her clothes cold, sticking to her skin like too much lotion.

Her eyes open. The electricity is so vital, she can see a panoramic view of the desolation, the rock, and the vegetation. Saguaros stand, as they have for centuries, pointing to the churning sky, welcoming its juices on outstretched arms. The wind grows stronger until its force becomes that of another human being, pushing her away, into the rock, yet holding her still. Desert dust twists and leaps, pirouetting in the rain, winding up like a pitcher, then *pow!* releasing the ball of dirt into her face. She coughs. This dance of wind and water and earth stings her skin. Her fire smolders, steam rising from the ashes. She cannot keep her eyes open. The dust is thick and churning, made into paste by the rain.

She didn't know if she had been born "that way." She couldn't remember giving her sexuality much thought. She knew she wanted a baby. A man was necessarily part of that plan. She didn't know it could be better. She didn't know how very empty she was until Melissa touched her fingers, bringing her spirit to the surface like a diver too long underwater. Suddenly, she knew what she had been missing, and before she could take control of the situation, she had been swallowed by it, the decision made for her.

She expected an amicable, peaceful divorce. She got that. She expected custody of her baby, and when she didn't get that, she began choking and scrambling. She pushed at Melissa and clawed at her daughter, further convincing the powers that be that she was unfit. But they didn't understand. She didn't understand. Her daughter was not for trade. Her Toby was for life—her life. She was her birthright. Her ex-husband, a decent man, could not be a mother. She was unused to the jeering, the cries of pervert and the picketers who frequented what should have been a simple, private hearing. She could not adjust to strangers believing they had a better understanding of her life than she did.

She began to let Melissa touch her again, gently, her nerve endings bruised and throbbing. She wanted to regroup; she wanted to reenter the life she never thought she would have to abandon. "It's a choice," Melissa had told her after a long night awake. "You have to decide if you really want to make it."

Coated in a tepid layer of dust, she opens her eyes. The rain is cool now, and light, dropping softly on the muddy earth. She remembers forgetting to close her car windows and looks behind her, but she can't see through the layers of black. She's not even sure she's looking in the right direction. In the morning she'll know. A few white, unpartnered sheets of lightening flash a farewell. She sits in a puddle, not noticing the dampness through her already-drenched jeans. She rocks onto her side, her knees resting on her arms. In the morning she'll be dry enough to pick up Toby and Melissa and head south.

Like Blood

KATHRYN WILDER

KATHRYN WILDER, 39, is a fourth-generation Californian who left the ranch country of California's central coast to pursue her education at Northern Arizona University in Flagstaff, where she received an MA in English with an emphasis in creative writing. She found that her writing changed with the move—lavender skies, red earth, wide green rivers, and yellow light on canyon walls caused her to slow down and touch place. She has been published in Northern Arizona Review, *and has been a columnist for the* Flagstaff Women's Newsletter *for two years. She lives and writes in a log cabin in the pines northeast of town with her dogs and cats. Her children, Kenney and Ty, live in her heart even when they're not living with her.*

YOU HAVE TO UNDERSTAND, beef is my life. Me and my husband T, we breed it, raise it, sell it, eat it. My mom and dad did that before me and so did his, and so did most all our grandparents.

I woke up early that day and went to the window to see the morning star in what Dad and I called a hunter's sky—a sky that made shadows of mountains, and made canyons into rivers of promise when we'd creep through sagebrush we could smell but not see, moving into position before the deer came down to feed in dawn's light. But the sky at the ranch where T and I were working was corralled by ponderosa pines, and though I loved to put my nose in the bark and breathe in caramel, and to hear the wind coming long before it got to me, I missed seeing the morning star. I went back to bed but not to sleep, something restless inside me wanting out, and I lay there with the ranch I grew up on floating above me like clouds, or dreams.

The phone call with the news about the accident came later in the day. I knew T wanted to go, and God knows I wanted him to, but we couldn't both go—it was the middle of calving season and T had to help the boss with the calving. But I had to go, because somebody had to calve out Dad's cows. His big Beefmaster heifers especially—he'd bred them to an Angus bull who usually threw small calves but Dad was worried about them nonetheless.

T and the boss could spare me because I just drew day wages when they needed an extra hand, which was pretty often, so me and T had some money put away toward our down-the-road ranch, even though Dad kept telling me we already had a ranch if we could just wait long enough. I didn't like thinking about waiting for Mom and Dad to retire or die, so I kept putting my wages, small though they were, away in a savings account. The boss's wife watched Charlie when I cowboyed, but she didn't charge me anything for babysitting, said it was her way of helping out since she wasn't about to get on a horse. I never understood living on a ranch and not wanting to ride and cowboy, but I appreciated her help. And the extra money, though as it turned out Dad was right and we wouldn't need it.

It was a neighbor that called and I didn't understand exactly what had happened, only that Dad had gotten hurt in a dozer accident somehow and was in danger of losing a leg. I packed the old leather suitcase with the corners worn clear off—the one Mom had given me for my honeymoon trip, that she'd had since hers—with enough clothes to last me and Charlie a week, folding his tiny Wranglers and snap-button shirts carefully on top, thinking Dad would get a kick out of seeing his little cowboy all dressed up. I heard Charlie crying from the front room, and went in and picked him up, pressing our faces to the cold window where we watched T throwing my saddle, chaps, and ropes into the old Dodge down at the barn. The cold made Charlie's cheek turn pink, and his tears stopped flowing. I pulled him tight on my hip and went back to packing with him riding there. He liked me scooting around like a Kaibab squirrel, and he flung his hands out and squealed.

"Hold on to Mama," I said, reaching into the closet for my dress boots. Sometimes I wore them outside my jeans to show off the red leather with its black stitching swirling up to my knees, but as I set Charlie down to take off my work boots and put the dress boots on, I decided that that might not be a good idea today. I snapped the suitcase shut and Charlie clapped his little hands. When I picked him up again he reached around me as far as he could, hugging his cheek to my shoulder, and I felt a pinch in my stomach.

T drove up to the house and got Charlie and put him in the car seat for me, and his hug was waiting for me when I got to the truck. "Colette," he said, but I felt tears coming and I didn't want to cry, so I pulled out of his hug and onto the dirt road leading toward the highway and Dad.

TWO HOURS later, the big lady behind the desk at the hospital said Charlie couldn't go upstairs. I paged Mom, and me and Charlie flipped through *Outdoor Life*, Charlie pointing to pictures of bucks and bull elk, saying "Deer" and "Ek" at most of the right ones.

"There's the little cowboy!" I heard Mom say as she stepped from the elevator. Charlie climbed over the table full of magazines and ran to her. She scooped him up and hugged him while I picked *Outdoor Life* and *Sports Illustrated* up from the floor, and even though she didn't look at me directly I saw that her face wasn't as round as usual, and that the silver waves of her hair had flattened.

"How is he?" I said, reaching for *Time* that had slipped under the table.

"He's in intensive care. They haven't made up their minds yet."

Right then I really wished T was with me. He and Dad had always liked each other, and I figured T would know the right words to say. All I could think of was, Hang on to that leg! I found the stairs and climbed toward Dad, remembering the last time I'd been in that hospital—it'd been a year and a half since I'd given birth to Charlie there, on that other floor with babies crying in the nursery at one end.

When I stepped out of the stairwell onto Dad's floor, I heard the beeps and hums of life-saving machinery, and a voice on the loudspeaker calling for Dr. Milligan to come to the nurses station. I couldn't help but look into the rooms as I walked by, at the gray heads on white pillows facing televisions with the sound turned off. A dark-haired nurse pushed a cart out of one of the rooms. She smiled at me and I tried but couldn't smile back. I made the turn into the ICU, thinking I'd be able to walk right up to Dad's bed, and stopped cold. Someone asked me who I was there to see and pointed toward him, and without her help I couldn't have picked him out.

He lay there as pale and lifeless as the sheets covering him; even his eyes, normally the brilliant blue of the high desert sky, were washed-out. I could see the shape of bulky bandages under the sheets, and when I stared directly into his eyes I thought I could see the future.

"I'll take care of your cows, Dad," I said, my throat tight. "They'll be all right."

"I know, Collie," he said, squeezing my hand for a second with all his old strength. As I leaned over to kiss his forehead I couldn't tell through the tears swimming in my eyes if there were tears in his, too, but when I left I felt like I was leaving everything I knew behind me in that hospital bed.

I FOUND Mom and Charlie in the cafeteria, eating "cafeteria cardboard," as Mom called it. I told her Dad had gone back to sleep, and I hugged her quickly and headed out of town with Charlie as fast as the old Dodge would go. But when I came to the bridge over the big river I slowed to a stop right there in the middle of the road and watched the water roll and tumble away at the bottom of the canyon. Even at that distance, I could feel it moving through me—the river'd been running through my family for a hundred years, like the ranch I was going home to, like the love of raising cattle, like blood.

"There's the river, Charlie," I said. He strained against the straps of his car seat and smiled, and I gassed the truck toward the cliffs, and the vast flat made by the wash that was our valley, and home.

The ranch house felt the same as always but cold. Charlie willingly settled for a nap, cozying deep under the goose feather quilt on my old bed. As I built a fire in the woodburning stove I noticed things—the newspaper fanned out across the floor in front of Dad's chair, his moccasins half buried beneath it; the earth-toned Navajo saddle blanket Mom smoothed along the back of the leather couch several times a day lying crumpled up on the cushions; two coffee cups on the antique end table, a black wolf painted on one and a gray wolf on the other, both peering through yellow eyes; Mom's Levi's jacket thrown over the horseshoe hat rack by the front door, one arm leaning toward the floor, the other up high, dark stains splotching the front of it.

I picked up the cups—the black wolf held black coffee, the gray wolf's coffee swirled murky brown—and took them to the kitchen. After washing yesterday's dishes, I went back to the front room to check the stove, smoothed the saddle blanket in place, and picked up the newspaper. I took Dad's moccasins to his bedroom, set them by his bed, thought better of it and put them away in the closet. Only Charlie's face could be seen under the down comforter when I peeked in. Sleeping angel.

Warmth spread slowly through the front room. I meant to straighten Mom's jacket up, even out the sleeves like she always did, but the blood stopped me. Snatching the coat off the rack, I checked the pockets on the way to the laundry, threw it and the bloody handkerchief I found into the washing machine, and left them to soak in cold water.

I wanted to go out and check the heifers before dark, but I could hear Charlie's soft snoring. Warming my hands at the woodstove, I didn't want to see the picture that came into my mind of Dad in the hospital bed, tubes poking into him in every possible place, his face ten years older than the last time I'd seen him. I thought instead of me and T a few years ago, stretched out on the red and black Navajo rug, Mom and Dad off to a poker game. We'd turned so our feet were toward the stove because mine were cold even in socks, so I didn't see the lights coming up the long dirt road from the highway. T lifted his head during one of his pushes and said something like Holy Shit! and about ten seconds later I heard the door handle turning. I grabbed my pants and ran to the bathroom, flushing the toilet like I'd already been in there, but when I went to put on my jeans I saw that my panties must have fallen out somewhere. I pulled my Wranglers on anyway and straightened my hair and makeup, walking out like I didn't do anything wrong.

T stood with his back to the stove, his hands clasped behind him, and I saw an edge of black lace in his fist. Dad settled himself into his chair near the picture window, gazing at T.

"Who won?" I said, reaching my arm around as though to give T a squeeze.

"Nobody," Dad answered, his eyes twinkling like the sky behind him.

DECIDING TO unpack while Charlie slept, I went outside and grabbed the old leather suitcase from the faded green Dodge. A cold wind blew in from the west, which means a storm coming in this country, and with a storm come the calves. For some reason I never figured out, cows like to drop calves during or at the tail end of bad weather. Of course Mom had me during a blizzard and I had Charlie in the middle of the year's biggest hailstorm, but that didn't give me any insight. Shuddering, I faced all the directions and prayed for easy calving.

Like a ghost roaming the house, the warmth of the woodstove had drifted into the room Charlie and I would share, the room that would later become his own. I took his Wranglers and cowboy shirts and put them in the top drawer of my old oak dresser, looking into the beveled mirror I grew up in. Pulling a blouse out of Mom's honeymoon suitcase—the red one with the swirly black stitching across the yoke that T got me to match the boots—I held it up to my chest, seeing Dad's blue eyes and Mom's round face. I never thought I was at all pretty until T told me so in tenth grade, and now what I saw was Dad's pain and Mom's worry in a face that seemed much older than my own. My mind wanted to think about what Dad would do without a leg—how he would ride, rope calves, rodeo, or even drive the damn dozer—but my heart couldn't allow it. Shaking the thoughts out of my head and the wrinkles from the blouse, I hung it up in the closet and lay down next to Charlie to wait for him to snuffle awake.

"Mama?" he said, touching my face, stroking my cheek like he would a cat.

"Hi, baby."

"We at Gwamma's, Mama?"

"Yes, we are. You have a good sleep?"

"Gwamma and Gwampa here?" he asked, his blue eyes shining as sleep slid away.

"No, baby. They're at the hospital, remember? Grandpa's hurt."

Charlie raised up on his elbows, his head poking out from beneath the quilt like a prairie dog's. "Mama cry?" he said.

"No," I said, making a smile break through. "Time to go check cows."

"My boots!" he said, standing up on the bed and pointing to the little red Ropers beside it. Charlie would not go check cows without his boots on.

FOUR DAYS at Mom and Dad's and the house got quieter with each one. I kept me and Charlie busy as best I could. We'd hike up to the water tank on the hill behind the house, and if I got Charlie busy building rock corrals I could hurry up the ladder on the side of the tank and sit on the tiny platform on top. From up there, I could see weather coming, clouds rolling in across the high desert from as far away as California, and if I snuck out when morning was still mixed with night like I used to when I was a kid, I could watch the morning star hover in a hunter's sky that covered the world. Dad had showed me how big the sky was from up there when I was a little girl, packing me up the ladder on his shoulders; I had shown T one moonless night; and I would soon show Charlie. But for right then, while Dad was in the hospital and T was at a different ranch and Charlie was too little, I kept that hunter's sky for mine.

We watched TV, too, and listened to Willie Nelson and Merle, and the phone rang some—Mom calling from the hospital, and friends wanting news and to offer help—but other than that the house sounded like a library. Except inside my head. Inside my head the noise was like the locker rooms in high school—the chatter never stopped. Sometimes it was so loud I didn't hear Charlie; once I didn't even hear the phone ringing until Charlie tugged at my knee saying, "Mama, phone; Mama, phone!"

Every day we went to the hospital, and every day we checked the cows and heifers. We did the other chores, too, feeding the horses and chickens, gathering eggs, splitting wood, tidying the house, but that never seemed to take more than ten minutes. I stopped soaking Mom's jacket after the first two days, deciding to throw it away instead. I took it out to the big trash cans Dad hauled to the dump on Sundays, and by the next day it had frozen in there. The dark stains stared out at me like eyes and I climbed in and jumped up and down until the other garbage covered the jacket. Then I pulled it out, shook it off, folded it neatly like Mom would and placed it back in the can, thinking that for sure I was going crazy, or had already gone.

Dad didn't want to look at me or talk much during my hospital visits, and I guess he couldn't what with the drugs dripping into his veins like a leaky faucet. I'd tell him the ranch news—who'd calved out and who was ready—and watch his eyes get hazier and his thinning body turn toward the wall. It seemed like he pulled farther away each day, and I'd think, Hang on, Dad, hang on! And I'd want to say something about how we could customize the Cat so he could drive it again; and trade the Chevy in for an automatic, no matter how much he hated them; and teach old Bulldog, Dad's retired rope horse, to respond to one real and one fake leg; and, hell, that he could humble himself and hunt from the damn truck! And maybe I should have said all that—maybe it would have made a difference—but the fear in me would get so big at my throat that all I could do was kiss him on a cheek the color of a December snowstorm, mumble, "I love you," wait for a minute hoping for an "I love you, too, Collie," and meet Mom and Charlie in the lobby downstairs when it didn't come. Then I'd hug Mom goodbye, and head back to the quiet ranch house and the noise in my head.

ON THE fourth day the call from Mom said that Dad's leg was infected bad. I called T even though I figured he'd be out on the ranch somewhere, and listened to the phone ring for a long time before finally putting the receiver down. I picked Charlie up and held him close, squishing his round red cheek against my wet one. "S'okay, Mama," Charlie said, his little hand patting my back. "S'okay."

I knew T would call again that night, and told myself it was okay to be alone, me and Charlie in Mom and Dad's house, all the parts of me that were connected by blood held together the way the river connects the country and the people it runs through. I made hot chocolate and Charlie and I sat together in Dad's chair, sipping out of wolf cups and fingering the chair's frayed arms.

Everything in the room held a scene from my memory. I could see Dad loading river rock into the bucket of the front-end loader, and him and Mom on their hands and knees fitting rocks like puzzle pieces into the frame of the hearth. I could hear him sneaking down through the sagebrush ahead of me to shoot the perfectly symmetrical four-point muley whose head now crowned the oak bookshelf he'd built. I could feel him racing up the arena behind me, yelling, "Atta girl, Collie!" as my loop fell flat and round over the steer's horns, wheeling two hind feet just as I turned the steer off, winning us the mixed teamroping championship.

"More?" Charlie said, the yellow-eyed black wolf suddenly interrupting my vision. A horse's whinny floated up from the barn.

"No," I said. "No more. We gotta go check cows." A big Beefmaster heifer had been springing pretty strong, her sides swelled out and bouncing with each step like a huge water balloon. According to Dad's records and her belly, she was due any minute.

"Boots!" Charlie said.

THE PICKUP bounced over the road heading south toward the calving field, the potholes lulling Charlie to sleep. When I was little we didn't have car seats, and Dad would lay me out on the seat next to him, his right hand resting on my shoulder to keep me in place as he drove. "Go to sleep, Collie," he'd say. "I'll wake you up when we get there." But sometimes he didn't, and I'd wake up mad when we got back to the ranch house. "You were sleeping so peaceful," he'd say, "like a little angel. I couldn't wake an angel."

Charlie's head fell over onto his shoulder, and his lips parted slightly. Through my thoughts I could hear his soft breathing, and I smiled at his innocence. We passed the rock outcropping where T had proposed to me, its lone juniper standing tall but crooked in the wind, and then the calving field spread open between sage-covered hills.

The heifers lingered near the corrals, which was a good thing because I could see right away the big heifer was in trouble. She stood off to one side under an old cottonwood near the sometimes-creek, and as the pickup rolled over the cattleguard into the field she arched her back, her sides tightening and her tail lifting, one dark hoof parting the loose skin beneath it.

"Damn," I said.

Charlie stirred, raised his head to drop it on the other shoulder, didn't wake up. I eased the Dodge as close to the corral as I could, cracked a window so I could hear him if he started to cry, and stepped out into the cold.

The heifers were used to Mom and Dad working around them, and didn't spook as I opened the gate into the corral. Before I even asked they ambled toward the gate, the big heifer among them. "Dad's spoiled you rotten," I said, smiling at pictures of him hand-feeding hay to his cows. I'd often teased him about it, but I'd always been grateful.

As soon as the big heifer passed through the gate, I stepped in front of the others, cutting them off. "Sorry, girls," I said, "no time to play." And I thought about how I talked like Dad while I sorted the heifer off. She didn't like being singled out and started to get huffy, and I remembered how I felt in the hospital with Charlie trying to come out and I didn't blame her.

I finally clanged the gate of the squeeze chute shut behind her, and, hating to do it, pulled the lever which tightened the bars of the chute against her ribs so that she couldn't jump forward or back and break my arm. As I tightened the bars she pushed, and I could see that the hoof belonged to a back, not a front, leg. Breach. Shit.

Throwing my jacket over a cedar post and stepping behind the heifer, I pushed my sleeves up and my hand into her, and the heat of her struck me after the cold air outside. I followed the course of the calf's leg and a rush of panic washed from my stomach into my throat as I realized the second leg wasn't there. Double trouble. I should have tried T again, I thought; he could have been here in another hour. But I knew I might not have even that much time—the hoof sticking out was dry.

In the tightness of the birth canal I followed the one leg to the calf's hip, my fingers sliding along slick fur, until I felt the second leg pointing forward. Tears pushed up behind the panic in my throat. I can't do this, I thought. I was up to my shoulder in the heifer, my cheek resting against her warm red hide. Beyond the corrals, the field, the sage-and-juniper hills, the sky shifted and changed in strange gray shapes. "You gotta help me," I said.

The heifer grunted and pushed, and the calf's rump slid toward me. If Dad were here, I thought, remembering other times, and I knew I had to get the second leg parallel with the first or turn the whole calf around. I strained into the heifer as she groaned and strained against me. The mucous helped me forward until the heifer stopped pushing and the calf slid deeper into her, my hand slipping on the hot jellied placenta, my arm cramped from the strain, from her muscles clamping down on me.

"Come on, heifer, help me!" I begged, and she bawled long and low with another big push and I knew life hinged on my efforts and I pushed, too, reaching into her depths, my arms not long enough, not man's arms, but I got it, got my fingers wrapped around the hock and the heifer pushed and I slid forward enough to grasp the bone below the hock and bend the hock and ease the bent hock backwards.

I prayed for time and strength and breath, easing the hock around. The calf started slipping away and I hung on, hung on to everything I had with everything I've got, my body straining as if in my own labor, my shoulder mashed into the heifer's rear, my cheek against her tailbone, feet braced behind me, not feeling or smelling or tasting any of it; not remembering pulling other calves with Dad, not remembering the results; not hearing Charlie cry out as he slid into the world, or woke in the pick-up to find himself alone; or was it Dad's scream in the hospital; or mine as Charlie tore through me; or mine now as I pulled the leg backward to join the other one and felt the shudder of life slipping away.

I KNEW I'd lost the calf and I almost lost my grip, but the heifer was quitting—I could feel it; I could feel myself saying, "I'm done," after Charlie's head ripped through me, and the room rallying against me, a football game roar: "Go Collie!" and I'd had to suck in and push, push Charlie out of my body and into my life. I had to get the calf out to save the heifer.

I groped about and found my grip on the leg. I pulled slowly at first, and when she felt the calf moving inside her the heifer joined me and pushed, and the calf slid and she paused and I joined her and then she pushed again. And I pulled, each hand on a leg, feet braced against the chute, body leaning backward, watching the heifer doing the same, hearing her strain, remembering, knowing, and with a giant effort the heifer pushed and I pulled and the calf slid all the way out. And I fell back on my butt and the calf landed on top of me, slimy and warm and deep dark red.

The weight of death heavy in my lap, I hugged slick fur, resting my cheek on wet fuzzy forehead, short red calf hairs and long stringy blond hairs curling together. I picked up the calf, its head drooping over my arm, its eyes closed, sleeping angel. Struggling under ninety pounds of dead weight and the wonder about the weight of a dead leg, I carried the calf into the corral for the heifer to grieve. I let her out of the squeeze chute, showed her the calf, and turned away as she started trying to lick life back into it. I'd bring her some hay later, after I got back from the hospital, let her mourn overnight, and dump the calf in a ditch for the turkey buzzards and coyotes tomorrow or the next day. By then its spirit would be long gone, and the heifer would know it. And, I decided—cows and fear and death dry on my teeth, the river and a hunter's sky tight in my heart—I'd go ahead and tell Dad we'd lost one.

The Plain of Nazca

Cathryn Alpert

CATHRYN ALPERT, 42, lives in northern California with her husband, two sons, and an adorable chihuahua. Formerly a professor of drama at Centre College in Kentucky, she now writes full time. Her stories have appeared in such places as the 1989 and 1991 volumes of O. Henry Festival Stories, Best of the West 5, Touching Fire: Erotic Writings by Women, ZYZZYVA, and Puerto del Sol. Although she resided only a short time in the desert, its magic seeped under her skin. "Once you've lived in the Southwest," she says, "it stays with you forever—like a dislocating dream. Or stretch marks." Her first novel, Rocket City, set in New Mexico, will be published in 1995 by MacMurray and Beck.

PUT THE TOP DOWN," said Samantha. It was always an order for Malcolm, never a request. Malcolm did as she commanded, not one to argue with what little success he'd had with her in the last fourteen years. The black vinyl shell arced up and away from the car's metal hull, billowed with hot air, crested and folded in on itself like the retracting wing of a beetle. Samantha closed her eyes and turned her face toward the sun. Wind, heat, and light, like a salve, beat down on her, smoothed the tiny furrows that just this year had established themselves on the outskirts of her smile—tenuous lines radiating upward and downward from a single point of structural weakness.

"Zzyzx Road," said the sign up ahead, a landmark of sorts in the Southern California desert. Samantha had passed it many times, driven by it on her jaunts to and from Las Vegas. There were times when the road beckoned to her to turn down it, see where it led—perhaps to the lost town of Zzyzx.

The sign grew larger. Still hours from L.A., she had plenty of time to think about her future: The old friends she would look up. The job she would seek when she got back home. She felt Malcolm's gaze as tears streamed from the corners of her eyes straight back into her hairline, tears she hoped he would assume were from the glare off the asphalt, the rush of hot, dry wind. She wiped at her face, forced a smile.

Malcolm smiled back. "Do you trust me?" he asked, out of the blue. Beyond the road sign, the linear slab of interstate narrowed to a vanishing point somewhere on the distant horizon.

Did she trust him? What a strange question. Was there anyone she trusted more? "Of course," she answered.

Malcolm slowed. "Are you sure?" His dark curls whipped at his forehead like tiny snakes.

What was going on? It was not like him to be coy. "Of course I'm sure," she said. He was her best friend. She'd known him half her life and he'd always been there when she needed him. Whom *could* she trust, if not Malcolm?

He slowed further and turned left onto Zzyzx Road. His fingers held tight to the steering wheel; his brow knit into a solid, worried line. His look was intent: head forward, shoulders hunched, elbows bent at acute angles—his whole posture geared toward a single purpose he seemed unwilling to disclose.

They headed south on Zzyzx Road, which led to other roads, which led to nowhere. Malcolm seemed to turn down all of them—paved roads that gave way to dirt roads that intersected other dirt roads that ran in straight lines over endless desert floor. Roads that crisscrossed at odd angles; roads that ran parallel to one another. From the air, they must have resembled the great Plain of Nazca, scored with miles-long, decussated arteries, rumored to have been an ancient alien landing field high in the Peruvian Andes. A place where peculiar forces were said to be at work. Where compasses spun counterclockwise and light bent in unpredictable directions.

The car bounded over stones and holes. "Where are we going?" she asked.

"Trust me," answered Malcolm.

WHEN THEY came to a crossing that looked like every other crossing in this strange network, Malcolm stopped the car. A cloud of dust whipped back on them as the El Dorado's tires came to a halt in the colorless dirt. Samantha held her breath until the air cleared, revealing a three-hundred-sixty-degree view of rocks and scrub. Insects buzzed, invisible. Birds circled. She worried about Malcolm not finding his way back to the highway.

Malcolm turned toward her, drew one foot up on the car's seat and pulled off his sunglasses. "Show me your scars," he said, and for the second time in as many months a knife went through her.

Show him her scars? Was he serious? She couldn't show anyone her scars—especially Malcolm. She tried to speak but her thoughts would not form themselves into words. She laughed. Shook her head, incredulous.

"Show me," he said. "I want to see what he did to you."

Samantha looked up at the vast, cloudless sky, wishing she were anywhere but here—wherever *this* was—with Malcolm, whom she thought she could trust not to do things like this. "No," she whispered, hoarsely. The wind blew warm. Dry. Quiet as sleep.

"You said you trusted me. Either you do, or you don't. Which is it?"

"I trust you. I just—"

"Then take off your blouse," he said, more a request than a command.

This couldn't be happening. Not with Malcolm. Didn't he realize she could no sooner take off her blouse in front of him than parade naked down Sunset Boulevard? "Let's get out of here," she said, more a command than a request.

Malcolm leaned back into his padded door. "Show me," he said. "Show me." His voice was tender, the way she imagined he would speak to a lover.

"Start the car," she ordered.

Malcolm didn't move.

"Start it."

Nothing.

"This isn't funny," she said, but her words were lost on the wind.

Malcolm pulled his keys from the ignition and tossed them into the surrounding desert. They disappeared with a sharp jangle. Now he stared at her, his brown eyes large, determined. "Do you trust me?"

"Stop asking me that."

"Then take off your blouse."

Did she trust him? How much? Enough to believe he wouldn't reveal to anyone what her body looked like now? Enough to believe that afterward he would still love her? She peered down into the dirt at the herringbone pattern of fat tires, tracks left by some vehicle that had travelled this road before them. A truck, or a Jeep. Where, she wondered, had it been headed? Malcolm shifted in his seat as she glanced up at him. His mouth twitched. He was probably as nervous as she. Maybe more—it was scary changing the rules.

"Why do you want to see?" she asked, her voice no more than a faint whisper. Malcolm didn't answer, just stared at her, twitching.

She started with the top button.

HE HAD never liked Gene. He was mean, he said, he could see it in his eyes, so watery blue that the irises got lost in the whites. Samantha had dismissed Malcolm's warning as easily as she'd rejected those about other men with whom, she imagined, he'd felt in competition. One by one she'd trot them out for his approval. One by one he'd find some fault, some latent peccadillo that was certain to manifest itself in time. No one was ever good enough.

She expected Malcolm thought *he* was good enough, although he was shy and had never made advances. He'd been safe company all these years, an ear to bend when the men in her life behaved; a shoulder to cry on when they didn't. And now he was being brave. Asking her to remove her blouse. Asking to see her scars.

Samantha paused after the last button. Having worn no bra, she barely separated her garment's two front panels to reveal a small section of scar, not yet white, which ran diagonally between her breasts.

Malcolm blinked; his lips parted. He stared hard, until Samantha drew the halves of her blouse together like a proscenium curtain. Okay, she said to herself. Okay. Now she expected Malcolm to hunt for his keys. To drive them out of this place where, with any luck, the imperfection she'd exposed would never again be mentioned.

But Malcolm remained seated, stretched one arm over the back of his seat and leaned his knee against the steering wheel. "There's more," he said. "Show me." His tone was final, the look in his eyes resolved.

"I can't," said Samantha. A fly buzzed angrily against the windshield, though the top and all the windows were down.

Slowly, Malcolm leaned forward, reached out, slipped his fingers into the opening in her blouse—careful not to touch skin—and paused, just long enough for her to remove his hand if she chose to do so. He pulled the near front panel toward him, exposing her left breast—the outline of which she had seen him contemplate for as many years as she had known him—and the red gash that traversed it.

Samantha could not look at Malcolm, but stared, blankly, at the scene beyond the dashboard. Watched a hawk circle down from the pale sky. Land on a bush. Bob until the branch steadied. What was Malcolm thinking, looking at her? Why didn't he speak? How long was he going to gape at her mangled breast?

"There's more," he said, clearing his throat. His voice was tight and broke between pitches, as it had that first summer she'd known him.

Turning to face him, Samantha fixed her gaze well beyond his features on an indiscernible focal point safely distant. She sat motionless as he peeled back the other panel of cotton to reveal her right breast—whole, undamaged—and the raw, fluted wound that plunged arrow-like from the base of her ribs down into her jeans. Malcolm stared. Samantha looked straight through him. The wind held open the front of her blouse.

Gently, Malcolm ran his hands up under the white fabric and slipped it off her shoulders, down the length of her arms so that now she sat bare to the waist before him. The feel of his fingers startled her; in all the years she'd known him, she could not remember a single instance in which he'd deliberately touched her skin. Now he was undressing her.

He placed his hands on her shoulders, held them there momentarily. Strong. Steady. She drew in her focus to catch the look on Malcolm's face—not one of shock, nor of disgust, but a look she'd seen a thousand times as he glanced across their table in a restaurant, or over at her in the front seat of his car. He looked pleased, which was not what she expected.

"Can I touch you?" he asked. The wind blew her hair off her shoulders, smelled of wild onion, warm. He was already touching her, but she knew what he meant. Could he *touch* her? Touch *her*? Alone in the desert. No one for miles. Malcolm, who loved her and had never asked for anything. Malcolm, who had come to carry her home.

He removed his left hand from her shoulder, placed it beneath her unmarred breast where the scar sank into her white skin like a furrow. He ran his finger down the length of it, as far as her jeans permitted, probing its depth, exploring its ropy texture. Not at all what she thought he'd meant by touching her. Had she misunderstood?

Malcolm shifted his gaze upward to her face. Lifted her chin. Drew his fingers lightly over her lips, her eyes, the tiny lines around her mouth. Whispered, "Take off your jeans."

Perhaps she had not misunderstood.

With his middle finger, he traced the full length of her other scar, the one that crossed her sternum, ran up and over the mound of her breast and came to a twisted closure directly above her heart. He traced it twice. Leaned over and kissed it. Moved his lips over the jagged red. Cupped her broken breast in his hand.

"Impossible," she whispered, but Malcolm drew her close to him and encompassed her in his arms. He stared straight into her eyes, blue-gray and terrified, and she stared into his and saw—not the familiar Malcolm into whose eyes she had gazed a thousand times and seen nothing. Not even her own reflection. But some distant place, lit by alien light.

Strange, yet familiar, this point in space where parallel lines converge.

Out There, in the Hills

DELLA FRANK

DELLA FRANK, 45, a full-blood Navajo, is from Aneth, Utah, near the Four Corners area of the Navajo Reservation. She has a BS in elementary/bilingual education, an MA in reading in a content area (reading specialist), and an MA in guidance and counseling. She is currently working toward another master's degree in educational administration. Her publications include stories and poetry in numerous anthologies, and a book entitled Stormpatterns: Poems from Two Navajo Women. *She is a Title IV Coordinator with Gallup-McKinley County School District in New Mexico, and an educational specialist. She has three children.*

DEAR FATHER, I REMEMBER how you told me a strange story about a white "being" one very quiet evening   out there   on the mesa   amongst the hills   plants among the trees   the desert rocks.

There   in the canyons   of Utah   where the *Diné* People wandered   roamed long before   there   where the *Diné*   People lived in harsh lands   cold winter lands— centuries before your time, my father, during the month of March of 1926, the year of your birth   before the lands became an issue around here: I say, leave Earth Mother alone, silence.

Dear Father, I remember how you told me quietly   that the local dogs had gathered early that day   how they had barked fiercely   toward the later evening how you had gone outside to see the cause   how it was so silent, halt: I say, Face it head on.

Dear Father, I remember how you had told me quietly that you had seen a tall "being" standing there   among the wood pile   how you felt afraid yet: You had stood your ground   how you had stood in place there   looking at the white being   looking back at him   The white being had huge white wings and dark piercing eyes   He had looked directly into your heart   your mind   your eyes: Silence, I say: Speak to it.

Dear Father, I remember how you had told me about how you noticed that your heart had picked up rhythm   a beat   a stir   You tried to yell at the being   to tell it to go away   that you were not ready yet   you had gone out there in the early evening hours   you had stood proudly, proudly: I say, approach him directly.

I remember how you told me that during the twilight hours   you had gone out there   you had gazed up at him   in turn   he had gazed down at you   you had gone back into your house   the house on the hill   the dogs had continued to bark   hastily   late into the evening hours   while you sat   quietly   inside your home: thinking   reflecting   you were determined that "he" was harmless   you had also worried that   perhaps   it was witchcraft, witchcraft: I say, Seek out a medicine man.

I remember how you had told me that you had prayed for it to go away   you had waited quietly   that night   for your family to return   the night   the night   the night of moons   stars   the night of sounds   your family had come home in the night   in the night   you were still sitting there   quietly thinking   reflecting   the light from the moon filtered into the front room   you sat, you sat: I say, Get down on your knees and pray.

I remember how you had told me that you had walked into the front room observing   your family   you had approached your wife   quietly   you had reached out and touched her round smooth shoulders   you had looked directly into her eyes from here   you stood   you stood: I say, Embrace your wife.

From here

Come to the night, the night that dances many canyons

From here

Come to the night, the night that sings many languages

I remember how you had told me that each minute passed slowly   like the sands of an hourglass   you slept soundly   you found it harder and harder to breathe clean breath   you continued to lay there   turning   gently   on your side   you were sure that it would pass   like before   in the distant past   you lay there, lay there: I say, Get up and walk forward.

Dear Father, you worked so hard   in your lifetime   your lifeline   out there   in the thick, thick woods   in your youth   yet you were paid very little money for your labor labor there among the woods there among the hills there among the mesas of Colorado, here far up as from our bare hills of Utah the endless dust the dust you had to breathe as Mom prepared the evening meal for you for me in the early morning hours the twilight hours you in your laughter your youth you had lifted me high up in the air squealing I had felt so happy! you had laughed also loudly proudly you had done this, my dear father, come to me.

I remember how you used to get up at the crack of dawn the early morning hours just to haul water from the nearest well I remember now how it appeared to be a miracle just to have any kind of water at all there on the lands bare lands of Utah the section that is forgotten, my dear father, go to the river.

The land where the *Diné* were located, got relocated, times before in the distant past when my grandmother was but a young vibrant girl wearing her moccasins singing her songs carrying her gourd I remember now, of these things.

(Chanting, drumming . . .)

Dear Father, I remember how you watered your tomato plants the last summer you walked the earth of the Indians how you watered your plants very early when dawn was still captured in the hills . . . I remember how the tomato plants grew twice their size that summer when you passed on the joy was there among us your children but you were not there then and the goats roamed the lands of Utah, I remember of these things now, my father, go into the hills.

The night is warm you are on your side on your bed looking contented you are breathing quietly a lone cracker lies by your side Outside the desert winds moan their agonies lightning lights up the nighttime sky the canyons stand in place shadows outline the hills bare of trees . . . the moist air air we speak of you we see impending rains we see the waters coming . . .

Dear Father, I remember the first time you had discovered that you had asthma I remember how you asked me to walk with you to go into the thick woods the forest lands of Colorado I was little then I wondered back then: Why, my father? I remember how you ran from tree to tree out there in the dark dark woods I remember how you had me wait for you out there in the stillness of the darkness how I saw bluebirds fly by how I saw golden eagles encircle my young body there in the mountains, my dear father, come to the red desert rocks now.

You were a proud man you were proud of your home you had wanted to build a fence around your home you were proud of your tall tall trees you had planted trees around your home   back in the sixties   you had wanted to plant more trees, more trees . . .

Sometime   in the night   your arms became numb   yes   there among the winds the rains   the desert leaves   there   very very slowly   very very slowly   your arms had become more numb   They had that familiar ache   that familiar dullness   you've felt this feeling before   your breathing became shallow   your lungs had filled with fluids the winds scattered dust   in all directions   that night   slowly   oh so slowly   you began to stir   you moved sideways   you stumbled into the front room   the ladies had slept quietly   to the side   caught in their dreams, my father, my father, come to the road.

From here

Come to the night: the night that speaks many voices

From here

Come to the night: the night that cries many tears

Dear Father, it rained the night you passed away   on   on to the other side   it rained I listened carefully   that night   I listened carefully   the day after   I listened carefully into the next night   I listened carefully   counting the drops   I lay there   in the back room listening to voices   strange sounding voices drifting from the kitchen . . . I heard my little brother crying his last tears   silently, my dear father, come to the mountains.

From here

Come to the room: the room that holds many memories

From here

Come to the room: the room that holds many voices

Dear Father, you told everyone   anyone   who would listen that your right arm was becoming numb   that you didn't feel anything   though   you continued to tend to your sheep   your goats   out there   on desert lands   you continued to walk your miles   you continued to gather your horses in   days before, my dear father, go to the lands of your forefathers.

MY YOUNG sister, Juanita, here   come away from the rivers   there   here   go there hold your father gently   it is you who held him that night   the night he took his last breath, remember this, my young sister.

My young sister, Juanita, here   come away from the waters there   here   hold your mother's shoulders   speak to her directly   She is feeling lost   your mother is standing there   at the door: *"Nihima lah Ha'at'iih Nih?"* What is your mother saying were his last words, remember this, my young sister.

My young sister, Juanita, remember how you held him gently   with your mother the night he slumped over in the front room   remember now, how   you ran into the front room   wanting to hold him   *"Yeego Shiinota',* Hold me tightly,"   he had said to you   remember this, my young sister.

My young sister, Juanita, remember these things for they will take you   to the canyons of Utah   the desert floors of Arizona   the high mesas of New Mexico   the Rocky Mountains of Colorado   remember this, my young sister.

My young sister, Juanita, you have the great need to sprinkle the yellow corn pollen within the Four Sacred Lands   the mountains   you have the great need to sprinkle the corn pollen along the roads he had walked   he had traveled   in his lifetime   paths to greater lands   from here   paths to greater stars   paths to greater galaxies   you have the need to do this, my sister.

You are on a land   far away from here   your wife/our mother   she still walks her canyons   the hills   the mesas   of Utah   looking for you . . .

My mother   she still stands in the doorway   wanting to see you   you in your other land   your land   amongst the nighttime skies   the galaxies   the stars   the eagles   they have come   they will continue to come, from here.

You are on a land   far away   far away from here   from here   There amongst the Tawaoc Mountains   there to the eastern skies   here amongst the arroyos of desert lands   there within the Four Directions   the Four Sacred Ways of the Diné Life.

Dear Father, it has been eight years since you passed on   since you left us   since you took your last breath   there in the hills   amongst the thunders of Utah   here where I sit   here where I reflect upon your years   with us   your children of Utah lands . . .   Near the Four Corners area . . .   I see you in my eyes   my mind   my heart, I see you,

there, out there, in the hills. . . .

Tight Places

RUTH I. KERN

RUTH I. KERN, 51, "followed her bliss" twenty-four years ago when she loaded her two small children and her cat into her car, hooked up the trailer, and left Long Island for Arizona. She has found that the desert and the heat are where she belongs. She lives in Phoenix, where she has directed an on-sight senior nutrition program, initiated a Meals-on-Wheels program for shut-ins (including inmates), directed a food bank, and become increasingly interested in the archaeology and anthropology of the Southwest. Although her nonfiction has been published in a variety of magazines, she didn't become a fiction writer until four years ago. Her stories have placed in several national writing competitions, and she is at work on a historical novel.

THE YOUNG NAVAJO SITS in my front doorway and chants a greeting to the rising sun, "Our Father." I know he's struggling for *hózhǫ́,* inner balance. I sidle past him, my eyes averted, careful not to disturb his quietude as I leave for work. Shadow, my black and white cockapoo, lies at his feet. She lifts her head and gives me a low whine of greeting as I pass. Reuben places his hand on her back and Shadow snuggles into his bare feet and stills. A mysterious bond unites them that I can't comprehend. The dog, loyal to me for seven years, skittish with visitors, unfriendly to every date, has now apparently shifted loyalty to this Indian lad. I broke the rules for county employees when I signed Reuben out of Cross Roads, a recovery house for alcoholics in Peoria, and spirited him away to Phoenix three weeks ago.

I start my car and look back towards the condo. His arms are still raised to the sky. I remember how we drove the twenty-three miles to my condo, the thump of the windshield wipers the only sound in the car, Reuben stone-still next to me, a bundle of clothing at his feet, his fingers holding tight to the art supplies I'd bought him a week earlier. Even from my driveway the facial wounds he suffered during a bar fight still glow an ugly wine red. Thirty-eight sutures tattoo his brow and lip, a reminder of a broken beer bottle across the face. His coal-black hair, an unruly mane, is held in place by a stained sweatband. Though his hair nearly reaches his shoulders, his bangs are cut short across his forehead. He looks much younger than twenty-two. A waif in tight jeans and T-shirt.

My inspection rounds include the rural halfway house I found him in. Fifty-seven street winos, toothless, coughing, wrinkled, scarred from street and jail fights, march reluctantly to AA meetings twice a day. No place for a smooth-faced Navajo boy raised on a reservation. For a month I visit him in those cramped barracks. In my six years as a community service worker for the county, I've never dealt with an Indian client. I read his report. Twenty-two years old, full-blooded Navajo. No address. No phone. No job. Refused to name any next of kin. Six arrests in two years. Drunk and disorderly. Brawler. I sit across from him at an AA meeting while men stand up sing-songing, "My name is Bill and I'm an alcoholic . . ."

Reuben sits close to the door ready to bolt if confronted. I can smell his fear. I know his heart pounds, that his mouth is dry. I try to imagine him in the mountains where you can smell the rain coming, his raven-wing hair flying in the wind, a shepherd boy herding sheep, gathering piñon nuts. Endless space. No boundaries of property lines and fences, only red cliffs and yellow meadows. I peer over at him. He never moves. Nothing makes sense. Grandfather Sky and Mother Earth embracing, traded for a walled-in city of dead-ends, bar brawls, sleeping in alleys, a life of unshaven, smelly men puking into gutters. I glance uneasily about the room at vacant eyes, wet brains, open sores, shaking hands wrapped around a chipped coffee mug. I squirm in discomfort, wanting to shield him from this brutal world. This can't be his destiny, too. Not this little-boy face under black bangs, with his thin, malnourished body and the delicate artist fingers that draw on any scrap of paper they can find.

I devise his escape. I bring him gifts of paper, chalk, charcoal, and paints. With these I draw him to me like the Pied Piper of Hamlin. But behind those hopeful eyes lies suspicion. I'm whitey, the enemy. But he has no way out. He comes.

I park the car under the carport. He gets out and slowly follows me toward a row of brick condos. He hesitates at the door and checks for direction. "East," he says, breathing a sigh of relief. "This is good, Alis."

A fortunate turn of events. Our smiles meet, then embarrassed we quickly go inside. I give him the spare room. More walls, I suddenly realize. He says nothing as he disappears into his new prison.

I offer him food, clean clothes, drawing material but we have little to say to each other. On the few occasions we speak, it is friendly enough, polite, but the words are edged in wariness. Our only common ground is the dog.

He draws feverishly for hours at a time, painting landscapes full of sheep; a Navajo woman weaving; the same woman spinning wool; the same Indian woman a dozen times. Is this his love? I wonder. I have nothing tangible to hang onto, no case studies to refer to that would explain what this Navajo is thinking. While he showers I slip into his room and pick up the drawings, carefully studying them for clues about this man-child, locked into a life now with a thirty-eight-year-old white woman. When he's not painting he's playing his harmonica or walking the boundaries of my block-walled yard, Shadow at his heels. He does the same in the house. I come home each day to rows of footprints in the plush carpet.

No one at work asks about Reuben and I am relieved. No call comes from the halfway house demanding a supervisor's questions. One less drunk to worry about. They are relieved, I'm sure, that they don't have to deal with an Indian alcoholic.

I arrive home late. Father Sun has fallen behind the mountains to the west. The moon, a white half-circle in the sky, hangs there reluctantly. A sprinkling of stars struggles to be seen through the valley haze. It's warm for the first of March—just a slight chill hangs in the air. I see the arcadia door is ajar. Several insects are buzzing about the kitchen. Annoyed, I move to close the door tight when the sound of harmonica music wafts towards me. I peer out into the darkness. Reuben lies on the dead grass blowing an unrecognizable tune, face under the great dipper, Shadow's head on his belly.

He doesn't see me. I back off. Exhausted by the long day and by the strain of this strange standoff with my houseguest, I get ready for bed. I fall into a half-sleep, restless with dreams of drunks and Indian shepherds.

The temperature falls the next day and the rains come. Toward evening I light a fire in the fireplace to take the chill off the room. It is Sunday. I read the paper and doze. Sensing a presence I start awake. He's squatting next to me. I force myself to full consciousness. He wants something.

"Yes?" I swing myself into an upright position.

He ignores the question. Instead, he gathers his knees to his chest, wraps them in his arms, and stares into the crackling fire.

An aura of expectancy washes over me, the same feeling that comes before a storm. A knowing something is about to happen. I gasp for air and realize I've been holding my breath. I join him on the floor; the heat of the fire flushes our faces. Time slows, then stops like my breathing. Shadow snuggles between us. Our hands move over her curly fur, touching suddenly. He does not flinch, nor pull back in distrust. We're on holy ground. Sacred space. I'm making contact with a mountain spirit. Be careful, I warn myself, don't break the mood with silly conversation.

After I add logs to the fire for the third time he speaks. "My mother wailed the day my draft notice came. She embraced me," and, remembering he speaks to an outsider, he politely adds, "the Navajo Way, arm about my waist, head lying on my shoulder." He taps his right shoulder as he speaks. His eyes say he feels the weight of her head, the pressure of her arm, her warmth, still.

"I am the eldest son of twelve children and, being the first, am her favorite. Some have said I see through my mother's eyes." Reverence surrounds the words *my mother* like a halo.

I see her in the firelight stirring mutton stew, child on her back. I am mute with respect. I can only nod my encouragement to continue.

"I return from boot camp at the beginning of summer, in the time for the rain ceremonies. But I am not happy. My orders say Vietnam. Twice I have a dream foretelling my death. Twice I see myself wounded in battle in that foreign place, my broken body stuffed into a body bag and piled with others to ship home."

The back of his hand reaches for his eyes; I know there are tears. I stroke Shadow to avoid embarrassing him with a stare. A thousand years of history sits beside me, sinking into me. I fuse with a people climbing up through four worlds into the fifth, and know a time when the world, not quite finished, waited for the mysterious power of motion to stir it to life.

He regains his composure and continues. "I arrive at Tonalea. My mother awaits me at the hogan entrance, dressed in her best velvet shirt and taffeta skirt, her silver and turquoise blazing in the sun. She is beautiful, my mother, even with her belly swollen with the thirteenth child, sixth by her second husband. My heart runs to her but I hold back, walking slowing up the slope surrounded by my brothers. I must not break step.

"Later, under the stars, we walk the slope alone. I share my dream. She listens hard but says nothing that night or the next. But I know she thinks of this each day as she weaves. My mother works her rug the old way. She knows to keep her designs open so not to weave her spirit in. I sit and watch, my mind on the upper right corner. When she finishes the pattern she will run one gray thread across the border to serve as a 'path.' While she works she tells me stories of finding good plants for colors. She tells me of her own mother, and her mother before her. She is proud of so many generations of expert weavers. She is full of stories. My sister Lucy listens and learns as my mother did.

"Only on my last day home, after the earth has cooled off under the stars, does she speak to the dream and then it is around it. She reminds me how the mist people climbed out of the first world and changed into men and beasts. She reminds me it was the wind that gave people life. How it breathed into our mouths and woke us. How it leaves us when we die. 'During the rain ceremony,' she told me, 'when I placed my stone offering in the hogan, I had a vision of you as an old man. The wind still lived in your mouth. My heart soared like a hawk. I knew my first child by the husband of my choice will come home again to his birthplace. It was revealed to me how this could be. You will not die in battle, I promise you, my Handsome Boy.'

"She uses her private name for me and I know that she understands my tight place. I want to give her a gift of thanks for the joy she gives me but I dare not. You must never repay someone who helps you through a tight spot. I must not insult my mother. I leave at dawn without a goodbye.

"Back at camp we pack our gear. My eyes burn with fever and my arm aches from the shots. The war settles heavy over the camp, it is no longer just talk, it is alive and clings to everyone. All the soldiers are jumpy and pushy. We will leave in two days.

"A telegram arrives. My mother has died in childbirth. I am to go home immediately, the officers tell me. I am to be discharged on a hardship. The men gather round me. Their words like a rush of wind in my ears. 'Lucky you, man. You're out of this place.'

"A white corporal grumbles in my face, 'Yeah, back to the easy life for you, Injun. Minorities get all the luck.'

"Luck? My home is empty. I can't breathe. I can hear the women weeping. I can smell the fires of her funeral pyre. I will never see my mother again. The sky closes down on me like the lid of a coffin. I run to a quiet place in the shelter of some trees and vomit. I slide down a tree trunk and sit there panting, my mother's last words ringing in my head, "You will not die, Handsome Boy.' And then I realize what she has done. "

He sees the question in my eyes.

"Our people say if you love someone enough you can trade deaths with them." His voice quivers then breaks. "I know my mother bargained to take my place. I have been in a tight place for two years over this." His head drops to his knees, his hair falls over his face, covering it.

His tight place is now mine. It presses down on my shoulders and chest until I can't bear the weight. I fight for the words to lift this off of me. I wet my lips, resisting the urge to reach out and touch him, put his head on my breast and weep with him. I want to say, your mother didn't die for you. She died from the burden of carrying thirteen children. What superstitious nonsense to think she could die in your place. It was only a twist of fate. But what I believe doesn't matter. He believes this. And how am I so sure I'm right? How do I know love isn't this powerful? His bent back rising and falling with sorrow says it is true. I am envious of his pain. No one in my life has touched me that much. But he must regain his life. He needs strong medicine and I feel impotent. Our Father, help me, I think. Moments tick by. I now know how far love will go and I am humbled by it. How can anything I say matter after that? But the words spill out anyway before I can stop them.

"Reuben," I say softly, as if praying.

His head jerks back. Dead eyes.

My courage almost fails me. I have to look away to continue. "Reuben, if this is so, that your mother chose to die in your place, and you know it to be true—do not waste her gift. Her life is yours now. Use it well."

That's all the words I can think of. I dread seeing his eyes but I have to look. A small light glints in them but I can't be sure it isn't firelight. I stoke the dying embers.

He mutters something under his breath about a sing, a Shooting Chant.

I spin around. "What?"

He gets up. "Navajo medicine is stronger than your white medicine," he says, and goes to his room.

I am alone. A log crashes off the andirons and bursts into a spray of glowing cinders. I have no interest in putting it right. Defeated, I drag myself to bed.

For several hours strains of harmonica music float under my door. I drift off to sleep on the rising and falling notes. I oversleep and am late leaving for work in the morning. His door is still shut.

I come home after a long evening meeting to empty closets and rooms. No Reuben. No Shadow. Just silence as vast as a canyon. It comes to me as I stand there surrounded by emptiness, why eagles cry as they lift and fall on cushions of air. Not even an eagle can stand such crushing loneliness. "Traitor," I scream as I throw the mail against the wall. "You ungrateful drunk. I gave you shelter and food. And you leave without a word of thanks. But worst of all you stole my little dog!" The urge to jump in my car and drive through the Deuce, checking alleys and parks, fills me. A wino will sell anything he can lay his hands on for a drink. He will sell my dog for a bottle of Thunderbird. But I go nowhere; it would be fruitless to go out into the night, and dangerous alone.

I march back into his room. What else will I discover missing? But there is nothing else gone—just his things and the dog. I sift through the litter in his wastepaper basket for clues—about what I'm not sure. I smooth out several papers on the carpet. Sketches. The first three of the woman weaving, his mother, I know now. The fourth is my face staring back at me. It's so honest I'm uncomfortable, yet something about the eyes is wrong—yet familiar. I'm too aggravated to think. I shove the drawings into my back pocket and go heat a TV dinner in the microwave. In bed, sleep refuses to come and release me from my thoughts. The emptiness of the silence is a reminder of my betrayal. I go sit in my front doorway listening to the hum of traffic and await the sunrise. The hurt and anger insulate me against the chill. I sulk, ashamed that I was conned by an alcoholic, taken in by a child's face. I doze fitfully, head against the jamb.

A car muffler backfires and I start awake. The sky glows lavender, then bright pink. The sun has not yet made an appearance. The changing hues of the sky cast a spell over me. I forget my aching back, my cramped legs. I lean back and something pokes me in the spine. I pull the drawings from my back pocket and smooth them out across my thighs. In the faint light I reflect on the sketches. It comes to me why my portrait disturbed me. He has made our eyes the same—his mother's and mine. With great respect I lay the drawing beside me and raise my arms towards the east. I squint at the sun, Our Father, his forehead now visible between two gray mountain peaks. A starling cries out, another answers. Then songbirds join in.

The sun is rising on the Reservation, too, I think. I close my eyes to red mountains and blowing sands, sheep dropping young. I can smell spring coming on the Blue Wind. Reuben appears, driving a herd of sheep across the horizon, Shadow at his heels. No boundaries. No fences. Clouds for a ceiling, grass for their feet. I hope that's where they have gone, my two runaways, to find a medicine stronger than mine.

Strays

LUCIA BERLIN

LUCIA BERLIN was born in Juneau, Alaska, in 1936. As a young child she lived in mining camps in Montana, Idaho, Arizona, and Kentucky; her adolescent years were spent in Santiago, Chile. Her undergraduate and gradutae degrees are from the University of New Mexico. She lived for many years in Oakland, California, teaching writing at the San Francisco County Jail, and now teaches at the University of Colorado in Boulder, where she resides. She often sees place as an actual protagonist in her work. She has published several short story collections, including Angels Laundromat; Phantom Pain; Safe and Sound; Homesick: New and Selected Stories; *and her latest,* So Long: Stories 1987–1992.

GOT INTO ALBUQUERQUE FROM Baton Rouge. It was about two in the morning. Whipping wind. That's what the wind does in Albuquerque. I hung out at the Greyhound station until a cab driver showed up who had so many prison tattoos I figured I could score & he'd tell me where to stay. He turned me on, took me to a pad, a *noria* they call it there, in the south valley. I lucked out meeting him, Noodles. I couldn't have picked a worse place to run to than Albuquerque. Chicanos control the town. *Mayates*, they can't score at all, are lucky not to be killed. Some white guys, with enough long joint time to have been tested. White women, forget it, they don't last. Only way, and Noodles helped me there too, was to get hooked up with a big connection, like I did with Nacho. Then nobody could hurt me. What a pitiful thing I just said. Nacho was a saint, which may seem hard to believe. He did a lot for Brown Berets, for the whole Chicano community, young people, old people. I don't know where he is now. He skipped bail. I mean a huge bail. He shot a narc, Marquez, five times, in the back. The jury didn't think he was a saint, but Robin Hood maybe, because they only gave him manslaughter. I wish I knew where he was. I got busted about the same time, for needle marks.

All this happened many years ago or I couldn't even be talking about it. In those days you could end up with five or ten years for just a roach or marks.

It was when the first methadone rehabilitation programs were starting. I got sent to one of the pilot projects. Six months at La Vida instead of years in "la pinta," the state prison in Santa Fe. Twenty other addicts got the same deal. We all arrived in an old yellow school bus at La Vida. A pack of wild dogs met the bus, snarling and baying at us until finally they loped off into the dust.

La Vida was thirty miles out of Albuquerque. In the desert. Nothing around, not a tree, not a bush. Route 66 was too far to walk to. La Vida had been a radar site, a military installation during World War II. It had been abandoned since them. I mean abandoned. We were going to restore it.

We stood around in the wind, in the glare of the sun. Just the gigantic radar disc towering over the whole place, the only shade. Fallen down barracks. Torn and rusted venetian blinds rattling in the wind. Pin-ups peeled off the walls. Three- or four-foot sand dunes in every room. Dunes, with waves & patterns like in postcards from the Painted Desert.

A lot of things were going to contribute to our rehabilitation. Number one was removing us from the street environment. Every time a counselor said that we laughed ourselves silly. We couldn't see any roads, much less streets, and the streets in the compound were buried in sand. There were tables in the dining rooms and cots in the barracks but they were buried too. Toilets clogged with dead animals and more sand.

You could only hear the wind and the pack of dogs that kept circling. Sometimes it was nice, the silence, except the radar discs kept turning with a whining petty kneeing, day and night, day and night. At first it freaked us out, but after awhile it grew comforting, like wind chimes. They said it had been used to intercept Japanese kamikaze pilots, but they said a lot of pretty weird things.

Of course the major part of our rehab was going to be honest work. The satisfaction of a job well done. Learning to interact. Teamwork. This teamwork started when we lined up for our methadone at six every morning. After breakfast we worked until lunchtime. Group from two until five, more group from seven to ten.

The purpose of these groups was to break us down. Our main problems were anger, arrogance, defiance. We lied and cheated and stole. There were daily "haircuts" where groups screamed at one person all his faults and weaknesses.

We were beaten down until we finally cried uncle. Who the fuck was uncle? See, I'm still angry, arrogant. I was ten minutes late to group & they shaved my eyebrows and cut my eyelashes.

The groups dealt with anger. All day long we dropped slips in a slip box saying who we were angry at and then in group we dealt with it. Mostly we just shouted what losers and fuck-ups everyone else was. But see, we all did lie and cheat. Half the time none of us was even mad, just shucking & jiving up some anger to play the group game, to stay at La Vida and not go to jail. Most of the slips were at Bobby, the cook, for feeding those wild dogs. Or things like Greñas doesn't weed enough, he just smokes and pushes tumbleweeds around with a rake.

We were mad at those dogs. Lines of us at six a.m. and at one and six outside the dining room. Whipping sand wind. We'd be tired and hungry. Freezing in the morning and hot in the afternoon. Bobby would wait, finally stroll across his floor like a smug bank official to unlock the door for us. And while we waited, a few feet away, at the kitchen door, the dogs would be waiting too, for him to throw them slops. Mangy, motley, ugly dogs people had abandoned out on the mesa. The dogs liked Bobby all right but they hated us, baring their teeth & snarling, day after day, meal after meal.

I got moved from the laundry to the kitchen. Helping cook, dishwashing, and mopping up. I felt better about Bobby after awhile. I even felt better about the dogs. He named them all. Dumb names. Duke, Spot, Blackie, Gimp, Shorty. And Liza, his favorite. An old yellow cur, flat-headed, with huge bat-like ears and amber yellow eyes. After a few months she'd even eat out of his hand. "Sunshine! Liza, my yellow-eyed sun," he used to croon to her. Finally she let him scratch behind her ugly ears and just above the long ratty tail that hung down between her legs. "My sweet sweet sunshine," he'd say.

Government money kept sending in people to do workshops with us. A lady who did a workshop about Families. As if any of us ever had a family. And some guy from Synanon who said our problem was our cool. His favorite expression was "When you think you're looking good you're looking bad." Every day he has us "blow our image." Which was just acting like fools.

We got a gym and a pool table, weights and punching bags. Two color televisions.

A basketball court, a bowling alley, and a tennis court. Framed paintings by Georgia O'Keeffe. Monet's *Water Lilies*. Soon a Hollywood movie company was coming, to make a science fiction film at the site. We would be able to work as extras and make some money. The movie was going to center around the radar disc & what it did to Angie Dickinson. It fell in love with her and took her soul when she died in a car wreck. It would take over all these other live souls, too, who would be La Vida residents, us. I've seen it about twenty times, in the middle of the night, on TV.

All in all the first three months went pretty well. We were clean and healthy; we worked hard. The site was in great shape. We got pretty close to each other and we did get angry. But for those first three months we were in total isolation. Nobody came in and nobody went out. No phone calls, no newspapers, no mail, no television. Things started falling apart when that ended. People went on passes and had dirty urines when they got back, or they didn't come back at all. New residents kept coming in, but they didn't have the sense of pride we had about the place.

Every day we had a morning meeting. Part gripe session, part snitch session. We also had to take turns speaking, even if it was just telling a joke or singing a song. But nobody could ever think of anything, so at least twice a week old Lyle Tanner sang "I thought I saw a whip-poor-will." "El Sapo" gave a talk on how to breed chihuahuas, which was gross. Sexy kept on reciting the Twenty-Third Psalm. Only the way she caressed the words it sounded lewd and everybody laughed, which hurt her feelings.

Sexy's name was a joke. She was an old whore from Mexico. She hadn't come with the first group of us, but later, after five days in solitary with no food. Bobby made her soup and some bacon and eggs. But all she wanted was bread. She sat there & ate three loaves of Wonder Bread, not even chewing it, just swallowing it, famished. Bobby gave the soup and bacon and eggs to Liza.

Sexy kept on eating until finally I took her to our room and she collapsed. Lydia and Sherry were in bed together in the next room. They had been lovers for years. I could tell by their slow laughs that they were high on something, reds or ludes probably. I went back to the kitchen to help Bobby clean up. Gabe, the counselor, came in to get the knives, to lock them up in the safe. He did that every night.

"I'm going to town. You're in charge, Bobby." There never were any staff members at night anymore.

Bobby and I went out to drink coffee under the chinaberry tree. The dogs yelped after something on the mesa.

"I'm glad Sexy came. She's nice."

"She's OK. She won't stay."

"She reminds me of Liza."

"Liza's not that ugly. Oye, Tina, be still. It's almost here."

The moon. There's no other moon like one on a clear New Mexico night. It rises over the Sandias and soothes the miles and miles of barren desert with all the quiet whiteness of a first snow. Moonlight in Liza's yellow eyes and the chinaberry tree.

The world just goes along. Nothing much matters, you know? I mean really matters. But then sometimes, just for a second, you get this grace, this belief that it does matter, a whole lot.

He felt that way too. I heard the catch in his throat. Some people may have said a prayer, knelt down, at a moment like that. Sung a hymn. Maybe cavemen would have done a dance. What we did was make love. "El Sapo" busted us. Later, but we were still naked.

So it came out at morning meeting and we had to get a punishment. Three weeks, after cleaning the kitchen, to strip and sand all the paint around the dining room windows. Until one in the morning, every single night. That was bad enough but then Bobby, trying to save his ass, got up and said, "I didn't want to ball Tina. I just want to stay clean, do my time, and go home to my wife Debbi and my baby Debbi-Ann." I could have dropped a slip on those two jive names.

That hurt bad. He had held me and talked to me. He had gone to a lot more trouble making love than most men do and I had been happy with him when the moon came up.

We had to work so hard there wasn't time to talk. I would never have let him know how bad it hurt anyway. We were tired, bone tired every night, all day.

The main thing we hadn't talked about was the dogs. They hadn't shown up for three nights.

Finally I said it. "Where do you think the dogs are?"

He shrugged. "A puma. Kids with guns."

We went back to sanding. It got too late even to go to bed so we made some fresh coffee and sat down under the tree.

I missed Sexy. I forgot to say that she had gone to town to the dentist but had managed to score, got busted and taken back to jail.

"I miss Sexy. Bobby, that was a lie what you said at morning meeting. You did so want to ball me."

"Yeah, it was a lie."

We went into the meat locker & held each other again, made love again but not for long because it was freezing cold. We went back outside.

The dogs started coming. Shorty, Blackie, Spot, Duke.

They had gotten into porcupines. Must have been days ago because they were all so infected, septic. Their faces swollen like monster rhinoceros, oozing green pus. Their eyes were bloated shut, quilled shut with tiny arrows. That was the scary part, that none of them could see. Or make a real sound since their throats were engorged too.

Blackie had a seizure. Hurtled up into the air with an eerie gargle. Thrashing, jerking, peeing in the air. High, two, three feet into the air and then he fell wet, dead, into the dust. Liza came in last because she couldn't walk, just crawled until she got to Bobby's feet, writhed there, her paw patting at his boot.

"Get me the goddam knives."

"Gabe's not back yet." Only counselors could unlock the safe.

Liza pawed at Bobby's foot, gentle, like asking to be petted, for him to throw her a ball.

Bobby went to the locker and brought out a steak. The sky was lavender. It was almost morning.

He had the dogs smell the meat. He called to them, cooed to them to follow him across the road to the machine shop. I stayed under the tree.

When he was in there, when he finally got them all in there, he beat them to death with a sledge hammer. I didn't see it, but I heard it and from where I sat I saw the blood spattering and streaking down the walls. I thought he would say something like "Liza, my sweet sunshine" but he didn't say a world. When he came out he was covered in blood, didn't look to me, went to the barracks.

The nurse drove up with doses of methadone and everybody started lining up for breakfast. I turned the griddle on and started making batter. Everybody was mad because I took so long with breakfast.

There still wasn't any staff around when the movie trailers started pulling in.

They began working right away, checking out locations, casting extras. People were running around with megaphones and walkie-talkies. Somehow nobody went into the machine shop.

They started one scene right away . . . a take of a stunt man who was supposed to be Angie Dickinson driving down from the gym while a helicopter hovered around the radar disc. The car was supposed to crash to the disc and Angie's spirit fly up into it but the car crashed into the chinaberry tree.

Bobby and I made lunch, so tired we were walking in slow motion, just like all the zombie extras were being told to walk. We didn't talk. Once, making tuna salad I said out loud, to myself, "Pickle relish?"

"What did you say?"

"I said pickle relish."

"Christ. Pickle relish!" We laughed, couldn't stop laughing. He touched my cheek, lightly, a bird's wing.

The movie crew thought the radar site was fab, far out. Angie Dickinson liked my eye shadow. I told her it was just chalk, the kind you rub on pool cues. "It's to die for, that blue," she said to me.

After lunch, an old gaffer, whatever that is, came up to me and asked where the nearest bar was. There was a place up the road, toward Gallup, but I told him Albuquerque. I told him I would do anything to get a ride into town.

"Don't worry about that. Hop in my truck and let's go."

Wham, crash, bang.

"Good God, what was that?" he asked.

"A cattle guard."

"Jesus, this sure is one godforsaken place."

We finally hit the highway. It was great, the sound of tires on the cement, the wind blowing in. Semis, bumper stickers, kids fighting in back seats. Route 66.

We got to the rise, with the wide valley and the Rio Grande below us, the Sandia mountains lovely above.

"Mister, what I need is money for a ticket home to Baton Rouge. Can you spare it, about sixty dollars?"

"Easy. You need a ticket. I need a drink. It will all work out."

El Ojito del Muerto

(Eye of the Dead One)

MELISSA PRITCHARD

MELISSA PRITCHARD, 45, a California native, lived in New Mexico in the seventies. She returned to Taos in 1988 and purchased a pair of red cowboy boots and an overweight spotted horse named Pal. The horse stayed in Taos with her ex-husband, the boots are somewhere in the back of her closet, but the personality of the high-spirited girl to whom she reconnected remains intact. Her work has appeared in such noted anthologies as Prize Stories: The O'Henry Awards *and* Best of the West. *Winner of the Flannery O'Connor Award for her book* Spirit Seizures *and author of the novel* Phoenix, *Melissa teaches in the creative writing program at Arizona State University. Her second collection,* The Instinct for Bliss, *will be published in 1995 by Zoland Books.*

OBEDIENT TO BLITHELY IMPERIOUS daughters wedging her into an orchid prom dress, the oldest tourniqueting a lace dresser scarf about her throat, the youngest hopping on the bed with Tinkerbell makeup, blotching frosted lavender above the eyes, fuschia on and off the lips, bulls'-eyes of rouge over the cheeks, the conclusive irony of a rhinestone tiara clamped on her middle-aged head, amusing her. Indulgent to children she adores, resigned to a life she had hoped to love.

With theatric pomp for so small a circumstance, they lead her, white half-slips on their heads, black polyester skirts belted against their chests, draping in stubby columns to the floor. Nuns. Freshly enrolled in Catholic school, her daughters compulsively act out ritual, impose doctrine. Tchaikovsky's *Swan Lake*, gargling and tinny, accompanies them from the Fisher Price record player to the arched entry of an adobe living room where Alan, her husband, and the young Hispanic man are re-mudding a corner fireplace.

Her youngest tugs her, trepid and embarrassed, off the top step, while the oldest makes trumpeting sounds.

"Hey Dad. Check out Mom. We made her beautiful."

The young man turns to see. Their father crooks his head out of the fireplace, smiles, asks about lunch.

Orchid taffeta rustles under the baggy, knee-length gray sweatshirt as she serves lunch. She watches the young man dump half a jar of salsa on his hamburger, hears him say he'd like to take off work tomorrow and go hunting. She observes Alan, an ecologically hypersensitive man, in his favorite T-shirt, "Don't Eat Anything with a Face," hypocritically vegetarian, scarfing down two hamburgers.

Perched on the counter, she swings her feet, swishing the taffeta loud, on purpose.

"Gee, I'd like to go. What is it you're hunting?"

"Deer."

Alan scrapes his chair back.

"Well, you two go hunting, shoot up a storm, though I'm adamantly opposed to the decimation of wildlife, and I hope you don't come across anything but trees, rocks, and roadkill, all that's left out there anyway."

He hikes up his pants, grins or grimaces, she can't tell most of the time, leaves the kitchen. From the living room, they hear him belch hugely before answering the phone, fielding yet another business call. Alan is a wildly successful tile manufacturer.

The young man brings his plate and her husband's to the sink, rinses them while looking at her, the frowzy dress, virulent makeup.

"Thank you. Lunch was excellent."

"You're quite welcome. I noticed you like salsa."

"Did you mean it about going hunting?"

"Yes, I really do want to go, but only if I don't have to kill anything. Have you heard of *Waiting for Godot?* It's this play where one of the characters, Vladimir, says 'Habit is a great deadener.' He's absolutely right. Since my last birthday, I've been breaking habits. If I go, I'll just watch, I'll be a hunting voyeur."

"That's fine, I'll come for you tomorrow at 4:30, so we can get to the mountains by first light. You have wool socks, gloves, long underwear?" He is scanning her body. "I have an extra pair of camouflage pants I got at the flea market, and an orange vest. I'll bring those for you."

"Do I bring the VCR? Just kidding. Can you imagine, home hunting videos?"

"No, that's OK. I'll bring everything."

SHE SETS out the girls' lunch, then watches them awhile from the living room window. They are kneeling inside the walled garden, beside an oval of fresh-dug dirt, profiles uptilted in morbid prayer. Her oldest intones from Alan's childhood Catholic missal, now an occult prop. Her youngest grips an unlit pink dinner candle. The pet cemetery is heavily overrun in the month they have been here. One cat, a road victim. Two birds, cat victims. And four lunch bags of shrivelling pet shop mice, tied and swaying like homemade ornaments from the arthritic crabapple. She won't ask, doesn't want to know. Children assault animals with wild swings of adoration and neglect.

SHE WATCHES out the same window, this time seeing his truck, headlights ploughing like twin stars up the driveway lined with brittle, naked elms. Her husband and children are asleep at the farthest black end of the hallway.

She has trouble with the camouflage pants, has to come out of the bathroom; he kneels to unknot and retie strings that gather around the ankles. "Long underwear?" She nods, embarrassed. He stands up. He has to touch her hips to secure the canteen, the hunting knife in its leather sheath. They whisper.

"What?"

"I feel like a female guerrilla."

"What's this?"

"What's what? Oh. An altar. The girls made it." She hands him a stick of incense. "They like playing church. Weddings with no groom. Funerals. Mostly funerals."

They walk out to the truck; purple-black, freckled with white mud, punched in numerous places. Red bandannas with black electrical tape bandage the broken taillights. In the truckbed are two chunks of cedar, a rotted tire, length of rope, plastic water jug, tricycle wheel, and four or five beer cans. She knows this even in darkness. Once when he had left it on their property to go fishing with friends, Alan had discovered her, sitting, just sitting in his truck. She'd made a lame excuse about getting out of the heat, which Alan distractedly, good-naturedly (naive for all his intelligence), accepted.

She gets in on his side, the other door broken, sidles under the steering wheel. The seat's caved in, stuffed with blankets and towels. Clumsy in her hunting regalia, she knocks the glove box so the front piece drops, hangs by a hinge. Receipts, cards, feathers, a box of bullets, she catches some in her hands, scoops the rest from the floor, apologizing.

Handing her the rifle, he gets in, slams the door. The truck clanks, rattles like a junk drawer; the heater abrades her face with silty, hot air. The gun is anchored across her lap, a Winchester 243, an elk etched into the oak butt, she traces it with her thumb. In the green and violet light off the dash, she watches him stick the incense where black vinyl has peeled down to bile-colored foam.

Heading into the mountains, in his truck, with its Clearasil-tinted interior, broken speedometer, needle gyrating, (Mach 10, we're at Mach 10, he says) . . . the highway a black current beneath the torn gear boot, candy wrappers, work gloves, rolls of electrical tape, toilet paper, sun-rotted parrot feathers fanning out of the visor, cat prints arrowing up the windshield, a yellow apple mushing against the windshield, binoculars, bullets, a Chinese noodle mix, the whole inside stinking of soured sponge, overheated plastic, and dead, crumbling styrofoam. He is telling a joke about two drunk mice and Elvis Presley.

"Coffee?" She lofts the thermos. "We can share from the cup-thingy on top."

"Sure." He navigates a dirt road sculpted with potholes and washboard gullies, saying he graded this road for the Forest Service two years before. Compressed against the roadsides are gothic, violet spires of ponderosa, streaks of white aspen. He is looking at her.

"What are you thinking?"

"How I was a member of the Canadian and American Wolf Defenders League, the Wild Horse and Burro Association, the Cousteau Society, the Sierra Club, how I had Save the Whale, Save the Turtle, what else, oh, Save the Dolphin stickers on my old station wagon in Illinois. I'm an environmentalist, so I'm feeling guilty. I'm also a conflicted vegetarian."

"Conflicted?"

"My mind rejects meat but my stomach won't."

"Well, we're not out here shooting animals for the sick thrill of it. My family's always hunted for survival; we use every part of the deer, the elk."

"You're saying you're not a sport hunter?"

"You bet. I'm not one of those guys who flies in not knowing wildlife from his own ass."

"I love deer. Actually I love armadillos. I was going to buy an armadillo, until somebody said they can give you leprosy. Can you believe it?"

He hits a deep gully and they both fly off the seat; her head grazes the ceiling and she slops coffee all over.

"Oops. Your pants, sorry. Camouflage works. They should make children's clothes out of this stuff."

He laughs. They've reached the mountaintop, fishtailing across a wide, grassy clearing. Behind a low, dark hump of mountains, light flows like spilt water, blurring perfect seams of fuschia, tangerine, violet. He stops the truck, and they sit together in an odd, detective-type silence.

"Look. There they are."

Gracefully he draws the rifle off her lap, rolls the window, pushes the barrel out, sighting. She doesn't see a thing, then four deer swiftly bearing down on the truck, passing in an elegant, dreamy arc. He draws the rifle in.

"Does. Flushed out from those woods over there."

"Do people shoot does?"

"Last year, one guy shot one from his truck, split her straight up the ass, got out, dragged her to the side of the road, took off. Idiot. Yeah, it happens."

The sun is on the mountain, the grass, the barbed fences steadily brightening.

"What do we do now?"

"Keep looking. Plus I'll teach you to shoot so you can go after your first deer."

"God, I really don't think I can do that." But she feels shamed by the eerie, sickening wish in herself that he accepts as natural.

The truck grinds, crawls. Once in a while, they pass hunters in other trucks and everyone waves, solemn, oath-like. She feels slightly bored, having imagined hunting as a sort of stalking through woods or crouching behind individual trees, not cruising in a truck, staring out dirt-crazed windows into greenish-black pools of trees and hazy stubble of oak, visually straining after a white flash of deer tail.

"Do they know? The deer?"

"That we're looking for them? You bet. They'll stash under rock ledges, or go with the elk after elk season's over."

"All I know is so far we've seen four does and entire herds of neutered beer cans."

They start counting cans. By the time they get to a hundred on both sides of the road, they're down to the highway, the sun on the center stripe the exact gold of fallen cottonwood leaves. Across the highway, a tarnished brass meadow holds cattle in matte, blackened clumps. He heads the truck up another Forest Service road, sunlight soaking the air, varnishing the sea-blue pines, hitting into flat red earth, pocked with white stone. Out her opened window, the air is thin and smells of turpentine. He stops, reads aloud a historic marker. *1540, Coronado's scouts, 1598, colonists used this road to settle New Spain. El Camino Real. Oldest road in the United States of America.*

The dirt road, thin as a hall, this oldest road, is piled and gouged with boulders. The truck shrieks up an increasingly precarious angle of ruts and clefts. Striking a partly submerged rock, it bucks, lists hideously to her side, stops. He yanks the brake, gets out, disappears by the tire on her side. She hears his voice.

"You're not gonna believe . . . "

"The tire came off . . . " She's joking.

His face comes up, a puppet in the stage of her window.

"Correct. We're thrown."

THEY ARE now peculiarly stuck on the oldest road in the United States of America. She helps as he calls for rocks to prop up the wrenched tire, directs him as he coasts the truck backward, downhill, swerving into a flat, weedy area, sits beside his camouflaged legs thrust from under the truck, leather boots sprawling up, hands him pliers, baling wire he happened to have. It's the steering rod mechanism, he's seen one of his uncles fix the same thing on his truck with wire and pliers.

"Did you know Hispanics buy parts cheap and can fix anything?" his voice muscles, cheerful, from under the truck.

"Nope. I didn't know that."

"Cheap parts because we don't have any money. Fix anything since we're smart. There. That should get us back to town."

Famished, they eat everything in his pack. Ham, cheese, oranges, Cheez-Its, peanut butter, green apples. He army-knifes an orange in a zig-zag design . . . there, a flower, presenting one pretty half to her. Lays Cheez-Its on the rough mountain grass, one corner against another, a flat formation of cracker butterflies. He shows her how to hold the Winchester, sight down the scope, pull back the trigger, shows her how to aim at an animal. A deer.

In the stifling truck, bumping cautiously, they pass a prim geometry of bicyclists in glistening black shorts, white helmets, colored flags snapping precisely. Her husband, Alan, is a bicycle racer. Competitive, ardent. She used to go to races with him, thinking at first how handsome he looked, later, how morose with competitive lust. Often he won. In Chicago, The Museum of Science and Industry had a gigantic human heart you could walk into, pressing buttons to hear the heart talk, explain itself. Her daughters used to pull her in and out of that heart, over and over. Right now, she remembers this.

She spots it first, standing on the highway's edge, in the restrained, verdigris light of early evening, so utterly still as to make her think it is false.

"Oh God."

He swerves the truck onto the gravel shoulder. "OK. Put your gun out the window, sight the way I showed you, and pull the trigger."

"I can't."

"Do it. Just the way I showed you."

She sights, seeing it in the little scope, a wire-thin cross over the concealed heart.

She misses, hits the neck. The deer stumbles, regains itself, weakly runs.

"Go after it. I'll find you. Go. Take the gun. You may have to shoot again, the way I showed you."

COMES UPON it in a sparse grass clearing, collapsed, doesn't understand whether to shoot or not. Dropping to her knees beside its head, she sees its antlers, white- tipped candelabra, the gorgeous eye fearful, her face miniaturized in its glazing surface. The breathing sounds hoarse, choppy, blood raveling from the earth side of the mouth. Her own breathing alters, suffers. She feels coarse, reverent. As a child, she'd rehearsed small, sweet cruelties on pets; now her daughters tenderly bully weaker creatures. She is exultant, stricken.

Standing above them, unsheathing his knife, he stoops to yank the deer so its exquisite head and sorrel neck slant downhill, slices the throat. Blood forming uneven collars around rocks, thickening, collecting, cherry red, stinking. Its eye open, hind legs kicking, still fleeing, tongue swelling between teeth. From the throat a marbling flood of air and blood.

He sits on his boot heels, wipes the blade edge along grass.

"Now we wait awhile for all the blood to drain. Want something to drink?"

She shakes her head.

"You all right?" Reaches over, sets a blood hand on her shoulder. "You're doing good. You feel sick? Quite a few people get sick at first, it's nothing to be embarrassed about. Wait here, I'm going to the truck to get a soda."

SEATED IN the company of death, blood thinning into arterial, still-exuberant rivers. She's been reading a book about medieval Spanish nuns, their journals, poetry. Reading about nuns chronically, tyrannically bled to take out the devil's afflictions. Affliction malefic in the blood.

He drinks his Coke, takes his knife, cuts its testicles.

"You can turn these inside out to cover gearshift knobs. People do that," he tells her. Hacks off what he calls 'stinkers' from the ankles, removing anything that taints the meat. Two of his thick, brown fingers spread in a V, two of his fingers and the knife cutting from the anus, the stomach left whole with its fermenting grasses, gutting to the throat. Opens its front legs, hauls out the esophagus, the lungs ripped from the rib cage, flung, grayish-pink, into sunlight. Harvesting intestines with square, bloodied hands. Steam climbs out from the deer, and a stink from gases caught between ribs and intestines. Lungs, guts, all the deer's arcane interior dumped out for scavenger birds, the deer's dark, complex interior broken and humid junk.

He halves the heart, and she pours water from the red and white plastic jug, laving the heart like a great, dark, broken bowl. The rinsed halves slide off his hand into a plastic bag. Disk of flat greenish liver, wine-colored kidneys, put with the heart, *asa duras*, he says. Delicious. His arms are brilliant red past the elbow. She floods water into the exposed cavity of deer, polishing the hollow of it.

Purpose graces his body, the shape of lowered head, the long hair, its curls like obsidian, with its bits of blue and red, the concentrated curve of spine, the deer's wildness perished and gone into him. Inordinate blood, red haze on the evening, the gray, languorous guts, the smell. She plants her two arms into the deer, into its pearled wreathing of ribs, arms chinese red and thick-smelling, her arms, her skin like his, purged of affliction.

He ropes the antlers and front feet together, and they drag the deer up through shrub to the road. Two hunters come by, help lift it into the truck bed. They speak Spanish, and do not look at her, which she thinks is politeness, respect, or hostility.

When he cleans her arms with a strip of torn shirt, both of them look at her arms smeared with blood. She thinks she has never seen her arms before, not really, their freckled pinkness, narrow wrists, work-thickened knuckles. Her hands look so much older than her arms, they embarrass her. She looks instead into his face, his eyes focus on her nails, wiping tendrils of deer's blood from the oval beds of her fingernails.

IN THE garage behind the house where he lives with his grandmother, aunt, and cousins, he uses rope to suspend the deer from a beam, begins to slice the hide, peel back the cape, exposing the meat. Like taking off tights, she thinks weirdly, obliquely, sitting on an old oil drum in one corner of the garage, eerily lit, like a bar, with one small ceiling bulb. A cousin comes out from the house to help, she hears this cousin, in Spanish say *amor,* nod towards her. She hears him on the other side of the door laughing, saying no. She hears her husband's name.

She is wondering how to interpret this place she has so idealistically moved to, the hacienda she and Alan will restore, the horses they will buy, the tiled pool they will build in the courtyard, embellished with huge clay pots of trailing red geranium. Her Mexican coffee table with its precise arrangement of books on the Southwest, on southwestern interior design, on southwestern landscaping, on New Mexican history. She just purchased another expensive book on Spanish door and window designs. And yesterday, she'd purchased two *ristras* of lacquered chilies to hang on either side of the massive front door. And now, sitting on this oil drum in a small, cluttered garage, facing the stucco house he has grown up in, old cars thrown and dismembered around the dirt yard, the clothesline, with jeans, T-shirts, dishcloths neatly pinned. The deer hanging between the two young men, in their worn shirts and jeans, expertly dividing the animal from itself.

Outside the house, he rubs his arms under the hose, chipping the dry blood, the water gray, wintry.

"Would you like to have supper with us? My aunt will want to cook the *lomo,* the part I told you about that runs along the spine. She uses butter and a little brandy; it's excellent."

"I should call home." She had been going to say call my husband.

"Oh, there's no phone. We can go to my neighbor's and call."

"Well, no. I suppose I'd better get home."

"You sure? Let me wrap some meat for you to take home to your family."

She cannot imagine her children, the little nuns, with hunks of deer meat in their roseate mouths.

She waits in his kitchen, near the back door, while he cuts the meat near the sink. The house is overly warm and smells of pine cleaning products. The TV is on in a room off the kitchen, and she hears the same news announcer she'd listened to in her kitchen in Illinois. A cedar crucifix hangs above the clean, white sink. He wraps the foil, his hands careful. She notices how he attends to what is before him.

"There. *Gracias a Dios.*" He grins sweetly. "We always thank God when we receive a deer for food."

Her heart, blocking her whole chest, keeps her from saying anything brittle or amusing. Back in his truck, they bump out the little rutted dirt driveway, sitting close because of the hunting equipment on her side.

"So. Did you enjoy your day?"

"Oh yes. Very much." Dull, so stupid. She who is known for wit in crisis has gone aphasic. She cannot breathe beside this man she scarcely knows.

"Do you mind if I hold your hand awhile?" He says this, his hand already on hers.

They drive to her house, down the long elm-lined driveway. The house, sprawling and huge, is dark.

She feels how close behind her he stands as she twists the key until the front door opens. She's self-conscious about the ornamental *ristras* beside the door, after seeing the homemade one in his kitchen, unlacquered, used for cooking.

She reads Alan's note, left on the kitchen table, while he opens the refrigerator, puts in the deer meat.

"Oh. They've gone to Albuquerque to see one of Alan's bicycle friends. He says he'll call in the morning—"

He hadn't even signed the note to her.

The girls left drawings; the oldest colored her in the pink prom dress, the youngest drew two heart heads, lopsided hearts with human features and stick bodies.

PERHAPS THERE are times when one's fate is predestined by those acts that came before, leading, maplike, to the present. During the long and irreversible span of devastation and betrayal to come, during the time when she would come to look upon her husband, her face the empty eye of the deer, she would ask over and over how she might have resisted, might have gone some uncomplicated, purer way.

AND IN those moments it took to lightly throw her upon the bed, guard, then guardian, purchasing her with beautiful eyes, with hands earlier gone inside the deer now opening her legs, hands now inside her, looking in a hard, bold, natural way no one had ever before looked upon her flesh, hands, body, eyes. In those moment her face surrendered its careful artifice, its years of artifice and taught pose, her face the deer she had killed, its spirit gone into his. So carefully placed as a vase upon the becalmed and lonely surface of her perfect life, so lonely, so careful, in her own life, doll in wife-clothes, doll in mother-clothes, doll in a pink dress, doll in camouflage, now so humbly naked, herself in a white bathtub in the ivory bathroom, an ivory candle in its dull brass stick on the watery ledge of the tub, his thick legs wedged against hers, his hands smoothing her back with ovals of soapy washcloth. No one since her mother had washed her back so tenderly, so gravely.

Head down, neck vulnerable, she mentions the beauty of the deer, the finality of its death. The only death, until now, she has ever caused.

"But death is necessary for new life. *La muerte es necesario para la vida nueva*," he says softly, rinsing her back with cupped hands, candlelight leafing her breasts and stomach, pulling her against him, showing how he cut and quartered the exquisite deer, his hands, callused and skillful, pushing her forward, her spine arching, slitting tender areas along the spine, cutting with the imaginary blade her cleansed, white skin.

She tries defending herself, the safe life she has built, but her humor is weak, lost in dangerous context, deeper feeling.

"So, are you done with killing the deer, and me as well?"

By answer, lifting the water-heavy hair, dropping it along one shoulder, moving his lips down the damp, surrendered neck, with the ungovernable authority of love, the godlike affliction of desire.

What I Never Told You

REBECCA LAWTON

REBECCA LAWTON worked on rivers throughout the West from 1973 to 1986, spending ten of those seasons in Grand Canyon. The entire time, she says, she was taking notes. In her off-seasons, she posed as a student, field geologist, ski lift attendant, cafe musician, landscaper, and winter kayaker. She holds a BS in earth sciences from the University of California at Santa Cruz and an MFA in creative writing from Mills College. Rebecca's articles, poetry, and fiction have appeared in research publications and small journals. Her river novel, Leaving Felliniville, *which takes place in the Uintah Basin of northeastern Utah, is under consideration for publication. Although her heart remains on desert rivers, Rebecca lives—for now—with her daughter, Rosie, among friendly neighbors in Sonoma, California.*

YOU CAME TO THE canyon just after the war and left when you had to, years later, when the sons of bitches we worked for let you go. Everybody besides them knew the river was the best place for you, with its side canyons and grottos—maybe the only place a guy could stand to live after two years in a strange jungle. What's a man supposed to do, get a desk job? After he's been trained to slit the throats of his sleeping enemies. After he's walked point in utter darkness, developed a sixth sense for trip wires. Other vets were going systematically crazy in those first years after the war, popping off a few relatives or a lover before doing themselves in. Even now, though I'm thinking you might have left sooner, I can't picture you eating microwaved meals in some darkened office, staring at some windowless wall. On the river you found your perfect niche.

Damn you anyway. Today I slammed down the phone after talking with the cops. I told the one cop he lied, that he didn't know you. I think I screamed at him—I don't know—for being wrong about you. He didn't know you were just out of place, that you belonged where you could live under the sky, use your knife every day, feel a rush of adrenaline in the roughest waves in the biggest rapids. You could work with ropes, coil them, tie them, pull and cut them. You could wear your boots, those green and black hightops you never took off. Even at night you wore them, your feet sticking toes-down into the sand past the end of your ground cloth. Nights when you fell asleep halfway down the beach or up in the kitchen, wherever you finished a bottle, I'd cover you with your blanket, but I wouldn't touch the boots. You said wearing them around the clock pulled you through more than one night raid, skirmishes other foot soldiers never survived.

You'd been on the river eleven years before I came there, fresh-faced, ready for everything. You were the veteran boatman; I was the eager trainee. I drew to you as fast as water runs off stone. Who could've resisted? I'd come to the canyon to learn the rapids, the names of side canyons, the best route through Lava Falls, how to survive the heat. You knew it all. You could show me. Since coming home you'd spent every summer rowing long days against the wind, setting up camps after dark, lining up for the bubble-line entry at Lava. You'd probably run every rapid a hundred times, all nerve ending and mumbled prayer, the same way you say you walked point. You may have lost your youth to the war, your virginity to an Asian whore, but your heart still beat hot and fast. On the river there was room for you. You swept like one more drop of water into the foam and waves and sharp falls that together pounded loud as thunder. You'd spent a decade under the dark sky and bright stars, watching the glow on far rims after the moon goes down. You had the distance in you.

At the oars you showed an artist's skill and madman's flair, detached from fear in a God-given way. To you the hairball entry at Crystal Rapids was the world's greatest cakewalk, a waltz with another great giant. I could only watch in awe alongside the other members of the crew. But being the only female, my unspoken awe worked two ways: I knew your hair curled at the nape of your neck, that you stood tan and tall, all parts intact. I knew about the difference in your eyes, their haunted and startled look. They drew me. I fought a growing urge to touch you—what to do with a man who tells scary war stories? When you caught me looking, you blinked, then smiled so dazzlingly wide I felt the hope of every angel crash in on my heart.

OF ALL places, we kissed first at the Flagstaff drive-in. Ironic, after what the police said today, but true. We'd spent all summer guiding on a real river, leading people through glades of single-leafed ash and cottonwood near clear-running pools. But we never kissed until we sat under the screen featuring *The Corpse Grinders*, on one of those asphalt bumps built up for cars so everyone can see the movie.

We'd driven out under a striped sky, crimson at the dark earth and lavender up higher, then indigo up under the first spread of stars. Just off a trip and smelling shower-clean, you looked handsome in a pair of clean jeans and light summer shirt; I wore a blouse and long skirt. We parked outside the chain-link fence and hoisted up a blanket before climbing over. At the right side of the lot, few cars had parked; we spread the blanket for us and a car speaker. Nighthawks dipped near lightpoles. We smelled sagebrush and popcorn on the night breeze. You left to fetch sodas as the title blasted onto the screen with a sappy blare of music; your laugh carried back to me from the refreshment stand. When you returned I pulled you to me; we giggled and huddled together as the corpse canners fed chopped human liver to rampant killer cats.

Soon you lay on and around me, rolling with me on the blanket and asphalt, your breath smelling thick and exciting of smoke and beer, dangerous and repelling. I kept my mouth open to kiss you. Your hands snaked under my blouse and skirt, felt calloused and rough on my clean skin, my breasts and belly.

"Oh la la," you whispered. I rubbed your boots with my toes, groped for your jeans, tugged open your fly. Inside were coarse, curled hairs, smooth skin. I dug deeper, then pulled my hand away too fast when I felt you, knowing I shouldn't. I tried to reach in again, but you rolled away.

You cried. "I can't."

I'd guessed that. You'd felt limp as string. I brushed tiny rocks from your hair, prayed to leave the hard ground of the Flagstaff drive-in. Maybe it would have gone better on some beach on the river, in the sand still warm from the summer sun. You sobbed quietly. I covered you in the thin camp blanket—it was yours, government issue.

Forget it, you told me, shaking your head; I could never have anything normal with you. If you loved me, I'd leave you, too.

I got that. You'd already told me about John from Twin Falls, who'd wanted to come home to raise quarter horses. And Henry from Rochester, who'd planned to manage his dad's hunting lodge. I knew you'd outlived your whole squad, all nine men blown away like leaves, not once but twice. The second time you'd made it by burrowing under the dead bodies of your buddies until the V. C. had swept through. If I'd pried more I would have learned the gory details: crushed intestines, fixed stares, pumping blood. Better men than you, you'd said—and here you were.

The credits rolled as car engines coughed and started up across the drive-in. We climbed back over the fence to walk to your truck, the Chevy Impala with a rack of old, sawn-off oars nailed together. We rode back to town and the crystalline streetlights on that clear August night. I spread my knees for you to shift gears; you kept your big hand on my leg. You dropped me back at the boathouse, though I'd said I'd go with you to Williams, to anywhere, maybe we could just drive all night and figure things out. But you dropped me off fast. No wonder your words stunned me: You were in love with me, you said. You quickly pulled the truck door closed. I watched your taillights under the other red lights in town, the blink-blinking aircraft-warning signals up on the Peaks.

BUT TRY telling all that to the police. Ask anybody, not just the cop I talked to, to take a heart as big as the world and give it some shit. Rough it up really good, then turn it loose and see how it does. Or just watch a star fall, or a bird blow to earth in a storm.

OUR LITTLE window slammed shut as fast as it had flung open, just as the summer season was ending. September pressed in, and fall touched the river. Little flocks of egrets moved upstream, on to somewhere. The pairs of ducks we saw didn't linger in pools; no more stopping and starting and letting us chase them downstream late afternoons. They flew right on through the canyon. I watched you watch the birds move on; the nights I had to cover you grew more frequent. I'd heard from the crew that you drank more toward the fall, maybe everybody did as dread crept in about winter jobs and colder weather. But you fell asleep out of your bag every night, curled up on the beach near a bottle, and seemed harder to wake each morning.

No doubt about it: Drink didn't improve your disposition. In that you were no exception. The crew knew to give you room on a hangover day, but the passengers didn't. And unfortunately you combined a hangover with our scheduled day at Havasu Creek. Talk about your worst combination: Havasu was the spookiest place on the river for you, the most reminiscent of the jungle, tangled with grape and arbors of cottonwood and willow. Other times at Havasu I'd seen you in a full sweat by the creek, first thing in the morning, just remembering. I'd seen your face covered in tears, you talking to yourself, features twisted, the only place I saw your dialogue with demons. Maybe if the New York lawyer's wife had snuck up behind you on a good morning at another creek, you'd have kept your job.

I didn't see what happened, but I heard it: twin screams, yours and hers. Later she confessed between sobs that she had run up tippy-toe behind you to tap on your shoulder, you who could always hear a man behind you or a whisper fifty yards away. But you were lost in the jungle that day. You'd whirled on her—tall in your instant ferocity—spun her, and held your knife to her throat. As soon as you'd done it you'd realized your mistake, as soon as the knife had pressed to soft flesh. Of the screams I heard, I remember yours, anguished and terrible.

You'd let her go. She'd squealed and run for the boats.

By the time I saw you on the trail, your fate had been sealed. First I saw your boots, through the wild grape, but the man wearing them was barely recognizable. You looked crumpled, your sun shirt torn and half tucked into your cutoffs. You turned to the creek and threw away your knife. It struck a midstream boulder, clattered, and fell into the turquoise water. I opened my mouth, and you whirled in the path. You stared and swayed, a world away.

I tried, but couldn't call your name. My mouth opened and closed, opened and closed, no sound coming out.

You squinted; I waved. Unsmiling, you peered, turned, lurched into a trailside ocotillo. You weaved and staggered down the path, hobbled out of sight, headed for the river and the boats.

IN EARLY December of that year, you started calling me. You didn't say much over the telephone, just giggled and said you were fine. You were sure you'd be back on the river for the next season. Some veteran's program was working wonders, you said, but I never found out where it was. Each time I asked for your number—each time you didn't tell me. Instead you said you loved me and hung up the phone. I wanted to say sweet words, too, but you were gone too soon, and the line went dead. When you called around Christmastime, you sounded blurred. After that, I heard only from the police, who said my number had been in your wallet.

Now I know you'd been living in your truck, maybe even since September. The last place you had a meal and a shower under one roof may have been back at the boathouse in Flagstaff. And it wasn't even the cops who found you. Two guys on a clean-up crew saw you in your locked car after hours at a drive-in in Bakersfield. They pounded on your window. They shouted at you to wake up, mister, the movie's been over for an hour. When they couldn't rouse you, they called the police.

The cop read me the coroner's report: adult male, veteran of the Vietnam War. Williams, Arizona, address. Thirty-six years old. Alcoholic seizure. Found in street clothes and combat boots.

The cop said, too, that the coroner was amazed you could wear any kind of shoe. "Pair of wicked bone spurs. Never could have passed selective service."

I told him your feet must have been normal, you'd been drafted. The war drove you crazy, if anything. I told him the truth, and slammed down the receiver. Soon as I did, I picked it up again. There was a lot I could tell them. They didn't know you slept with your boots on, face down mostly, that you worked on the river and could sleep anywhere, even in the cab of your truck. You had gone cold turkey and were going to work again next season. You had things to look forward to. You were in love with me.

It wasn't a cop's voice I heard then—just dial tone. No words. Just a whine lonelier than any sound I can remember, lonelier even than a river's hush when winter's coming. No voice from me, either. Just my mouth opening and closing, opening and closing, no sound coming out.

Rawhide

ARIANA-SOPHIA M. KARTSONIS

ARIANA-SOPHIA M. KARTSONIS, 28, lived in Wyoming for her first seven years, and has been in Utah for the past twenty-one. She is the former editor of Shades; a senior at the University of Utah, pursuing a degree in English with an emphasis in creative writing; a reader for Quarterly West; and a creative writing teacher at East Community Education. Her work has appeared in Weber Studies and Ellipsis, and she has recently completed a short story collection entitled A Tricycle, the Moon, an Angel. In addition to writing, she loves angels, finger-painting, and her three cats, Bronte, Schroedinger Taz, and Sneakily. She finds the landscape of Utah and the Southwest "haunted and alive, rich, full of beauty and contradiction, and, of course, stories."

DANNY AND I, WE were kids back then, pitching horseshoes in the yard. This happens to you when you run into a man who is difficult as a bum steer but a good man.

Dammit Danny, I loved you but anymore that's one thing I'm not sure you were, was a good man. I believed it like anything once but I don't know; and it has nothing to do with the stealing or the jail time, the day you threw a six-pack at me, or the way you'd pull my head back with a fistful of hair that grew wild and tangled as the hawthorn bushes in my father's front yard.

Daniel scared me sometimes. No, mostly Danny scared me. Something about him seemed translucent as if he was here and not here, all at once—a fingernail clipping, a slip of the moon. He was dark as a storm cloud, that Danny, depressed and thinking all the time. He made trouble for himself, and loving him was a little like loving fear, or a ghost.

Still, Daniel had a way, a way that made people who didn't think with their hearts as I did do it anyhow.

Here I got lost again in that swirling wind of leaves, gusts of autumn, breaths of goodbye all over him, pungent and raw like sex and dying.

Nothing hurt more than the way he stopped looking at me entirely. The way that cool gaze was all I had once and I would swim in it until I began to shake, my heart beating wild and afraid like a game animal.

Once when we were making love, once, and the only time to my recollection I ever heard those three words from Danny, "I fucking love you Gale, you know that?"

We were kids back then, I told you, and other things too, cat burglars and drifters. God how we moved.

There's a purity to motion for its own sake. Something pure and ancient as that coral earth and the heavenly bodies above it, avoiding the cities, meeting like wine-crazed, life-crazed gypsies to dance above the desert. The old aged sacredness to the scenes dashing by the window, scenes we'd place ourselves in after too much charred truck-stop coffee, looking for somewhere mineral-rich to lay down our restlessness for awhile, a place on the ground for a little sleep. Out here it was obvious. What had once been sea turned bone-dry, sure of itself and its rune-like symbols on fossils. It could take all the time there would ever be to grow wet, change itself back, and what next? I suppose we believed, Danny and me, that we'd taken in a bit of that antiquity through our pores from the long nights spent under the stars, searing in each other's arms. Maybe we thought we'd entered that endless cycle somehow. We were wrong. What we couldn't have known then, couldn't have slowed down enough to realize, was how like those ghost stars we'd become, Danny: already dead with light still arriving or me: white-hot and dying slowly. The two of us keeping vigil over the desert and burning ourselves out.

Utah, Wyoming, Texas, Arizona flashing along the window so fast sometimes I missed the borders, the signs that read "Welcome to Arizona" or "You are now leaving big, wonderful Wyoming." At Spirit Lake the fishermen say: "Cast a line in Utah and pull in Wyoming trout." Danny and I loved the fringes, too, places that kept us on the edge of two states at once.

Danny called Utah "Nature's Christmas" for the way it was all green and red, plush canyoned and sandstone desert, brittle and soft and aching at once. With Danny, under Danny, or arching over Danny, I imagined myself part of this land, a Looking Glass Rock with my shoulders pushed into the sand, my hips sloping down, or an Angel's Arch when I rode Danny against that enormous sky. Reaching Flaming Gorge at sunset, that burning gash set wild with its own orange heat, I can't imagine I'm the first to think the earth at this point is a woman's anatomy. It is delicate and graceful and full of fury.

That night overlooking the gorge on a high windy peak I found the lump on Danny's neck. The next week I spent threatening every god I could think of and Danny as well, who was harder to get to a doctor than a whole herd of rabid cattle.

Once in a getaway, Danny was shot in the arm. I swear he wore that sling for weeks even after he was better, the wound healed over. He loved the legend of it—"I've been shot," he'd tell anyone who'd listen. It was me to form the tourniquet, though it was just a flesh wound, I took pride in my makeshift bandaging. "Nightingale," Danny called me then, "my nurse with her name spelled in the wind." It was me nursing Danny back to health that time, the way I can't anymore, me nursing Danny cradled at my breast like an infant sucking everything out of me, until I was dry as the desert he loved so much.

Like everything else, Daniel insisted he could do this better, no doctors, no medicine, just herb wheels and rocks. He would meditate surrounded by his "power stones." Garnet, the warrior stone in his right hand, picture jasper in his left for answers, understanding. His medicine bag had others: apple coral for love, watermelon tourmaline for perseverance and there are more. I don't believe any of it, though I try to understand his need for ceremony now, ritual; the way he always stopped at Crazy Woman Creek for me, let me wash my face and hands in the cool water. We all have our sacred cows, this much is clear. This wasn't what he wanted, I know that. Danny wanted a studly death, a shoot-out or a barroom brawl, maybe. Ask what a woman loves in a man like this and the answer almost comes out of the question. It is that urgency, that fatalistic quality, a man like Danny follows everything to its inevitable conclusion, in bed and out.

For the crook Daniel always was, he had odd ethics, too. "Respect for the land," he believed, "those campgrounds, those mountains, aren't there to keep us suckling, they stand for themselves," Danny would say, "and they're pissed off."

"How long?" I asked the doctor, "how long?" Though in a case like this, long seemed to be the wrong word to use, long implied duration, years. Short seemed more fitting, or even swift when we're talking about a couple of months.

TONIGHT DANNY carries only volcanic ash, the stone for surrender, acceptance of fate. I'm no priestess but it's my voice Danny wants to hear.

"Tonight will ask more of us, that's all I know. More of us than it ever has, more than it ever could, last winter, for example, or in a small town. Lean into the night," I tell Danny, "press against it, through it even if you like. Just don't ask me to unravel any of it for you, it can stay tangled for all I care. The stars will keep their comfortable distance and the blackness will weave in and out of them. A black graph punctuated by light. I am remembering the night we used to dress ourselves in, when we'd creep feline-like out to do job after job in our bandit days. Tonight will ask you to accept everything, take it for granted (easy for you, I know). It will push itself against your mouth, your lips, and spill itself into you drop by drop."

It's an odd incantation, and although Danny, at the end of it all, wants a little witchcraft, a little magic, he likes his faith to be honest, grounded.

It is then that I take out the pocket knife and begin sawing away at that crazy strawberry hair of mine that hangs to my waist and drives Daniel wild. I don't stop until it's boy-short, uneven as all hell, and absolutely freeing.

I prefer to think of Danny as having a brindle-colored heart, neither all black or all white but marked with streaks of color. For a minute, before I turn away, I think of dousing his body with flames, leaving him branded on the skin of the land that has claimed him. I imagine him for a moment full-bright, on fire, scorching and scarring, his buckskin vest folding inward against him the way I once did. Then I think of his love for this place, how he would change so much of the world if he could, but not here, not the singing crimson stones, not a single grain of sand.

Maybe that's why I leave Daniel there. On that red sand with his healing stones on each chakra point and facing east with his face cast all silvery in the full moonlight. Maybe that's why I keep walking and don't look back to burn that image into my mind. Danny and my pile of long coppery-gold hair: a little fire burning on the sand. Maybe I just want them to find Danny that way, like a real outlaw. With a little luck, he'll be wanted in a state or two and they'll find him dead, escaped, and in some small way, with his crooked sense of justice, he'll have won. Danny would've liked that.

I'm not that woman anymore. The one I leave behind in the desert with Danny and that pile of hair. So, I desert him and that woman whose wild hair could be pulled back with his rough hands. Someday when I imagine it there might be fairies stepping out from behind the cactus and sagebrush and prickly pear, their wings phosphorescent in the full moon. There are no witnesses tonight, not even Daniel's lover, her back to him now and walking away, to dispute anything. There might be shooting stars and auroras and sparks flying from those stones in his clutched hands like prayers. Tonight belongs to Danny; who could say otherwise?

A Blizzard Under Blue Sky

PAM HOUSTON

PAM HOUSTON, 32, originally from New Jersey, has lived in many places in the West and has been a river guide and a hunting guide. Her story "How to Talk to a Hunter" was selected for Best American Short Stories 1990, and her short story collection Cowboys Are My Weakness won the 1993 Regional Book Award from the Mountains and Plains Booksellers Association. Her essays, interviews, and short fiction have appeared in such periodicals and magazines as Cimarron Review, Quarterly West, Mirabella, Mademoiselle, and Outside, and she is a contributing editor at Elle and Ski. She divides her time between the Rocky Mountains and the San Francisco Bay Area.

THE DOCTOR SAID I was clinically depressed. It was February, the month in which depression runs rampant in the inversion-cloaked Salt Lake Valley and the city dwellers escape to Park City, where the snow is fresh and the sun is shining and everybody is happy, except me. In truth, my life was on the verge of more spectacular and satisfying discoveries than I had ever imagined, but of course I couldn't see that far ahead. What I saw was work that wasn't getting done, bills that weren't getting paid, and a man I'd given my heart to weekending in the desert with his ex.

The doctor said, "I can give you drugs."

I said, "No way."

She said, "The machine that drives you is broken. You need something to help you get it fixed."

I said, "Winter camping."

She said, "Whatever floats your boat."

One of the things I love the most about the natural world is the way it gives you what's good for you even if you don't know it at the time. I had never been winter camping before, at least not in the high country, and the weekend I chose to try and fix my machine was the same weekend the air mass they called the Alaska Clipper showed up. It was thirty-two degrees below zero in town on the night I spent in my snow cave. I don't know how cold it was out on Beaver Creek. I had listened to the weather forecast, and to the advice of my housemate, Alex, who was an experienced winter camper.

"I don't know what you think you're going to prove by freezing to death," Alex said, "but if you've got to go, take my bivvy sack; it's warmer than anything you have."

"Thanks," I said.

"If you mix Kool-Aid with your water it won't freeze up," he said, "and don't forget lighting paste for your stove."

"Okay," I said.

"I hope it turns out to be worth it," he said, "because you are going to freeze your butt."

When everything in your life is uncertain, there's nothing quite like the clarity and precision of fresh snow and blue sky. That was the first thought I had on Saturday morning as I stepped away from the warmth of my truck and let my skis slap the snow in front of me. There was no wind and no clouds that morning, just still air and cold sunshine. The hair in my nostrils froze almost immediately. When I took a deep breath, my lungs only filled up halfway.

I opened the tailgate to excited whines and whimpers. I never go skiing without Jackson and Hailey: my two best friends, my yin and yang of dogs. Some of you might know Jackson. He's the oversized sheepdog-and-something-else with the great big nose and the bark that will shatter glass. He gets out and about more than I do. People I've never seen before come by my house daily and call him by name. He's all grace, and he's tireless; he won't go skiing with me unless I let him lead. Hailey is not so graceful, and her body seems in constant indecision when she runs. When we ski she stays behind me, and on the downhills she tries to sneak rides on my skis.

The dogs ran circles in the chest-high snow while I inventoried my backpack one more time to make sure I had everything I needed. My sleeping bag, my Thermarest, my stove, Alex's bivvy sack, matches, lighting paste, flashlight, knife. I brought three pairs of long underwear—tops and bottoms—so I could change once before I went to bed, and once again in the morning, so I wouldn't get chilled by my own sweat. I brought paper and pen, and Kool-Aid to mix with my water. I brought Mountain House chicken stew and some freeze-dried green peas, some peanut butter and honey, lots of dried apricots, coffee and Carnation instant breakfast for morning.

Jackson stood very still while I adjusted his backpack. He carries the dog food and enough water for all of us. He takes himself very seriously when he's got his pack on. He won't step off the trail for any reason, not even to chase rabbits, and he gets nervous and angry if I do. That morning he was impatient with me. "Miles to go, Mom," he said over his shoulder. I snapped my boots into my skis and we were off.

There are not too many good things you can say about temperatures that dip past twenty below zero, except this: They turn the landscape into a crystal palace and they turn your vision into Superman's. In the cold thin morning air the trees and mountains, even the twigs and shadows, seemed to leap out of the background like a 3-D movie, only it was better than 3-D because I could feel the sharpness of the air.

I have a friend in Moab who swears that Utah is the center of the fourth dimension, and although I know he has in mind something much different and more complicated than subzero weather, it was there, on that ice-edged morning, that I felt on the verge of seeing something more than depth perception in the brutal clarity of the morning sun.

As I kicked along the first couple of miles, I noticed the sun crawling higher in the sky and yet the day wasn't really warming, and I wondered if I should have brought another vest, another layer to put between me and the cold night ahead.

It was utterly quiet out there, and what minimal noise we made intruded on the morning like a brass band: the squeaking of my bindings, the slosh of the water in Jackson's pack, the whoosh of nylon, the jangle of dog tags. It was the bass line and percussion to some primal song, and I kept wanting to sing to it, but I didn't know the words.

Jackson and I crested the top of a hill and stopped to wait for Hailey. The trail stretched out as far as we could see into the meadow below us and beyond, a double track and pole plants carving through softer trails of rabbit and deer.

"Nice place," I said to Jackson, and his tail thumped the snow underneath him without sound.

We stopped for lunch near something that looked like it could be a lake in its other life, or maybe just a womb-shaped meadow. I made peanut butter and honey sandwiches for all of us, and we opened the apricots.

"It's fabulous here," I told the dogs. "But so far it's not working."

There had never been anything wrong with my life that a few good days in the wilderness wouldn't cure, but there I sat in the middle of all those crystal-coated trees, all that diamond-studded sunshine, and I didn't feel any better. Apparently clinical depression was not like having a bad day, it wasn't even like having a lot of bad days, it was more like a house of mirrors, it was like being in a room full of one-way glass.

"Come on, Mom," Jackson said. "Ski harder, go faster, climb higher."

Hailey turned her belly to the sun and groaned.

"He's right," I told her. "It's all we can do."

After lunch the sun had moved behind our backs, throwing a whole different light on the path ahead of us. The snow we moved through stopped being simply white and became translucent, hinting at other colors, reflections of blues and purples and grays. I thought of Moby Dick, you know, the whiteness of the whale, where white is really the absence of all color, and whiteness equals truth, and Ahab's search is finally futile, as he finds nothing but his own reflection.

"Put your mind where your skis are," Jackson said, and we made considerably better time after that.

The sun was getting quite low in the sky when I asked Jackson if he thought we should stop to build the snow cave, and he said he'd look for the next good bank. About one hundred yards down the trail we found it, a gentle slope with eastern exposure that didn't look like it would cave in under any circumstances. Jackson started to dig first.

Let me make one thing clear. I knew only slightly more about building snow caves than Jackson, having never built one, and all my knowledge coming from disaster tales of winter camping fatalities. I knew several things not to do when building a snow cave, but I was having a hard time knowing what exactly to do. But Jackson helped, and Hailey supervised, and before too long we had a little cave built, just big enough for three. We ate dinner quite pleased with our accomplishments and set the bivvy sack up inside the cave just as the sun slipped away and dusk came over Beaver Creek.

The temperature, which hadn't exactly soared during the day, dropped twenty degrees in as many minutes, and suddenly it didn't seem like such a great idea to change my long underwear. The original plan was to sleep with the dogs inside the bivvy sack but outside the sleeping bag, which was okay with Jackson the super-metabolizer, but not so with Hailey, the couch potato. She whined and wriggled and managed to stuff her entire fat body down inside my mummy bag, and Jackson stretched out full-length on top.

One of the unfortunate things about winter camping is that it has to happen when the days are so short. Fourteen hours is a long time to lie in a snow cave under the most perfect of circumstances. And when it's thirty-two below, or forty, fourteen hours seems like weeks.

I wish I could tell you I dropped right off to sleep. In truth, fear crept into my spine with the cold and I never closed my eyes. Cuddled there, amid my dogs and water bottles, I spent half of the night chastising myself for thinking I was Wonder Woman, not only risking my own life but the lives of my dogs, and the other half trying to keep the numbness in my feet from crawling up to my knees. When I did doze off, which was actually more like blacking out than dozing off, I'd come back to my senses wondering if I had frozen to death, but the alternating pain and numbness that started in my extremities and worked its way into my bones convinced me I must still be alive.

It was a clear night, and every now and again I would poke my head out of its nest of down and nylon to watch the progress of the moon across the sky. There is no doubt that it was the longest and most uncomfortable night of my life.

But then the sky began to get gray, and then it began to get pink, and before too long the sun was on my bivvy sack, not warm, exactly, but holding the promise of warmth later in the day. And I ate apricots and drank Kool-Aid-flavored coffee and celebrated the rebirth of my fingers and toes, and the survival of many more important parts of my body. I sang "Rocky Mountain High" and "If I Had a Hammer," and yodeled and whistled, and even danced the two-step with Jackson and let him lick my face. And when Hailey finally emerged form the sleeping bag a full hour after I did, we shared a peanut butter and honey sandwich and she said nothing ever tasted so good.

We broke camp and packed up and kicked in the snow cave with something resembling glee.

I was five miles down the trail before I realized what had happened. Not once in that fourteen-hour night did I think about deadlines, or bills, or the man in the desert. For the first time in many months I was happy to see a day beginning. The morning sunshine was like a present from the gods. What really happened, of course, is that I remembered about joy.

I know that one night out at thirty-two below doesn't sound like much to those of you who have climbed Everest or run the Iditarod or kayaked to Antarctica, and I won't try to convince you that my life was like the movies where depression goes away in one weekend, and all of life's problems vanish with a moment's clear sight. The simple truth of the matter is this: On Sunday I had a glimpse outside of the house of mirrors, on Saturday I couldn't have seen my way out of a paper bag. And while I was skiing back toward the truck that morning, a wind came up behind us and swirled the snow around our bodies like a blizzard under blue sky. And I was struck by the simple perfection of the snowflakes, and startled by the hopefulness of sun on frozen trees.

Holy Dirt

LISA CHEWNING

LISA CHEWNING, 41, lives in Pittsburgh, Pennsylvania, with her husband, two teenaged sons, four cats, and one dog. She has a BA and an MFA in creative writing from the University of Pittsburgh, and her short stories have been prizewinners in several national contests and appeared in such publications as Beloit Fiction Journal, American Literary Review, and First, for Women. Although born and raised in Pennsylvania, Lisa has visited the Southwest every year for the past six and has found her heart in New Mexico. Her best writing, she says, has come as a result of the influence of the Southwest, and it is her plan to relocate in New Mexico when her children are in college.

ONCE YOU WERE AND once you were not. I lie on an outcropping of redrock and listen to the sounds of the high desert. I feel the heat, the red dirt and the jagged rocks under my back; I know the insects and lizards scuttle past me; I smell the sage. I wait. My eyes close against the white sun but even through my eyelids the light penetrates and burns. I feel my skin drawing taut and tender and imagine how pink I must be.

For three mornings you have watched me eating my breakfast alone at Pasqual's, your eyes so dark I cannot name their color. I see your dark skin, your black braid hanging down the middle of your back, and I wonder how your hair feels on your skin, how it would feel on mine. You have watched me, staring boldly, not turning away when I looked at you. As I sit under the sun on the High Road, I wonder if you will still look when my skin is tan.

I was not prepared for this country. Nothing anyone has told me prepared me for the desert, the open expanse of land, the mosaic of peoples. For three mornings I breathe the warm air from my hotel window and look to the hills and mountains that guard the town. I feel I have come home in a way I have never known before. I possess the land and am possessed by it, caught up in its heat and passion like a lover.

On my own I explore the city, its chapels, its treasures, while my husband conducts business, making the wealthy more so. I look into the familiar faces of the people under the portal at the Governor's Palace and do not understand what I see. I move outward, my circles expanding until they are farther and farther away from the plaza, too far to walk, too close to contain me.

You finally speak to me at Pasqual's and ask me how long I am staying in Santa Fe; do I need someone to take me places. I politely refuse, saying I am with my husband. "But he is not here now," you say with a smile.

"No," I say, "no, he is not here now."

Each afternoon I meet my husband, surrounded by his salesmen in the hushed high-ceilinged lobby of El Dorado Hotel, where I sip a cool drink and listen to them brag about their sales of the day. On the third afternoon, on the day you first spoke to me, I sit in a chair behind my husband and listen to what he names his "ten-year plan"; he does not know I am there.

In ten years our children will be teenagers and he can pay me alimony; he'll still be in his forties. He says I can go back to school or get a job or something. Maybe some older man will want me. My husband will be young enough to start over with a new young wife. When I hear these words, the room does not come crashing in on me; time does not stop. I become numb and frozen inside. I do not let him know I am there, that I have heard him. I slip out into the plaza and walk until dinner.

That night my husband and I eat at a restaurant named for a flamenco dancer, Maria Ysabel. In the entry is a poster of this dancer in a white dress with layers and layers, tier after tier, of ruffles, her black hair swept and tied up over one ear with an orange flower. There in the courtyard at a table under the vine-covered latticework canopy, I see another you and a woman with black curls that fall over her shoulders, fall onto her breasts. She is dressed simply in a long-tiered skirt, a sheer white blouse, and long earrings that brush her shoulders. She pulls an orange flower from the trumpet vine overhead and tucks it behind your ear. That other you leans across the table, over the burning candle, and kisses her. I turn away.

Walking back to our hotel, my husband and I hear music coming from the plaza. Ahead we see a throng of people: weekend tourists, ragged longhairs, children. Standing in the doorway of a shop are four musicians—perhaps Peruvian—dark-skinned with the shining thick blue-black hair of *los indios*. One plays a long goatskin drum hanging from his hip; he uses his hands, sometimes a stick. Another plays a mandolin, another a primitive panpipe, the fourth a pear-shaped acoustic guitar. The sounds they give are folk rhythms, mystical, thick, spiritual. The crowd of people listens and nods, sways and claps hands to the beat. A child with Down Syndrome, clutching a naked doll, hops from one foot to the other, falling when her movements pull her out of control. She laughs and gets up again.

A sinewy man with a ponytail and no shirt, his shorts low enough on his hips for me to see he has nothing on under them, stands behind a woman who looks like him, tall and thin with long hair. They sway together, his hips pressed into her buttocks, sway to music of their own rhythms. I feel a lurch in my stomach as I watch them. I turn to find my husband but he has moved to the edge of the crowd and stands with his back turned, looking out into the plaza.

I watch another couple. The woman is short and squat with long hair, a round protruding belly, and a broad flat face. The man is ugly with glasses and thick lips, the upper looking as if it is turned inside out with its exaggerated Cupid's bow. His lips are a shade of brown darker than his skin. He too is short and squat, thick-chested. They move together in the graceful, gliding rhythms of a traditional dance. Her stomach curves into the hollow under his chest, above his belt. They look as though they have been shaped and grown together for this very dance.

When the musicians stop, a man who has been squatting in the doorway to the store walks around the crowd with a handful of their recordings. I turn to find my husband. I gesture to the man, smile, raise my eyebrows, but my husband turns away. I know what he is thinking, that they are dirty, they are children. I pay with a twenty dollar bill and refuse the change. When we return to our hotel, I go to the bedroom and my husband sits in front of the television in the living room.

The next day at the cafe you watch me. You come to my table again and say, "Your husband is not here now, is he? Would you like to see the holy dirt? I will take you."

On the road to Chimayó to see the holy dirt we tell each other how we have come to be who we are. You labor with your hands and with your back until you have enough money not to for awhile. It is a long mountain road and you stop several times and tell me to look back, to see the redrocks, the sky, the sage, the Sangre de Cristos. I remember this was once the bottom of a great sea and I feel as new and as raw as these stones.

You tell me about Chimayó, about El Santuario where the holy dirt is. I tell you I have no faith, that I do not believe in miracles. You look at me and smile. You tell me about the crucifix that appeared in the ground, was moved three times to Santa Cruz but each time reappeared in Chimayó. This is where the chapel was built.

We enter the sanctuary; it is cool and smells of incense, wood, wax, and age. The golds and reds and greens of the *reredos*, the sacred paintings, are brilliant in their colors and primitive-looking. Votives in red glass flicker at the altar. You show me the *bultos*, the carvings in wood of holy men, gaunt with downcast eyes. I shake my head at the conviction and hope sculpted into this art.

You take my hand and step through the low narrow door into the *Santuario*. The walls are lined with crutches, photographs, baby shoes, artificial flowers, dog tags hanging over photos of young sons in uniform, letters of prayer, letters of hope, paintings, statues of the Virgin. I read a letter from a child who asks that his mother not die from the thing growing inside her. I see a pair of white satin baby shoes and a christening gown; pinned to it is the child's name and the dates of her life. Everywhere there is trust. Everywhere there is faith. Everywhere there is pain.

A young girl, perhaps fifteen or sixteen, carries a sleeping infant in her arms. The girl's mother and other women with dark eyes, brown faces, and black hair enter the last room, the room with the holy dirt. I hear the murmur of their prayers, the song of their tears. I look into the room. They are sheltered around the child and her mother. The eldest woman bends down to the dirt floor and scoops a metal teaspoon into the holy dirt. She transfers the dirt to her other hand, clenches it to her heart, and quietly prays. She rubs it over the infant's arms, her legs, and gently into her scalp; the dirt leaves a fine reddish powder on the baby's new skin. She steps back and the other women fill small containers with the dirt. They leave.

I step in and look down. A tiny window lets in a breeze, and a square of sun shines over the hole. It is only a hole, a hole filled with the red dirt of the desert. You step into the room behind me and I can feel you, smell you, taste you. You kneel and take the dirt into your hand. You offer it to me.

I shake my head, no, this is not for me. It will not work. You do not lower your arm. I see into your eyes of no color and I feel my heart break open, and all that I thought I was escapes. I cup my hand under yours and you let the holy dirt trickle into it. I reach inside my blouse and rub it over my heart.

When Redrocks Talk

LIZA BESMEHN

LIZA BESMEHN, 34, began her relationship with the Southwest in 1981 when she left her home in northern Minnesota to migrate west. On a tightwire trail in Canyonlands National Park, she ignored a four-wheel-drive-only sign and ended up sleeping beside her car. She awoke the next morning "on fire, in lust with the taste of dust on my mouth, in love with silence." Two days later a kind man in a four-wheel-drive rescued her, but the Southwest had struck its magic, and she's been here ever since. She lives in Salt Lake City, Utah, with her husband, Bruce; three sons, Josh, Luke and Dusty; and their cats, birds, ferret, and dog. A new writer, Liza has had work published in local newspapers and in Shades.

FRIDAY AFTERNOON I FALL asleep. I wake to find the desert in me, to the smell of sagebrush and dirt. It snuck into my bones while I slept. Took root while my eyes were closed. I open my eyes and see the full moon shining over Interstate 70 like a neon arrow. I sit up and hear them talking. Those wild red rocks with the wide open voices. They're shouting at me through the thick walls of my basement apartment. They're saying, "Now. Right now. Get down here now."

I sit on my bed, bewildered. This is insanity. I can't run off to the desert tonight. I have to be at work in less than two hours. I have bills to pay, kids to feed, people depending on me to show up, do my job.

I hear the wind whistle through a canyon. I put my fingers in my ears. The whole desert is talking at once. "What do you want?" I ask.

"Now," it says. "Come now."

"Now?"

"It'll be fun. We'll make music," the redrocks whisper.

My husband, Jess, walks through our kitchen door. He's home from work, greasy with labor. He needs a shower. He takes a peek at me and changes his mind. I'm listening to country music. I must have that crazy look in my eyes. The one that scares him. The look that says, "Buckle up, baby, it's gonna be a rough ride."

He tries to get away. He thinks that if he fixes the kitchen sink, I'll forget this talking desert. He plugs in a power drill. I put crackers in my pack. He reaches for a bag of screws. I reach for my flute, notebook, and pen. We stare each other down. "No," he says, "I'm not going."

"Fine," I say, "stay here."

We fight halfway to Moab. Jess gets so cranky when he thinks that he's ruining his life for a good time. I gladly ruin mine. It's what I live for.

By the time we're fueling the truck and buying coffee at Walkers truck stop in Wellington, Jess is beginning to forgive me. I think he even likes me again, but he doesn't trust me enough to try a chocolate-covered coffee bean. The package says, "Adult candy," so I bought it. He shakes his head and tells me, "Not a chance."

Driving south, the night is everything it promised. The moon is high, faking daylight, laughing at the snow on the ground. I can see the San Rafael Swell from the truck window. See it all black and blue and shadowy, rising from the white flats. Inside the swell you can find a black dragon painted on a pale wall. Put there by people who knew a different earth, worshipped a god who made more sense in a paradise that defies logic. The Colorado Plateau.

Moab, Utah, is about four hours from Salt Lake City, depending on how serious you are about getting there. On other occasions it has taken several days. Sometimes we make a right turn and find ourselves helplessly lost in the Book Cliffs, or the Swell, or stretched in the sun on the sandy banks of the Green River. Tonight, the full moon of February and nearly midnight, we're being careful not to make any right turns. We're going to Moab.

At the intersection of Highway 6 and Interstate 70, I get itchy-feeling. This is where I shed my urban coat. I slough off rush hour, jobs, payments, sirens, smog, and all that other "real life" shit that makes insanity a common frame of mind. This is the place that I always open my window, sniff the air for signs of life, find it sweet and full.

We turn east on I-70. The town of Green River sparkles. I'm tempted to exit. See if Ray's Tavern is open and serving burgers. I'm not hungry but I love the wooden benches and the smell of river water mixed with beer and oily smoke.

Jess keeps the truck on the road. I see his hands wobble on the wheel as we pass the exit. He's determined not to screw up his life. We have a plan and he's not budging. I admire his strength.

The interstate crosses the Green River. I reach over and blow the horn. Have to make sure the water is awake. Have to say hello, even if I can't stop to visit.

We wheel into Moab at 1 a.m. We check into a motel, unload our things. By 1:30, we're standing on red ground, celebrating the way the moon moves across the sky, the way pickers get stuck in our shoelaces, and the way silence can be worn like a heavy wool coat.

SATURDAY

ON THE surface of morning everything is right. A passionate blue sky is strapped to the backs of brick-colored cliffs. It's warm, sixty degrees, and breakfast is good, the toast unburnt, the coffee thick, black, delicious.

Below the surface, things are not so picturesque. Those demanding desert voices that convinced me to skip another day and come play are subdued murmurs now. I can't understand what they're saying and I'm not sure why I'm here. I should be home, washing clothes.

Jess looks at me expectantly from his side of the truck. I snuggle a little closer to the passenger door, pretend to enjoy the view. "So, where to?" he asks.

"You pick," I say.

"This is your baby," he reminds me. "Where do you want to go?"

The truth is, I don't know where to go. I can't tell him that. Not after I drug him down here on this cosmic adventure.

"Go where the rocks talk," I say.

Jess loves me. I don't have to explain to him the voices that pull me around the planet. He doesn't say so, but he knows that I'm lost. Whatever spirit it was that moved me yesterday has left me without a map. Jess knows that navigation will be his job, whether he wants it or not.

We ride quietly. He doesn't say where we're going. I don't ask. When we stop beside the Colorado River he is hopeful. "You want to look at petroglyphs?" he asks.

We get out of the truck and walk across the road to the cliffs that rise from the river bottom. The desert varnish looks liquid in the sunlight, poured onto the rock like blackstrap molasses. I scrutinize triangular people holding hands, making chains across the wall. The antlered head of an ancient man rivets my attention. Chiseled eyes gaze into mine. A fierce stare that makes the hair on my arms stand up. I wait for him to speak.

"Want to go?" Jess breaks the trance.

I nod. "Yeah, might as well."

We spend the remaining day a few miles off the pavement in a delicate slickrock wonderland. Jess finds fossils. Snails and the flowing shadows of aquatic plants are cast in stone. The desert is haunted. Each ghost has a story, a voice, a song. There is a melody that the wind amplifies. The rhythm of your own feet walking. Your own heart beating sets the tempo and lyrics come easy as a Mourning Dove's call.

Jess and I seldom hike together, preferring to spend our time alone and hooking up later with stories to tell. Today while I walk I listen for the desert to sing. I'm careful not to damage the cryptogamic soil or the fragile plants that are peeking above the arid ground, seeking spring. I see the season's first lizard bask on the limb of a grizzled cedar tree. I touch the scant moisture in the cool pink sand. Crumble it between my fingers like slipping poetry, sifting into space.

I stop to rest on a lonely hump of sandstone. For awhile neither of us say anything. I decide to risk conversation. "You want to know what my mom said to me last week?" I ask the rock. "She told me to be a hollow bone. She ran into those words in a book she's reading. She said they make sense."

I wait for the rock to reply. I sit cross-legged, fidget with the nylon strap of my day-pack. I sip water and soak sun into my hair. The rock doesn't offer a comment.

"In theory," I say, "they do make some sense. I understand the concept, but I'm not sure how it applies to everyday living. Be open, like a hollow bone. Let spirit pass, like wind, through me."

The rock that I'm sitting on doesn't seem the least concerned with my philosophical contemplation. It mumbles something about a hawk I'm missing, talking so much.

I shut up, look ahead, past the rim into sky. There is a red-tailed hawk circling. I think there is a message in her spiral dance across the sky. I try hard to be a hollow bone. I close my eyes and focus on my breath. I repeat the words, hollow bone, over and over. Nothing happens. When I open my eyes there is a hawk hunting in front of me. She's part of the landscape. Lovely, but not unusual.

A raven squawks. I squawk back. I listen for a message from divinity. I am alone in the desert with a hawk, a raven, and a rock. I expect to have a vision any minute. The minutes pass and the only vision I have all day is a perfect red desert melting off winter and whispering into spring.

SUNDAY

JESS AND I are broke. If we skip breakfast and don't drive too far, we might have enough money for dinner on the way back to the city. It's this thought that carries us into the neighborhood hills of Moab.

We're driving and chatting, admiring, or appalled by the new executive housing development in the pink-orange slickrock above town. We're on a street that's coiling up farther than we expected when I discover that we've accidentally made one of those right turns again. One of those spontaneous twists of fate that can't possibly be planned.

We round a corner, drive past the city dump, and I'm hit with a frenzy of excited voices. We've stumbled onto the rocks that shook me from sleep and insisted I come to the desert.

I grab Jess by the arm. "Can you hear them?" I ask him. "This is it. This is where the rocks talk. Jess, can you hear them?"

Jess opens his window to listen. "I don't hear anything," he says.

The pavement ends and the street turns to well-maintained gravel. A sign points to a trailhead. Tells us that we've found Moab's renowned Slickrock Recreation Area. Mountain-biking extravaganza. Wilderness extraordinaire.

I want to puke. The desert has cancer. Is dying a wretched death.

We park the truck a couple of miles up the road, past the paved parking lot and the painted-white-line mountain bike freeway system. We get out. Jess goes his way. I go mine.

I walk. The devastation is breathtaking. The gentle vista is improved with health-conscious America's plastic power-drink bottles. Pure mountain springwater jugs caress the land in ornate, decorative gardens. Dry washes now come with the added benefit of Jeep trails. Each twisted juniper has a campground with a fireplace and its own circular driveway. No extra cost for beer cans, dirty diapers, used toilet paper, cigarette butts, or plastic forks. All standard amenities. Part of the scenic wilderness package.

I sit in a shallow cave and gaze at modern-day pictographs. Black marker symbols painted on the windblown walls. A pot leaf, a rock climber, a downhill skier with a tasseled stocking cap, a hatchet. Twentieth-century rock art telling the tale of twentieth-century recreation. I wonder if the artists know the story they write on the pink wall, or if they leave the cave as ignorant as they enter it.

I'm suddenly overcome with the urge to rouse Ed Abbey from his comfortable desert grave and ask him, What now? What the fuck do we do now? Everybody loved the way you drove off the road and left beer cans as a tribute to the American way. But Ed, we have us a real problem here. Folks love Abbey's country. Love it to death.

I guess I know it's not his fault. I just can't figure out who else to blame. So I sit there, the wind blowing sand in my face. I watch a rabbit dart from sagebrush, a raven fly, dark clouds bank together for rain.

I sit here and feel sorry for myself for a long time. I don't need to see this. I've been playing in the desert for ten years without bumping into this crap. I think it's pretty crummy of the rocks to drag my ass down here for this. They promised a good time.

That's the way it is when you start listening to rocks. Sneaky bastards. They'll say anything to get you to do what they want.

I ask the rounded old monolith in front of me just exactly what it is that he thinks I can do about this mess.

"Be a hollow bone," he says.

Perfect Kiva

TERRY TEMPEST WILLIAMS

TERRY TEMPEST WILLIAMS, 37, is the Naturalist-in-Residence at the Utah Museum of Natural History in Salt Lake City, the place of her upbringing. A woman whose "ideas have been shaped by the Colorado Plateau and the Great Basin," she writes through her "biases of gender, geography, and culture." Her Mormon background and her intimate relationship to the natural world resound throughout books such as Refuge: An Unnatural History of Family and Place; Pieces of White Shell: A Journey into Navajoland; *and her most recent work,* An Unspoken Hunger. *A leader among writers and readers of the New West, Terry lives in Salt Lake City.*

IN A POORLY LIT corner of a restaurant in Moab, a woman draws a map on a napkin and slips it to a man. The man studies the paper square carefully and asks her a few questions. He thanks her. They pay for their meals and then part ways.

The man stops at a gas station, fills up his truck, then walks to the corner pay phone and makes three calls. Within hours, he meets five friends in Blanding, Utah, at the Rainbow Cafe. They conspire under the plastic jade lanterns, eating Navajo tacos and egg rolls.

"It's called Perfect Kiva. We'll camp on top of the mesa tonight, then hike into the canyon tomorrow. The site is on our right, up high, the third ledge down. I have the map."

THE SIX left Blanding in three trucks. The man with the map led them in the dark across miles of dirt roads that crisscrossed the mesa. In a sense, he had blindfolded them. That was his plan, and his promise to the woman in Moab.

Their camp appeared as a black hole in the desert. Each person drew out his flashlight and checked the ground for cow pies and scorpions. One by one, they threw down their sleeping bags and fell asleep. Dream time was kept by the rotation of stars.

Dawn came into the country like a secret. The six had burrowed so deep inside their bags that they emerged like startled ground squirrels after an eight-hour hibernation. The black hole of the previous night had been transformed into a bevy of piñon and juniper. A few yards beyond was a cut in the desert a quarter mile wide.

Camp was erased. Cars were locked. Water bottles were filled and packs put on. The pacing was brisk as they descended into one of the finger canyons. For two hours, they walked in and out of morning shadows, until, finally, they stood on the slickrock in full sunlight.

The man with the map studied cliffs, looking for the perfect alcove with the perfect kiva. Placing their trust in the leader, the others kept walking and found pleasures in small things like blister beetles and feathers snatched from the air by sage. The desert heat loosened the muscles and spirit of the group. Joy crept in and filled their boots. A few ran up and down boulders just to see if their courage could hold them. Others focused on birds—a lazuli bunting here, an ash-throated fly-catcher there. But the man with the map kept looking.

A raven flew out from the rocks.

"There it is!" cried the leader. "The third ledge down. I'll bet that's our alcove."

The six began to climb where the raven flew. They hiked straight up, some on hands and knees, through the sandstone scree, until finally, breathless, they encountered the ruins. Upright and stable, in spite of the thousand feet below them, the friends stood in wonder. They had entered an open-sided hallway of stone. Pink stone. Stone so soft that if held it would crumble.

There were figures with broad shoulders and wild eyes staring at them from inside the rock—petroglyphs that not only seized the imagination but turned it upside down. Animals with bear bodies and deer heads danced on the overhang. Walls made of dry-laid stones divided the ledge. Most of them had tumbled with time: no mortar had been used, just the careful placement of stone against stone to house the Anasazi.

Beyond the walls were mealing bins, standing stones that corralled the corn. The manos and metates were gone, but images of women chanting corn to meal were as real as the shriveled cobs piled inside the granary.

Perfect Kiva was more subtle. It was recognizable only by the fraying juniper bark that had shown through the eroded sand. The six sat outside the circle until calm. The kiva seemed to ask that of them. Five slabs of sandstone framed the entrance, which appeared as a dark square on the ledge floor. A juniper ladder with rungs of willow led to the underworld. They paused. The ladder that had supported the Ancient Ones might not support them. They chose not to use it. Instead, they jerry-rigged a sling out of nylon cording and carabiners and anchored it around a boulder. They moved the ladder aside and, one by one, lowered themselves into the kiva. Perfect Kiva—round like the earth. Hidden in the earth, the six sat.

It took a few minutes for their eyes to adjust. Cobwebs dangled from the wooden ceiling, most likely black widows spinning webs off the cribbed logs and pilasters. Walls bricked, then plastered, created the smooth red circumference of the ceremonial chamber. Four shelves were cut into the walls. Each was lined with juniper lace and berries. Two full moons, one green and one white, faced each other on the east and west walls. A green serpent of the same pigment moved on the north wall, west to east, connecting the circles.

No one spoke. The six remained captive to their own meanderings, each individual absorbing what he was in need of. An angle of light poured through the hole in the ceiling as the dust in the air danced up the ladder. They breathed deeply. It was old, old air.

The longer they sat in the kiva, the more they saw. There was a hearth in the center, a smoke vent to the south, eight loom anchors, and the fine desert powder they were sitting on. But the focus inside the kiva was on the *sipapu*—the small hole in the floor that, according to the Hopi myth, promised emergence. In time, each one circled the *sipapu* with his fingers and raised himself on the slings. They untied the rope from around the boulder and placed the Anasazi ladder back where it had been for as long as ravens had a memory.

A FEW months later, in a poorly lit corner of a restaurant in Moab, a woman speaks softly to a man.

"They took the ladder, put it in a museum, and stabilized the kiva. It's just not the same," she whispers. "They fear aging and want it stopped like an insect in amber."

He studies her face and asks her a few questions. He thanks her. They pay for their meals and then part ways.

The man stops at a gas station, fills up his truck, then walks to the corner pay phone and makes three calls. Within hours, the six meet in Blanding at the Rainbow Cafe.

"It's called theft in the name of preservation," he says. "The ladder is held hostage at the local museum. It belongs to the desert. It must be returned."

The friends move closer around the table.

"Tomorrow—," he says.

"Tonight," they insist.

DAWN CAME into the country like a secret.

Turquoise Canyon Sunset

PAT CARR

PAT CARR, 62, was born in Wyoming but grew up in Texas, mostly in Houston and El Paso. After teaching in El Paso for ten years, she and her writer husband Duane spent three years in Coudcroft, New Mexico, then back they went to academia at Western Kentucky University to send their youngest of four to college. They currently live on a small farm in Arkansas, but eventually hope to build on acreage they "just couldn't let go" near Deming, New Mexico. Winner of the Iowa Short Fiction Award for her book The Women in the Mirror, *Pat has published seven other books, including an archaeological study of Mimbres pottery entitled* Mimbres Mythology.

SHE'D SET OUT FROM El Paso early in the morning, but it took longer than she'd anticipated to search out the house set back on one of the unnamed dirt roads, took even longer to hammer loud enough for someone to answer her knock, and it was late afternoon by the time she actually found the old man. But he finally came to the door, stood there, his face the shade of oiled oak and his irises the color of dusty apple leaves, surveying her through the screen.

"I heard you had Indian artifacts for sale," she said without preamble. She'd become practiced in omitting the unnecessary civilities when buying artifacts.

He gazed at her with bland appraisal.

"Do you have any Mimbres?"

The possession of Mimbres pottery, for the most part illegally dug from government land, was almost impossible to get any dealer to admit to, and in this instance, the old man merely stared through the wire mesh screen as if he hadn't heard. He studied her for a few seconds.

"I got some Mimbres," he said at last. "Got 'em myself, from caves in the canyon mostly." He abruptly swung open the screen door. "Ain't for sale, but you're welcome to look."

She'd also become accustomed to appreciating other people's collections, and she climbed the frayed steps past the old man, who gave off a faint cellar odor, and went into a room that had been given over entirely to artifacts. Pottery, mauls, metates, trays of stone tools lined the dozens of wall shelves, spilled over onto the windowsills, the planks of the dusty floor. A narrow passageway, left between the rows of relics, gave the impression that it would become increasingly narrow as more and more artifacts crowded against it. Two ping-pong tables were the only furnishings left in the room, and they were crammed with pottery, stacked lip to lip over the playing surface. One of the tables held nothing but half-sphere Mimbres bowls.

She stepped carefully around the grimy pieces on the floor to reach the table, gazed down at the bowls, instantly engrossed, absorbed in a singular hiatus of space and time that excluded everything around her, that held her almost hypnotically each time she stood before Mimbres pottery. She found the bowls achingly beautiful, the sharp black figures on the white backgrounds as intricate, as distinctly original as any ancient Greek kylix design, as precise and immediately recognizable as any tombed Egyptian mural. She'd seen nothing from antiquity that could rival the stylized black figures so delicately, so painstakingly painted on the gray-white bowl interiors.

She reached down, her hand shaking slightly, and touched one of the bowls. Its rounded base tipped it into the next, and the thin pottery clicked with a sound of fine porcelain.

The old man came to stand at the end of the table. "That's a nice one," he said.

It was exquisite. A stylized black rabbit with long ears, long flexed legs, balanced in the smooth white hemisphere, poised for a leap through the four concentric bordering lines at the rim of the bowl. A startling white diamond, cross-hatched with tiny black squares, centered the rabbit's chest, symbolized its powers.

"I heard from Raphael Ortiz up in the village that you might know where there are some story bowls for sale."

There was a short silence. "I know where some are."

"I'm interested in them."

The old man gazed at her steadily with his pale jade eyes. "Latham's got some," he said after a pause. "He digs 'em up with a backhoe."

She stood for a moment, the strange flavor of metal on her tongue. "I'd still like to see the bowls," she said finally.

The old man nodded. "He's up at Jeffery's this week. Near a half hour ride's all."

He led the way back through the rows of pottery and stone implements, out to a canvas-topped, mud-spattered Jeep.

As soon as she climbed in, he gunned the Jeep across the gravel yard, hurtled over the cattle guard, and sped along beside the canyon. The path he took had once been a road, but was no longer passable except for the highest-axelled truck. Huge rocks had rolled near the tire tracks, lay boulder-sized, barely avoidable, and yellow flowered weeds grew a sturdy two feet high between the ruts. The ponderosa pines along the unused road had the girth of massive barrels, their bark scaly, warted, as if they'd stood on the mountain for millennia, their twelve-inch needles glinting in the paling sunlight as if they'd fossilized into glittering sprays of quartz.

She couldn't pass up the opportunity to see some of the fabled story bowls. Just to trace them down, to get someone to acknowledge the existence of the rare bowls that contained human figures and suggested Indian myths, was such a feat that she couldn't resist going out to see them. But how could she possibly buy pottery from someone who dug up ancient ruins with a backhoe? She knew no museum would have touched material vandalized like that, but their curators, lacking her ardor for Mimbres, could well stand aloof, could righteously and smugly reiterate that if there were no buyers, there would be no vandals.

The old man gestured vaguely toward the canyon. "Supposed to be veins of turquoise somewhere, but I never found any."

The cliff of dark stone dropped vertically, dramatically sheer to the empty river-bed. The water that the river once carried had polished the canyon face to the blocked and gleaming semblance of marble, and the perpendicular white striations in the bluish stone gave the effect of great dressed squares locked into a windowless wall. There too, in secret crevices, were supposedly ancient Mimbres dead, their skulls protected by, their spirits released through, the precious broken bowl.

The Jeep was enveloped in dust that hung colloidal below the canvas top, layered her jacket with fine powder, clouded the windshield into opaque glass. She tried to see through it as the old Jeep veered suddenly away from the canyon edge into the empty countryside where there was no sign of even the most rudimentary road.

They whirled across the open field for perhaps ten minutes, then the Jeep abruptly shuddered to a stop. The old man opened his door and got out while the motor was still shivering with inertia.

As she climbed down from her side, she couldn't suppress a grin of excited anticipation. "It's not very often anyone can locate story bowls," she said.

They weren't more than a few miles from the mountains and the canyon that cut through them, but the landscape had changed completely. Squat mesquite had replaced the towering pines; arid dunes, with gray-green weeds anchored to their sides like tufts of hair, had replaced the browning carpet of the forest floor.

"This here's Jeffery's land. State ain't got a say," the old man threw out cryptically as they set off across the desert.

He was leading her rapidly, but even in her quick stride that kept pace with him, she could tell they were crossing the ruins of an ancient pueblo. Ten centuries of blowing dust had buried the crumbled walls, but the very spacing of the mounds had given away the presence of the village. Pottery sherds littered the surface, showed in their fragments the black paint on the white slip of Mimbres ware.

"I've never actually been on a site before," she said as they went over a rise, down to a vast area in which the square outlines of pueblo rooms, dozens of them, were easily discernible.

She noted the ruined adobe walls at the same moment as she saw the backhoe.

Painted a garish chartreuse, its rectangular shovel was half sunk in the sand, ready to lift out a cubic yard of earth and adobe flooring from the thousand-year-old pueblo.

A wiry man in a billed cap, white T-shirt, and jeans relaxed on the tractor seat watching them.

"Buck," the old man called, just loud enough for the man to nod. "Buck, got somebody here who wants to buy story pots."

The one named Buck waited a few seconds before he slid down, slapped off his gloves, and turned toward them. *Disneyland* with its fantasy castle spires was emblazoned across his T-shirt. She saw that even with his cowboy boot heels, he was about her height.

"Got 'em inside," he said, and motioned toward a camper beyond the lime green backhoe. He stood evaluating her as a potential buyer, then nodded slightly as he went over to the camper, began wrestling with the triple row of locks he'd installed on the flimsy door.

A rose flush stained the sky and one lone cloud, arrested over the mountain, burst into a scarlet sunset flame. The mountain ridge began to empurple, and the pot sherds on the ground at their feet turned a faint mauve.

The final lock clicked open, and Buck began hefting cartons down from the camper. He carefully untied the ropes that secured the cardboard flaps and drew a series of bowls from their nest of newspaper.

There were white bowls with black figures hunting, swimming, carrying hatched baskets of four-footed fish, dancing with the humpbacked flute player, sowing, gathering, all arched in moments of stilled action, black against the pale slip. There were rare negatively printed black bowls with white figures of rabbits, geometrical butterflies, the horned water serpent. It seemed to her awed gaze that every ancient village activity was reproduced, that every ancient Indian ritual was depicted.

Bowls of all diameters, some with careful and minute kill holes, some fragmented and then repaired with twentieth-century glue, spread over the sand, became a pale amethyst in the sunset.

They were excruciatingly beautiful.

"Good, huh?" Buck looked up at her from the ground, untied a second box, took out another bowl.

Two figures danced in the white center, their ecstatic limbs the pure black of nudity, frozen in a moment of reaching hand to hand. The potter a thousand years before had caught in the joyful freedom of the dance an eternal love scene, black on white.

"But you ain't seen nothin' yet." Buck laid a second bowl carefully beside the dancers.

Two similar figures, attired only in a white bead necklace and an elaborate feather headdress, were engaged in obvious copulation, their sex organs scrupulously outlined with white. Their full-face eyes stared happily from the bowl interior as their profiles leaned tenderly into each other.

"You dig them all up with the backhoe?"

"Faster that way." He shrugged. "Market's good."

"Don't you destroy some?"

"'Bout half." Then he glanced up at her sharply. "You buyin' or not?" He turned to the old man watching them beside the camper. "I thought she was interested in some a them pots."

She stood there, her boots on the myriads of washed-to-the-surface pottery fragments, and willed herself to refuse, willed herself to have the necessary virtue to walk away. But her gaze was drawn back to the pottery, and the shadows of the two men faded as she stared down at the bowls laid out for auction, the bowls once so lovingly placed and killed over the skulls of the flexed dead.

"I'll take those," she said quickly and pointed at the two dancers, the lovers, the humpbacked flute player, the negatively painted horned water serpent. "How much?"

He didn't hesitate, didn't add anything up. "$3,700."

She glanced at his face that was rigidly impassive as he reached for the four bowls and started re-wrapping them in newspaper, laying them in one of the cartons he'd emptied.

She pulled her checkbook from her jacket pocket. She'd also learned when to bargain, when to accept the quoted price, and she knew he wouldn't refuse her check. She wanted all the bowls, wanted to sweep them all up in her arms, to carry them safely to her own cabinets, but she didn't have such unlimited funds, and she knew too that the more she bought, the faster he'd dig with the callous scoop of his back-hoe, the faster he'd destroy all of the culture, half the bowls buried beneath the floors of the ancient pueblos. And yet she couldn't not buy.

She handed him the check, which he barely glanced at, then stuffed into the pocket of his jeans while the old man lifted the box, carried it in silence back to the Jeep.

She didn't look at the sand-covered ruins as they drove away, but caught her lower lip slightly between her teeth and stared toward the sunset that had begun to fade, the mountain silhouette that had begun to blacken, to flatten against the sky as if it had been painted on the lavender curve of the horizon.

Officer Magdalena,
White Shell Woman, and Me

MARY SOJOURNER

MARY SOJOURNER, 54, is a freelance writer living in Flagstaff, Arizona. She has published a novel, Sisters of the Dream, *and two journals,* DreamWeaving *and* Sister Raven, Brother Hare, *in addition to many short stories and articles. Among the awards she has won are the 1990 Arizona Commission on the Arts Fellowship, and the 1993* Sierra Magazine *nature essay contest. She is currently at work on her second novel,* Going Through Ghosts, *which is "about the Vietnam War, how it touched so many of us, how it seared the earth." Her writing, Mary says, is her prayer of thanks to the place in which she is allowed to live.*

It wasn't until they locked Katy and me in the holding tank with the shoplifter and the public intox that I actually had my first spiritual experience. Up till then, it had gone pretty much to plan, *It* being the First Annual Uranium Mine Resistance Circle Dance and Blockade. Katy, a.k.a. Sparrow, and I were the only women to chain ourselves to the gates that protected the proposed mine site from the dangers of deer, elk, and mountain chickadees. Up there, right up near the Grand Canyon, in that green-gold ponderosa pine forest, with purple lupine and locoweed underfoot, beneath a high desert sun, she and I and the six men had stretched our arms along the wire and we'd all thought something like, If you're gonna get busted, this is the place to do it!

You might know how it can be with these things, how the circles form, how support people take your valuables and car keys, how everybody starts singing a round or two of inspired and outdated songs which each of us knows only parts of, so that our voices waver on the verses, and only on the chorus do they bust loose and soar and send shivers down our linked arms. And, of course, before all that brief and glorious solidarity, there are the meetings with that which Katy calls "terminal consensus," and the frantic phone calls, and the too-long press releases that go out one day short of too late.

And then, at last, there is the stepping out, the half-walk, half-dance to the twelve-foot-high chain-link fence. There are the wails of those who have come to mourn for the poisoned creatures of these Four Corners, and for the poisoned land, for Tuba City and Rio Puerco and Grants, and, if our cries aren't heard and heeded, Grandmama Canyon, herself. That's how we talk, that's how some of us feel, that the earth really is a woman, and She is being killed. I don't know if we're making that up, or if we're finally, like Katy says, just remembering what we once knew.

So there we all are, the woman got up as a raven and one as a raccoon. There's always at least one white kid with dreads and Tibetan bells. There are three sturdy housewives from the Pueblos; a withered, grinning Blue-Green Water People medicine woman in fuzzy bedroom slippers; six determined and appropriately dressed hikers from the birdwatchers' group, and then, almost as an afterthought, there are the sheriffs coming toward us, good old Joe Bob and Carl, the young cop, the one with all the community college human relations courses under his belt, and, smack in between them, Officer Lita Consuela Magdalena, her shining hair caught up neatly under her hat.

They held us awhile up there, Katy and me and the six guys. In the lull, in the nothing much happening, I was suddenly afraid. I could hear our circles singing. I could see banners waving in the fading sun. It didn't help enough. I bent and picked a few sprigs of sage and tucked them in my shirt pocket. That good, green, fierce scent vaporized a little of my fear.

"Thanks," I whispered.

Joe Bob got a message on his radio. He nodded, then he and Carl and Officer Magadalena cuffed us behind our backs.

"Orders from above," Joe Bob said sheepishly.

It took ten minutes for the hurt to start. I went inside myself, away from the pain, away from the steady and unwelcome knowledge of muscles in my shoulders I'd never cared to know about. I'm glad I learned to do that when things get bad, even if I learned it when I was little and it was necessary . . . even if that very ability has chased off more than one love in my life.

They loaded the guys into a waiting van and drove out the dirt road. We could see the dust plume rise up above the trees and get smaller and smaller till it disappeared. *That* was a strange feeling. In my stomach. Down in my knees. Officer Magdalena led Katy and me away from the gate. Katy and I sat on a big ponderosa stump, resting our aching arms on each other, taking turns, taking comfort till the squad car came. We squirmed in. Everybody cheered and waved good-bye. Officer Magdalena sighed, hit the gas, and we were off.

We rode the first forty-five minutes in silence. I watched the great, grandmotherly hump of Red Butte rise up on the horizon and fade away. I watched the ponderosa give way to squatty piñon and juniper. It was almost peaceful there in the car . . . the thin, dark scent of juniper drifting in through the open windows, the young aspens on the flanks of the Sacred Mountain starting to catch the first rose-gold of sunset. Much later, Katy and I would talk about that time, and we would agree that when you're as scared as we both were, when you're vigilant and surrendered, everything gets magical . . . the light and rock and sky you've seen for years are sudden miracles. I still hesitate to call that spiritual. It can be ordinary. It can be daily.

Officer Magdalena didn't say a word. About where the meadows stretch out like beaten silver below the Sacred Mountain, she turned on the radio and tuned in the oldies station that beams out of a rusted double-wide trailer on the outskirts of town. We've still got stuff like that out here, little hippie cafes, outdoor blues 'n' barbecue, bars where anybody can dance to good rock 'n' roll, anybody, burned-out, scrawny original Deadheads, nervous college kids in their natural fibers and mock psychedelic tees, even getting-older, built-for-comfort women like myself.

This station Officer M. tuned in plays Aretha and Creedence Clearwater and Cream and real blues, so, if you looked at it in the right spirit, the drive down, aside from the cuffs, was as good as it could get. Now and then, I'd look up in the rearview mirror and more often than not, I'd catch Officer Magdalena's cool brown eyes catching mine.

Katy fell asleep somewhere in the middle of "Chain of Fools." The shimmery feathers she'd woven into her braids fluttered in the air. I watched her eyes rove back and forth under her lids. She loves to dream. She believes we learn more in our dreams than we ever do in our waking life, and she says "Blessed be" whenever she parts from someone, and she has taught herself about the people out here, about their Grandmothers, White Shell Woman and Spider Grandmother and Angwusiwuhti, the Black-Winged, and the old, old Earth Mother that lives near Red Butte, under the proposed mine site, her belly, her uterus directly beneath where they would sink the shaft.

It was purple dusk by the time Officer Magdalena drove into the narrow alley behind the jail. Katy stretched and winced. Officer Magdalena didn't unlock the squad car doors. She glanced over. You could see the guys in the receiving area looking out at us.

"Listen girls," Officer Magdalena said, "I want to tell you something."

"Sure," Katy said.

"A lot of us are with you in spirit," Officer Magdalena said. She looked down at her hands. "We just have to be careful."

"We know that," Katy said. "Thanks."

Officer Magdalena grinned in the rearview mirror. "For what?" she said. "I didn't say anything."

I heard the doors unlock. Officer M. gently helped us out of the car and led us past a barrage of buzzers and clicking locks. Those clicks are loud as gunshots. They scare you immediately. They, and the fluorescent lights that shed icy green glare down on the receiving area, let you understand, in no uncertain terms, where you are.

We walked in, past maybe a dozen guys in yellow jumpsuits and rubber flip-flops. These dudes were sitting around on the benches that lined the walls. They were smoking and staring and waiting for something happen. Katy and I were the happening for the day. I got mad and Katy just smiled.

"Assholes," she whispered in my ear.

They didn't catch it and went on conjecturing just loud enough for us to hear about the young broad's butt and the old one's bad attitude till Officer Magdalena pointed out quietly that they were walking a *mucho* narrow line. She took off our cuffs. In that sweet moment of release, I didn't care about the guys not saying anything about my butt, the scary green lights, or the way my heart was going bonzai against my ribs.

Officer M. traded papers with the receiving officer, took us in the john one at a time, confiscated our bras so we wouldn't hang ourselves with them and led us to the ugliest door I've ever seen. It was metal. It was scarred. It held nothing but a tiny barred window and what seemed like a dozen locks. You couldn't look through it. You couldn't see the room until you were in it.

I stepped in and saw two women, two mattresses on the floor, and a toilet smack in the middle of it all.

"This is Liz and Katy," Officer Magdalena said.

"Can you get me a cigarette?" the older lady said. You could tell she was hurting bad. Her brown eyes were red and her dark skin was gray. She grinned. The younger girl just stared at the floor. She was wearing some kind of really great perfume. She'd set her high-polished cowgirl boots in the corner and her stockinged toes were blue with cold.

"Sallie, " Officer M. said, "I'll try." She turned to me and Katy.

"This is Sallie," she said, "and Philomena." The younger woman nodded and stretched out her hand. She didn't look up. I took her hand. Her grasp was a whisper.

"It's past supper," Officer Magdalena said, "but I'll try to get you girls some coffee."

"Oh please," I said. Katy laughed. Coffee's my communion. Officer Magdalena nodded and let herself out. How a door like that closes is a miracle. You learn more in that instant than you could ever imagine.

"She's one of the nice ones," Sallie said. She was still loaded. There was a blue bruise on her cheek. Every now and then she would touch it and she'd shake her head, the way you sometimes think you can shake off pain. She grabbed the toilet and pulled herself up enough to lean over it. When she gagged, nothing came. I could hear the air catch in her throat. I could smell her breath, the sweet wine, the vomit.

Philomena looked up. "I hate doing that," she said.

Katy nodded. She was buttoning up her flannel shirt against the chill. I followed suit, found the sage in my pocket. I crushed some between my fingers and passed it around. Sallie sat back down and cupped her hands for the sage. She breathed in deep and smiled.

"Yeah," Katy said, "once when I was fifteen I got messed-up drunk and my mom had me arrested and when they were carrying me to the cell, I puked all over 'em. They wanted to hit me. You could tell, but they didn't do it."

"How come?" Philomena said.

" 'Cause they knew my mom's ex, my good old Dad," Katy said. Philomena nodded.

"Hey," Sallie said, "that's how it is. You got a smoke?"

Somehow, Katy had smuggled in her makings, so she rolled a couple cigarettes and we settled down for Girls' Night In. I drifted in and out of the talk. I spend a lot of time alone, mostly by choice, and it was new to me, and good, how one woman's voice would rise up, another's chime in, then fade away into a comfortable silence, and then, gently moving into the silence, some more words, a little laughter.

"I'm a weaver," Sallie said. "Me and my husband, we got horses, too. We got our own place up Farmington way. He come down here to party. That's how I got *here*. Went lookin' for him. Stopped into Joe's. Next thing you know, fell off the damn bar stool. And *next* thing you know, busted for P. I." She shrugged down into her denim jacket.

"What're you girls in for?"

The question hung there between us. I looked down. White folks' privilege was what I was thinking, getting arrested on purpose, knowing that somewhere outside, forces were moving, calls were being made, bail was being easily arranged. I'd hassled that around in my head before I'd stepped out and I guessed I'd be wrestling it around for the rest of my life. Katy just sucked in a good lung-full of smoke, blew it out, and, as usual, kept it simple.

"We locked ourselves to the gate of that uranium mine up near the Canyon."

Philomena laughed. "Why'd you do that? Shit, I didn't even know there was one. Why'd you want to go and get arrested?"

"So the TV people would come," Katy said. "So the mine owners and the government would know not everybody goes along with their program."

Sallie stubbed out her cigarette and tucked the butt in her pocket. "My grandma died from that shit," she said. "My uncle Ray, too. He worked in it. They never told him nothin'."

"Well," Philomena said, "I sure wish I could trade places with you girls. I took my little cousin into the Fairmart and he wanted a box of crayons. I didn't have no money, so I just stuck 'em in my purse, no big deal, a buck twenty-nine was all. We get outside and this big old security comes up behind me and grabs my purse. I thought she was trying to snatch it, so I whacked her." She shook her head.

"Course I was a little drunk." She grinned at me. She'd made her eyes up perfectly, black liner stroked on just so, shadow all shimmery and soft.

"Ooooeee," she said, "my aunt's gonna kill me." I grinned back and nodded.

"You got kids?" she said, and right there, right then, I got whomped with my moment of light. I nodded again. I could hardly talk. I could hardly tell her about my daughter and her daughter, and how my daughter made up her eyes just so and how streaked they were that night she nearly died from booze and I was too loaded to help her. I could hardly tell her about the day my daughter came home clean and sober. And, the day I did.

I could hardly get out the words to name the feelings, the words that could make the knowledge whole. I wasn't seeing things. There was nothing psychedelic, nothing like the visions I hear some people describe. Nobody had colors glowing around her head and there was no big Grandfather God voice speaking. Those Las Vegas moments don't come to me. Blessed be. I remembered how Katy had taken me to a white-boy sweat lodge once, and while the guys were singing Navajo songs, hollering Paiute chants, all I'd gotten was drenched and dizzy, a longing for the midnight indigo sky, and the faintest glimmer that my people had done this. Me and my sisters and cousins and aunts had sat in the hot dark, had risen up out of a mountain cave and breathed in the cold diamond stars.

Truth is, I'm grateful to be spared those 3-D visitations. Whatever moves out there, whatever hums and dances in me, She knows I'm scared. She knows I've seen enough, heard enough to last a lifetime. She knows I can only take a little at a time. She knows to keep it simple and do it daily. So, as I knew the way Philomena's eyes were like my daughter's, and my daughter's like Katy's, and Katy's like Sallie's and mine and Officer Magdalena's, and that lady cop's clear tiger's-eye gaze so like my granddaughter's, I smiled.

"I do have kids," I said. "I've got three sons, a daughter, and a grandbaby. They're the reason I got arrested."

Sallie grinned. "Well, yeah," she said quietly. "That's the way it's supposed to be."

Olivia

RITA GARITANO

RITA GARITANO, 55, has combined the careers of teaching and writing for her life's work, believing that the dual careers are symbiotic. She has taught at high schools, community colleges, and universities, and found that teaching has involved her in the lives of others in a way that nourishes her creativity. Her poetry and fiction have appeared in a variety of magazines and six anthologies. She was an NEA creative writing recipient in 1987, and she received an Arizona Commission on the Arts creative writing fellowship in 1990. "Olivia" is from Speedway Boulevard, *a novel-in-progress about the impact of urbanization on residents of Tucson, Arizona, the first chapter of which was published in* Riversedge, Chicano Issue 3, *in 1993. Rita currently resides in Tucson.*

ALONE AT HOME AT night, Olivia sat knitting. She tossed the yarn about the needle point and drew it taut to make another stitch. Her movements were so rapid and precise, she was mesmerized as she stared at the needles and yarn flashing before her, so deep in a trance she wasn't conscious of the rattling at the door. When the door, swollen by the monsoon rains, groaned as it pushed open, she froze. This was too early for Manny to be home. And Megda had begun working late evenings on the four-day schedule for the city. Stifling her impulse to call out, Olivia's belly contracted as she held her breath. Someone walked in her kitchen, the steps slow and stealthy, the steps of someone stealing inside, the way Gloria sneaked into the house when she'd violated her curfew. But this couldn't be Gloria. Now she never came home at night, when their most furious battles had been fought. Now, Gloria only came to the house for her dutiful Sunday morning appearances.

If Olivia moved her head, she could see behind her into the darkness. But if she turned her face to the side to peer from the corner of her eye, she might be observed by this thief who had broken into her house. She might be bludgeoned to death and raped like the Corrales girl they found in the arroyo near Speedway. She heard her own breathing, and the pounding of her heart was so powerful she wondered if the thief could hear it, too.

"Mamma," the sound hoarse, not the feathery whisper of Gloria.

Stunned, Olivia swiveled her head as if she'd been struck. In the shadows, a man's white T-shirt glowed and above it was Lalo's tense face. His eyes black in dim light, he held his finger to his lips as a warning for her to silence her cries. He said in a low voice, "You're alone, Mamma." And it wasn't a question; it was a confirmation.

She beckoned for him to come into the living room light, where she could see him. He might be a vision in a nightmare; perhaps she'd fallen asleep and was experiencing a dream. Lalo was supposed to be locked away in some prison. After he violated his probation by using drugs, he was sentenced to at least a year in one of the many prisons Rey said were out on the east side, a place she'd never visited. This man who stood before her was tense and wary as a starving alley cat. He had the hungry look he'd had the last time she'd seen him. As she gazed out of the window of Manny's car while it flowed with the traffic down Speedway, they'd flashed by a hitchhiker; their son stood by the side of the road with his arm stretched out. The fleeting image of his dark eyes in his gaunt face had been so devastating she'd been unable to call out to Manny to stop, and when she turned to him, his eyes were fixed on the road before him. His concentration had insulated him from her painful vision. Perhaps she'd hallucinated. But Lalo's image haunted her, the question hovering like a stinging wasp: How had her son, her baby, her spoiled little prince, become this starved, frightened man, locked away from others to protect the world from his violence that exploded like a match being struck?

Olivia only went once to see Lalo when he was sentenced to the county jail as an adult. On visiting day, Manny had driven her all the way across town to a group of tall buildings, and a yard surrounded by a chain-link fence with swirls of barbed wire topping it. She was sick imagining her son locked inside. Manny went into a building with her and listened while she spoke in English to ask a man in a uniform about the procedure to see the prisoners and watched while she filled out the papers to request a visit; they waited thirty minutes before the prisoners were led through the steel doors to meet their visitors. Lalo glanced at his father, who nodded a silent acceptance of his son's shame, and then his mother. For a moment Lalo had gnawed on his lower lip, and then looked away. Women who must've been wives embraced the men who came toward them smiling. Families shook hands with the prisoners or patted them on their backs. But Lalo stared past Manny and Olivia and walked in front of them, so they silently followed. They sat in a yard on concrete benches among the other prisoners and their visitors. His shoulders hunched like a tortoise shell, Lalo leaned forward with his elbows propped on his knees and studied the ground. He kept his face turned from them, set in stony silence, only nodding a response occasionally. She asked how he'd been and what he did all day and when he thought he'd be coming home, but his terse answers made questions harder and harder to ask, so they all sat in silence. She wished she'd known she could bring him food, for the others were eating and some even laughed as if it were a picnic. When she asked if she should bring him some food next week, he turned to look at her. He said, "Don't come see me. If I have a visitor, the guard gives me a strip search."

She didn't know what a "strip search" meant and Rey was the only person who might. When he'd come to visit, she'd called him into the kitchen where they'd be alone. Even he seemed embarrassed when he said, "The guards make the prisoners take off their clothes, and check their privates to see if they're hiding any drugs or weapons brought by their visitors."

In the shadows of her lighted living room, Lalo's pupils weren't visible in his glossy irises. He warily glanced about him. She wondered if his body ached for drugs to course through his veins. He kept his hands stuffed in his jeans pockets, so his shoulders jutted forward and up. A blue worker's shirt flapped open over his white undershirt and Levi's, an outfit he'd never select to wear. Her son, the peacock who strutted in the flamboyant threads of his gang, was wearing the uniform of the jail where he lived. He was a skeleton, so tense the skin beneath his left eye ticked. He stepped from foot to foot, almost dancing as he spoke. "Mamma." His whisper was urgent. "Mamma, I need money. Cash. As much as you can—now."

Her heart hurt when she tried to speak. "I have no money." She had nothing to give him but the coins in the penny jar and the couple of dollars in the envelope where she kept her grocery money. This was Thursday, almost a week after pay day and all the money had been spent to pay bills, a chore she always performed as soon as Manny brought her his check. "I have only pennies and a couple of dollars."

Lalo ground his teeth and wrenched his head to the side. "Mamma, you want me to beg?"

Her breath escaped as though he'd hit her in the throat. Lalo was a greedy baby, a selfish child, a prince she could never satisfy. She'd been too sick to nurse him, too weak to care for him, to sick to fight him. She'd taught Gloria to mother him. Only five, only a baby herself, Gloria dressed Lalo and carried him and cooed to him and put the bottle to his lips the moment he began to cry. Shamed by the sight of her baby girl caring for her infant brother, a mother's obligation, Olivia had grown silent and withdrawn. Gloria had always given Lalo whatever he wanted as soon as he asked for it. And he'd always asked for more than the family could give. So nothing he got was ever enough. And he never believed they gave all they could. When Lalo's desires were denied, he'd run to his mother, the person who should be the source of his nourishment. Whenever she refused him, he stared at her, his eyes smoldering with angry accusation as if he believed she'd abandoned him just to be cruel.

Olivia braced her arms against the arms of her chair and pushed her spine against its back. She'd go in the kitchen and get the envelope. She'd get the penny jar from Manny's side of the dresser. If she showed Lalo these simple pieces of evidence, he should believe her.

He'd turned from her. His shoulders were broad, far more powerful than hers; his luxuriant hair, thick and straight as an Indian's, was knotted with a rubber band and fanned down his back. He stared at Manny's TV that muttered too low to hear what Johnny Carson said.

She wondered if Lalo planned to steal his father's favorite possession. She hoped Lalo wouldn't steal the TV, for she could never tell Manny; it would be far too painful to tell such a shameful tale. And the secret would be as painful to carry as one of her stillborn babies. She silently prayed: *Oh God, oh God, oh God, come to Lalo now and make him right.* But her mind made her words stop. Only God could save Lalo, and God had never answered her prayers for her son.

"Jesus Christ," he murmured. "Jesus Christ," he hissed, and his hands were out of his pockets and he was shaking his fists at the ceiling. "Christ!" he screamed. "Nothing. They've got nothing but this fuckin' shitty TV."

Clock of Changing Color

ELLEN WINTER

ELLEN WINTER, 32, drove Southwest in 1987 to attend the MFA creative writing program at the University of Arizona in Tucson. "I'd never been west of the Mississippi," she says, "and by the time I saw my first prickly pear I knew I'd made a big mistake. I complained about how brown things were, the way the seasons blended into one, and the sky—it was always so blue." After completing the program, she moved back East like she'd been longing to, and found that she couldn't stop writing about the Southwest. She now lives in a ramshackle adobe on the outskirts of Tucson with a black cat and an Australian shepherd. Ellen is completing a collection of short stories, several of which have been published in places such as Ladies' Home Journal, Cosmopolitan, *and* Puerto del Sol.

I'VE LIVED IN THIS house since 1952. It was built forty years before that. The house has spent half its life with me, and I've spent two-thirds of my life with the house. It'll go on without me, I suppose. The house—a bungalow, really—is considered "historic." I'm just old.

Things have changed and they haven't. The house is much as it's always been. During his stay here my husband Arnie enclosed its two porches. After he died I opened them up again. I'd like to say I took a sledge to the walls myself, but the truth is I hired a carpenter with the money Arnie left me. He tore down the walls that brought darkness to my kitchen, carried away wood that spread gloom through my halls. He had the delicate touch of a jeweler; the nails he pulled were straight enough to use again. With the porch walls gone, air and light streamed into the house, scrubbing it clean of shadows that had before gathered like corner dirt. What if the wind was hot as the breath of a panting dog? The potted plants swayed and the curtains fluttered, and it seemed to me that the house was shifting about like an animal in its den, settling in for another long period of waiting.

The neighborhood has changed, of course, riding a wave of ups and downs typical of neighborhoods built at the turn of the century. When Arnie and I moved here as newlyweds this was a family neighborhood. The railroad heyday was over, but descendents of trainmen still lived in the small brick and adobe houses that huddled together as if they could hide in each other's shade. There were corner stores with plate glass windows where kids bought pop. Now the storefronts are boarded over. There's a Dairy Mart at Fourth and Twenty-Second, and a drive-through liquor store at Cushing and Stone. I use the car to get groceries at Safeway.

There are still families here, but they live in houses with flaking roofs and crumbling foundations, close to the tracks or busy street corners. They are often headed by a mother only. Mexicans have pushed north from South Tucson, and a few daring lawyers have pushed south from downtown. There are graduate students from the university, and artistic types drawn by low rent and history. In the dusky hours of morning and evening, vagrants shamble their way down the narrowest streets in a daily migration from park to park.

It's the kind of neighborhood where young women hike their long, full skirts to slowly pedal one-speed bikes. I find myself watching those women with a certain envy, not sure if it's the bike I admire (and the ability to ride it—my bony knees will never push a pedal again) or the lazy nonchalance with which these women reveal themselves. I imagine the breeze must feel nice on their perspiring thighs.

A bike-riding woman lives in the duplex next door. She chains the bike to her part of the porch when she comes home from work. As soon as she is in the place the music starts up. Her name is Larinda. I know this because her boyfriend, who acts like his car will never start again if he shuts it off (he may be correct in his judgment) hollers for her when he picks her up. "Larinda baby, are you ready for me or what?" he calls, gunning the engine and shooting exhaust into the street. Soon enough she appears in the doorway, looking like a gypsy in her swishing skirt.

After I tore down the walls that enclosed my porches, I started planting vines. I had no real preference—any kind of vine would do. I have honeysuckle and bougainvillaea, passion vine and tombstone roses. The vines wind together like yarn tangled by an errant cat. They spiral around the porch railing, trail like water from the edges of my roof. Light passing through their webbing makes lacy patterns on the gray planks of my porch. Sitting on my glider I can see and hear much. But from the street I am only a shadow.

I moved to Tucson from Prescott in the fall of 1950. I came to attend the teacher's college at the university. My family never really expected me to graduate, but after what happened going away seemed like the best thing. I'd been through Tucson on my way to Mexico, so I knew what to expect when I got here. I met Arnie at a mixer they had for us. He worked in the mines, though his father was a rancher like mine. I suppose I thought he was nice enough. I remember the way his hand trembled when he took mine in it to dance. I remember thinking that it mattered to him what I thought of him, and being impressed by that fact.

Arnie was always courteous. What he lacked in kindness he nearly made up for with good manners. He sent flowers, was on time when he picked me up for dates. I learned later that he thought he was getting more than I had to offer. He assumed I was from "good stock" as he put it, since my family was able to send me to school. He was shocked when he saw my father's patchwork outbuildings and peeling paint. He'd imagined my father a sort of rancher-statesman—someone with influence in the community.

Arnie didn't meet my family until after our elopement. I made sure of that. I didn't meet his until the Thanksgiving after our marriage. I felt right at home on their hardscrabble ranch in Thatcher. I couldn't understand what it was about my father's place that made Arnie sputter and fume.

Things weren't so bad at first. As I said, Arnie was courteous. He was impressed with me in a way, and impressed with himself for winning me. After he saw my father's ranch he made some adjustments to the story he told himself. Instead of seeing me as the daughter of someone with influence, he came to see me as a woman so lovingly dedicated to the younger generation that she'd sacrifice everything to teach. This after I'd dropped out of school to marry him. Arnie saw things the way he saw them—there was never any reasoning with him.

Arnie bought the little house on Herbert Avenue because it was in the Armory Park district: the best neighborhood in town when Tucson was barely a speck on the map. The house was nice enough, small but solid. I could have told him what would happen to the neighborhood, pointed out that bigger houses were being built east of the university, but of course he never asked and I'd learned by then to keep my opinions to myself. Marriage with Arnie was like a ride on a two-seater bicycle: he in front with the wind in his hair, me behind with his back for a view, pedaling more than my share.

The porches were enclosed to make room for the children. Arnie did it himself, though he wasn't particularly handy. He was practical but not inventive; the rooms he made had only a window apiece that let in little light. They had high ceilings like the rest of the house, and Arnie went on and on about the bunk beds they'd hold, putting his arms around me from behind so he could rub my stomach, which was flat as a board and firm to the touch. Over time my stomach changed, but not in the way he'd hoped, taking on the heft and consistency of dough that refuses to rise. I know, I baked a lot in those days and had my share of frustrations.

Housework was my forte. I scrubbed floors on my hands and knees, polished wood and glass until they glistened seamlessly. When everything was clean as I could get it I took up handiwork. Silly things at first: a cover for the toaster and matching pot holders, a doll whose dress cleverly concealed a roll of toilet paper. After awhile I started quilting. I was good at it, too. Before long I was working intricate patterns of my own design with smaller and smaller pieces of cloth. It was as if I were out to discover how tiny a piece of cloth could be and still have its color affect the outcome of the whole. I was deft. Looking in the mirror I saw my face gathering at the middle, pulled together by many hours of bending over work with an expression of rapt concentration. I saw that everything about me was moving toward a center, not radiating from me to others like it should.

Arnie kept his peace for a long time, loving me twice a week in a determined fashion. For a while he massaged my stomach vigorously in way that wasn't altogether pleasant, saying I needed to increase my circulation. Once or twice he suggested I prop my heels on the wall over my head, but I wasn't up for that sort of silliness. You see I knew all along that the juices running out of me were at fault. I knew but I couldn't say.

Arnie was a hard worker, and we never lacked for food and clothing. Still, when it became clear that I wasn't going to hold up my end of the bargain he became stingy in a focused way, doing what he could to make my work harder. Long after other women on the block had washing machines, I was still making twice weekly trips to the Laundromat. If I were like the others, Arnie told me when I mentioned it, I'd have something besides laundry to carry.

By that time our house looked like something out of a magazine. Everything was clean and in its place. The curtains matched the bedspreads, the towels matched the rugs, the furniture had matching slipcovers. There was a single-minded neatness to the place. It was unnerving; there was none of the tangle of happily entwined lives.

And so I began luring the cats. It was easy enough; most of the families in the neighborhood had a pet or two and sooner or later a litter of kittens came along. I favored females, and gave them names that hinted at wrongdoings to come: Malverne and Felonia, Trixie and Spite. The cats wove through the house, their trails connecting dark hiding places to windowsills and cubbyholes with a view. They snuck into our bed, only to be tossed fat-furred into the night by Arnie. He never admitted they were mine, though they yowled at doors and snagged at screens with their claws. I kept bowls of food beneath the front steps. After a while Arnie began sleeping on the enclosed back porch, claiming their cries and the feel of their fur against his legs were more than he could abide. When he caught them in the house he'd stamp his foot, sending them scuttling into shadow like vermin.

Arnie wasn't one to directly accuse. But little by little he let me and anyone else who would listen know that it was my fault. Once at a Christmas gathering I over-heard him talking to his brother. They'd snuck off to the back porch—the blue room, decorated in a jaunty nautical mode in anticipation of seaworthy boys. They had a bottle of scotch I wasn't supposed to know about. "She ain't right," I heard Arnie say as I made my way down the hall, the liquor releasing a slang he usually managed to contain. "I can feel it in her, something tight and hard she's squeezing closed. I could pump gallons in there and not a drop would get through." There was a pause, a space in which they most likely raised their glasses to take self-righteous slugs of liquor. "She just lays there," Arnie added.

I stood as if my pumps had anchored themselves to the floor. My heart was pounding. Partly it was the indignity of being evoked that way—sprawled spread-eagled beneath Arnie. Partly it was fear that one of them would choose that moment to leave the boys' room and find me lurking in the hallway. But mostly it was a helpless rage over what I knew and could never say.

THERE ARE fall days in Arizona when the sky increases its blue with each passing hour. Looking at it you feel as if you've taken a too-deep breath and held it, your lungs stretched to a sweet ache. It was on a day like this in my nineteenth year that Jack and I saddled up horses and went for a ride.

Jack was a ranch hand, a wetback, as my father called them. His given name was Joaquin. He'd taken the name Jack as if it could bleach the brown from his skin. He'd been with us since early summer, helping with the cattle and living in a shed out back. My mother fixed him a plate at dinnertime, but he didn't eat with us. Each night he'd return the plate spotless, and each night I'd wash it again at my mother's insistence. That's when I saw him up close, though he moved around me all day, passing from corral to shed, riding fences in the distance. As the plate passed between us, I'd try to arrange for my fingers to touch his. That moment, a moment when he might or might not glance up at me, pulled me through interminable days.

I never knew much about Jack—how old he was, the name of the town he came from, whether or not he had a woman waiting. I knew only what I saw: shy brown eyes, a manner of moving that was both humble and graceful. He could make a horse do anything, and was quiet in a powerful way, like a far-off mountain. My father and brothers squabbled like barnyard fowl.

It was a lie that convinced Jack to ride with me that day. I told him I wasn't allowed to go alone. My father frowned on women riding, but there wasn't a rule about it for me to break, only the promise of manly mutterings and exchanged looks. We left in the morning with a packed lunch. I was glad that it was early and that we had the whole day, which with the sun just beginning to warm my shoulders seemed an awfully long time.

Jack rode beside me, not ahead in what my father and brothers considered their rightful place. The gentle way his pelvis rocked in cadence with his horse's gait made me lightheaded. All morning I watched his hands, one holding the reins, one resting on his thigh. He kept a light tension on the bit, a steady connection between his fingers and the horse's mouth. Late in the morning the trail we were riding began to switchback into the mountains. I leaned forward over my horse's withers, enjoying the feel of them working beneath me. The sun was hot on my hair, my shoulders, my thighs, and after a while the horse went liquid, carrying me like a bobbing cork. I removed the tie from my long braid, allowing it to unwind on its own as if by accident.

Jack and I didn't say much, our separate languages a barrier not easily crossed. We made occasional comments on the world around us: a hawk on a faraway branch, the bouncing tail of a jackrabbit. It was hard to talk about things that couldn't be pointed to, and I lost concern for all but the immediate. Maybe that's why I did what I did, though it's possible that even then I knew I'd need a day to remember, something I could hold on to like a picture of myself in a glamorous and unlikely dress.

We stopped to eat on a high plateau, turning the horses loose to search among rocks and prickly pears for tender traces of green. Jack and I passed a canteen. Our brushing fingers fueled the trembling in my knees. His eyes were on the place where my loose hair flapped against my shoulder.

We spread a blanket on the ground and ate the leftover chicken I'd packed the night before. He watched the horizon as we ate, neither speaking nor glancing my way. Something about the careful way he chewed let me hope he thought of me. I tried hard to think of something I could say or do, something that would make him smile into my eyes and acknowledge me. More than anything I wanted him to see me, to take me in like the view.

Jack reached for the last piece of bread. Soon it would be time for me to gather the things I'd spread before us. I'd fold the blanket, neatly matching corners, my hopes halved with each doubling of cloth. This was the day we had; I couldn't imagine stealing another. I looked back the way we'd come. My father's ranch was too far away to see, lost behind the curving side of a mountain. Above us the cloudless sky grew bluer, a clock of changing color.

And so I closed my hand over his. It was that simple. He turned to look at me. His eyes were like water viewed from above, full of shifting shadows and unrecognizable reflections. He must have seen something in me that reminded him of his own loneliness. He brought his fingers to my hair. And then he made love with me, so gently that afterward I would wonder if I had fallen asleep and dreamt it. I was filled with a warmth like liquid sunlight, teased into shuddering like dry grass blowing in the wind.

Jack had the good sense to leave that night. My father said it was what he expected. What he didn't expect was the way my stomach began to push at my dress a few months later, as if the secret I held inside me were growing and wanted out. They sent me to a relative in a faraway state, where the baby was taken from me. Never meant to be, I told myself. The baby was like a blown bubble, magically swelling to suddenly disappear.

When I got home silence greeted me, but whispers lurked in every corner. The ones who spoke to me directly—my mother and aunts—said I was lucky. I could start over again with a clean slate. They tried to erase what had happened, to cover my memories of Jack with ugly remarks about the way he'd bullied me. But tucked away out of view were marks on my belly, silver lines that would always remind me of his touch. To me they were like the trails of feathers.

And so if Arnie had known as much about women's bodies as he liked to think he did, he might have guessed that I'd once carried a child. I saw the doctor eyeing my stretch marks curiously when I went in for my yearly exam, but he was too polite to say anything. They didn't bother with tests and procedures back then. The men simply decided amongst themselves that there was something wrong with me. I was kept quiet by the power of what I knew, though there were times when I longed to set loose that disruptive information. I think I would have enjoyed watching it send the ideas Arnie had about me scattering like my cats did at the stamp of his foot.

ARNIE DIED several years ago. Somehow I knew he would go first. I was serene in my knowledge, believing always that I'd someday have the little bungalow to myself. Now it's peaceful here. There are days when I don't even bother to put on shoes. The threads I clip from my sewing gather in clumps on the floor, where they're batted about by cats.

Along with Arnie went part of my reason to tell. There's no longer a need to vindicate myself. The daily reminders that I'm not the woman I should've been are gone. And though it's true I've never been comfortable with children, other small things are drawn to me. Cats are pulled from corners, and hummingbirds lose themselves in the tangle of my vines.

There are people to talk to: the mailman, the paper boy, and Larinda-next-door. They call me Mrs. Luckmann, all of them, though I would much prefer to be called Lucy—the name of the girl I was.

Sometimes I think I'd like to tell someone about that blue-sky day long ago, when I climbed a hill I'd never wander again. Larinda is the one I most often imagine telling. But when I call her to my porch railing what I usually end up talking about is cats: hers and mine, the flying fur of their fights and the nighttime yowling. The secret—not of what I did but of who I was—has been mine for so long that a part of me is reluctant to share it. Bare-skinned in the late afternoon sun I knew the absolute certainty that is desire. Even after Jack turned away from me, embarrassed or sorry, I was sure. I looked back the way we'd come, saw the way the shadows reached for us in the fading light. It would be dark before we got home. I knew this, but I was unafraid.

With Fire

DEBRA HUGHES

DEBRA HUGHES, 38, was born in a town in the southern quarter of New Mexico, and grew up outside of Albuquerque in the bosque next to the Rio Grande. She has lived in places outside the Southwest, but not for long. The land here, "its changes and rifts and blank spaces," feeds her soul and her writing, which has been published in the anthology Tierra: Contemporary Short Fiction of New Mexico, *and in* New Mexico Humanities Review *and* Blue Mesa Review. *She has taught at Ohio State University and in many writing workshops; she co-directed the 1992 Santa Fe Writers' Workshop; and she is currently an associate of the Western States Arts Federation literature program. She lives in Santa Fe with her sons, Austin and Merritt.*

A SMALL CROSS RISES, a sliver of white next to the mailbox posts across the road. This cross is from my neighbor's hands. He is a man who thinks and dreams so much that his head is wrapped in fire. He stands under his portal and watches the horizon to the west purple then thin out to evening gray. It is as if part of him leaves, evaporates as the sun notches its way down. When it comes to this, there in life the blue of fire flares, twisting oxygen filaments into combustion.

I think that a whisper might steer him back: one breath of moisture. Just how many wet molecules can I breathe out in that whisper?

I live on the other side of a coyote fence built of young pines with the bark still intact and zig-zagging on top like a saw. I look through cracks in my fence where two poles never join. I wonder what he sees. Sometimes, I turn and glorious colors are written in the sky. The orange, the pink, even the purple, scrolled as if placed there by him, the lines so shaped and edited. There's that letting out sound as if a deep breath were welling from the earth. He just stands with his gaze arched over the fence to way out there. And I want to bring him back, extinguish the flame.

This sort of thing doesn't happen. Am I some fool? I could never waste myself like he does. I can't even let go of a wish or dream. And as I watch him, I tell myself there is no difference between bodily heaving one's wings and standing with a head afire. That's what it is. Bits are leaving, taking one form into another. This divergence. I want to tell him: *Hold on! Hold on to me,* I want to say. But then, as if to remind me of just where I am, my body speaks instead. I feel the tremors run through my legs. My head shakes. I look through the tiniest pinpoint of space, down through the tunnel for my sitting stump. I focus. There it is. I pour myself through my chest. I must set one foot in front of the other, and at times that takes my mind, my whole mind. I do not let one moment of concentration escape.

Seated, I can be. Later, the night comes and his door closes. I navigate. There are rocks to step over, a hose and sprinkler to avoid. There are days like this.

OUR HOUSES were built one month apart in this new development outside of town. There were times when I'd sit on my stump, a rootless piece of wood hauled here from my last home, to watch the men bend to adobe brick. He would roll up in his car and walk his lot. I could see everything then. The land between us was flat as a map and with markings so similar it took a measuring stick to differentiate. With hands in his pockets, he walked the compass points staking his acre. Then he stood on a spot and gazed west. That happened to be where he placed his house. More men came, bending to the mud and heaving it. From my stump, I watched. *"Eee, Chingale,"* they would curse as the walls rose from the ground. Then came our coyote fences, and our worlds were ours.

Yet I find myself pressing my cheek against the brown stubble and long twisting hairs of bark-wood covering those saplings. The spirals tickle the skin on my face and catch my hair as I look between them. Many times he is not there. And I am alone peering through, and it is then that I feel so foolish. An old woman looking at nothing. It is then that I feel the thickness of a rock spread through my stomach into my heart. Instead, you'd think I'd feel something like he might; the one so willing to let himself go.

It was just last month that I first went to his house. It took the restlessness of bullet holes to bring two neighbors together. I had gone to my mailbox along the road and he was there.

"My God," I said.

"Get used to it," he said. There they were. Bullet holes. That's what amazed me. Holes, like patterned anagrams of hatred, sheared right through the little wooden cross. "Some teenagers. I heard them last night. Some joyride." It's where his dog, Pilar, had been hit by a truck: one of the workmen late to the job. A skid and pop. My neighbor made the *descanso* and put it along the road, in the custom of the people here, marking where Pilar's spirit had left our earth. A resting place, usually adorned with red and pink plastic carnations. Up to then Pilar's had been simple, plain.

He asked me into his house.

"Lets you know what other people think of you, doesn't it," he said standing back so I could enter.

My God, I thought. I sensed that the bullets had seared the dog's spirit. Pulling a gun on the unknown, I felt the threat so. We were silent, the kind of silence that is so heavy you want to rip through it, but I had no way of stopping it. He fixed tea and we sat on his back porch. Shadows played across his face. Did he know how much I had watched? I squirmed at the thought of his knowing. He looked out at the west. "But it's much, much more," he said.

I looked out where he did half expecting to see something, something big like a huge black cloud approaching. There was nothing.

"I'm not quite sure I follow," I said.

"The aim is at anything," he said.

"Oh. Yes." I pieced together what he was referring to. Walls first, then a dog, then memories. The very men who had cursed our walls had sons. Anger was genetic I had heard. The thought of bumping up against heredity took a slight edge off as something contained, explained. "You will be okay?" I sipped my tea. Oh, to reach out and place my hand on his chest. It was a gesture I held at check. An almost fruitless move, what would he do with it? What would I? I imagined my hand evaporating upon touching his body.

Hold on. Hold on to me.

Behind him, in a tropical scene on his canvas, leaves protruded, diminishing the town in the background.

He looked at me as if for the first time.

I felt such embarrassment at what he saw. I had seen him look out there. As he watched, the light would change as if the very mountains and clouds performed for him, and there were times when even their show seemed inconsequential. To have this scrutiny running over my face. *My beauty*, a voice once polished me like silver. I am that no more. Could it ever be his voice?

I turn back. Serene blue air; green tropical leaves pulled from some jungle; water lapping at desert sand where a sea could never be. There's always a way through which air can flow, can feed combustion, a hole, a squiggle running from the canvas heart to its edge. The back door out, I figure. This man, this man, I think. Another one lost in existential play, another whose feet would rarely touch ground.

When I looked back at him, it was the absence of light in his eyes that told me it was time to go. He would not release one bit of himself in my presence the way he did when standing alone in his backyard. "I'm sorry about Pilar's *descanso*. Thank you." I pushed myself up out of the chair. He moved and offered his hand. A flush of anxiety that age could laugh at passed through me. I felt him. I felt him so close.

IT HAS been that way ever since. I would be the wiser, I know, to turn my back. But I haven't. Some foolish woman yearning for passed away moments. There was a day, I know there was a day when this man would have walked near and kissed me. Now, each day I'm drawn. Even the light between two fence posts is what I walk to willingly. With spring, I work the ground into the promise of a border along my fence. My hands, my arms move the shovel slowly. I crack through *caliche* and overturn clods of dirt so inhospitable it's hard to imagine that even a weed could anchor its roots in them. I pick up the pieces of *caliche*; they are fists clenched. My illusions of green vines with trumpeting flowers face a battle. Yet each late afternoon I lower myself to my knees, then sit sideways and with a three-pronged tool like a claw I loosen the dirt and mix in mulch. I water the ground and rest my hands in dark mud. Such white fingers there. They ache in the cool, wet dirt. This border. I know, it's ridiculous. Such work you put yourself through, I say. And I plant the vine cuttings.

The little *descanso* stays, and on my trips to the mailbox I see he has tied fetishes within the holes. A silver *milagro* of a dog is in one. Smoothed rocks and herb bundles dangle in the wind. Surprised at this show of sentimentality I bend and touch one of the fetishes, a black heart-shaped rock, smooth as a river-washed stone.

The cross gets it again. This time, one side arm is blown off.

Again, as if curfew were raised, he asks me in.

Leaning within the frame of the door, he waits. I will be there, I say to him inside my mind. Patience. In asking him to have it, I strip myself of my own and my body works against itself. I focus on my legs, on calming the tremors that run through them. When I'm down to this again, to get from one spot to the next I pour myself through the tiniest pinpoint of space. I cry within, *Don't give up.* He stands in the doorway. In this time his phone could ring. He could forget I'm coming. He could change his mind. He could forget. My mind locks like a stopwatch that counts the seconds, the minutes as they fly, and I can't seem to move. Flames shoot around him.

Just one breath would stop it. But I cannot summon that now. Were I also to be wrapped in flames. Briefly I covet the thought of release. I begin to see this door, like the crack in my fence, where I rest between my own tight grip and losing myself to a feeling so unknown, so completely overwhelming.

"I guess I'll put up a new one," he says, leading me into the house. The reel of the stopwatch halts and time as we know it resumes.

There on the easel is his latest. From the colors of the clothing, I take the man to be Guatemalan. Thick leaves hang in bunches from his shoulder. One eye is cocked down. In the center of the other eye's dark iris is a river of blue. I trace its banks, keeping my finger just barely above the canvas. The banks take a slow curve.

"Where can this fellow go?"

"Why do you ask?"

"He must dream . . . of where the water could push him."

"If that's what you want him to do," he says, sitting.

I didn't anticipate the setup until it was too late and I am quiet. So is he for awhile. Now I'm a part of it. *What you do with yourself,* I say to him in my head. *Pushing yourself away. The little that attaches you. This river of yours . . . you won't even let yourself fall in. You miss the banks, too. Hold on. I am here.*

"Don't you see?" He closes his eyes and tilts his head back.

What do you mean? I shout inside my head. Oh this body of mine. So cloistered I am within it. *Move! Move to him.* My feet seem to plant themselves even more staunchly to what's beneath me. I simply cannot move. And if I were, to rest my fingertips over his eyelids, to press kisses there, he would without doubt be gone. What is my business here, after all?

"I frame people's fantasies." He was almost resigned, maybe sad. It was then that

I realized how doors, even the cracks between the fence poles, aren't necessarily the passageways of comings and goings, but harbors of ambiguity. So inured in his scenes, yet he burns. Up to now I had thought his was one man's flight of freedom. I look again at the man in the painting with his dark skin, orange for eyes, and one with a river of blue. I see no flight. There is no movement. Each brush stroke within that river: so still, I can feel it now. The banks within the Guatemalan's eye press with tension. No one's fantasy could change that. I could float, if my mind would take me, far away on that water, but I snap back to the cocked eye, the downward glance, and I feel the weight of the harvested plants hanging over my shoulders and pulling down.

I clasp my hands in my lap. "This is all so lovely," is all I can say, and it rings out of me like a false alarm. I am an old woman. Oh, remember, I tell myself, I am an old woman who has never been anything but alone.

"Damn these kids for coming around and blasting the holy hell out of Pilar's *descanso*." His chair scooted across the floor behind him as he stood and then paced the floor.

"Yes," I say. "It's unfair."

"Oh, no. I didn't say that," his eyes shot back to me. "It's more than that. It's more than the kids and their fathers and their fathers and my dog. Yeah, I'd like it to end. But where would it be different?"

"There are places . . . "

"Where?" He walks to the sliding door and looks out with one hand on the glass. "You don't know, do you?"

"No. I don't," I said. I hesitated for a moment, and in that moment I wanted to slip back to my own home. "I better go, now." What is he telling me? I wonder. As I rise, he is there. His hand steadies my arm, so I balance to his gentle touch. What would it be to love?

Once in my own home, I am dreadfully tired. I move close to my bedroom wall, and put my hand, my cheek against the plaster so cool and smooth it feels wet. I breathe in its touch and the earthy smell, like rain on dry ground. Safe here, I care not to move even toward the crack in my fence.

The next morning, I garden before the sun gets too hot. As I work the soil free of weeds, I hear someone on the road in front. I go to my gate and open it. I see a boy, no older than seven, positioned. He blasts away at the little cross. It's a bee-bee gun. I unlatch my gate and step from behind it. I focus on the boy and his gun. His cheeks so full and round with youth I want to laugh and say, boy, you are too sweet to take on such anger. But at the sight of me, he tucks his gun under his arm and runs. I check the *descanso*. Indeed, what's left is riddled with dents.

Who do I think I am? My presence and my neighbor's so desperately unwanted that this simple place of rest has become the local front line. Is that what he was asking? Can we simply affix ourselves to a place or even a person with all of our good intentions?

I walk back to my garage for some wire. The one-armed cross needs steadying. I return to the roadside and wrap the wire like lace around the cross's middle and along the arm. Carefully I weave around metal and rock hearts, a hammered silver dog, dried bundles of sage, and silver coils of a brain. I stop my wire here and finger the milagro. It should be no surprise that he acknowledge the miracle of his dog companion and how its sweet licks and nuzzles pulled him out of the place where he lives so much.

In the weeks to come the cross remains one-armed and it flourishes. On my trips to my mailbox, I see more fetishes, a plastic flower, "Pilar" painted in gold. This animal spirit so glorified, it seems to me that love is growing along with it. Had the dog been present would love have been as evident?

My border greens and tendrils of vines curl their way up my fence. I water nightly when the sun is low and the air cool. I bend and pull from the ground bind weeds, sinewy strands of leaves and pale purple flowers, which I soon discovered thrive in the crags of these dirt clods. They wrap around my vines and would choke them if I let them grow. I spread fertilizer like birdseed and the vines trumpet with blossoms the brilliance of fire. Nightly I look through the fence crack, but my neighbor is not there and I turn back. I feel such weight that I must cross my yard to my sitting stump, placed here so vicariously. I would like it next to my border much better than smack in the middle of my yard. But I had not known then when I built the house and when the men carried it in. I would dare not ask them to move it for fear that it, like the *descanso*, would become their next target. So I sit some distance away.

One evening while dragging the hose out, I stop to take in the thickening growth. The fence, now practically hidden, is ablaze with orange, heavy blossoms. I drop the hose and walk without hesitation into them. The succulent petals rub my cheeks and body and I press into the vines and wish for one moment. My chest clenches inside like tamped-down earth, like those clumps of dried clay I've dug from this garden. They've lodged here, right here where these petals touch. I press further into the vines. If only this body could twist and twirl with such elegance. If only this body could let go. The desire stabs at me so. Then I feel it, as if the stiffness were melted, that my arms encircle my waist.

The gate rattles and I push myself from the vines. Wiping their moist touch from me I walk to the gate and open it. He is there.

"I know it's been weeks, but I've meant to tell you. Thanks for the wire." He stands looking suddenly like a boy with clear untroubled eyes. "They've left us alone for a while, at least." Then as if reckoning with hope, his years come back to him and arrange themselves around his mouth and in his eyes. The "much-much-more" that he had spoken of earlier is on his horizon again. "You are good."

He touches my cheek with his fingers: so careful, so gentle, so compelling a touch.

"What is this?" he asks, rubbing his fingers.

I take his hand and fingers. They are orange with pollen. I slide my hand over my cheek to see.

"You're streaked with the stuff," he laughs. "Look at you." He brushes his hands over my arms and hair, then cups his hands around my face. We stand like that, caught in the equilibrium of the moment. "I cannot do this," he whispers, withdrawing his hands.

"You can," I say to him. "You can."

I watch him walk away with the white *descanso* of flowers and glittering trinkets rising in the distance. As if trained on a rubbery cord he is catapulted back to his frameworks. Though he had left, I feel as if he stands at my elbow. Oh, this ambivalence, it hurts like nothing else. So protected he and I are, without even the nerve of the boy; here in our in-between, where the losses of the little cross allow us to exaggerate our affection.

What would it be to love? Is it this disappointment? I feel partly in time and partly in the out there where I have watched him look for months. I walk back to my yard and I stand. I feel heat. Around me springs a circle of flames, and I feel no urge to tamp them out. I must remember this. *My beauty.* The blossoms whisper. I press myself against the flames and push, throwing my arms up. They pull me. *My beauty.* I must remember this.

Not Just Red

JO ANN FREED

JO ANN FREED, 63, grew up in a small Mormon town in Utah. She is the mother of four sons, and she and her husband live half the year in Utah and half on an island in the Puget Sound. Her nonfiction has appeared in Network *and* Rodeo Zone; *she has co-produced a Utah public radio show, "Western Women Speak," and has conducted many personal oral histories regarding women's issues. She has a bachelor's degree from the University of Utah, a master's degree from New York University, and received an MFA this year from Vermont College—this time in creative writing. "Not Just Red" is her first published fiction.*

THEY DROVE SLOWLY THROUGH the rural southern Utah town near Zion National Park where they would hike tomorrow. A sign said "Bumbleberry pie, our speciality." Vinnie pointed toward the next right turn, which took them down a lane lined with scrubby desert tamarack. She wanted Ted to see her grandmother's childhood home, deserted for years but still standing. Two stories, the house was made from blocks of pink sandstone just like the cliffs behind it, in plain sight but almost camouflaged. Pink against pink.

"Park here so we can walk around it." In truth, she wanted to touch the house and feel the soft heat of the sandstone against her palms. When, as a child, she had been brought here to visit, she had rubbed her fingers against the grainy pink stone next to the front door, and stroked it onto her cheeks, pretending it was rouge.

Ted came around the front of the car, his old trusty Landcruiser, and looked at the house, stretching his arms out away from his chest. "What's with the two pathways? And two doors? Did they have duplexes in those days?"

Married for five years, and each for a second time, they were still learning things about each other's history. She had explained that Zion was named by Mormon pioneers who thought of Utah as a new-world homeland. Already, he had heard of polygamy, and thought it a novelty that he, a third-generation Vermonter of stern parentage, had married a former Mormon of equally rigid upbringing. She had been apprehensive about bringing him to Utah to live, but she had missed both the northern Utah granite and this gentle sandstone, farther south and warm.

"One man built it for his two wives," Vinnie said. "Polygamy."

The red sand paths were choked with weeds dusted red. The sagging wood-planked veranda was caulked with more red sand. Handmade, the house was straightforward and strong. The only relief from its squareness was a touch of wooden fretwork ornamenting its windows like lace.

Hasps and matching padlocks sucured the front doors. Vinnie pushed both locks up and down and shook the shackles, making sure the house was locked. Through the small front windows, they saw bare rooms, a broken-down chair, and a few boards. Vinnie imagined her grandmother in one of these rooms, in a long black skirt with bustle, a high-necked shirtwaist, hair piled on her head, waiting for her future groom to take her away from here. She had found a photograph of this woman among her own mother's things when she died.

"Her name was Lavinia. I'm her namesake."

Standing on the veranda, she felt the afternoon sun radiating off the stone walls. Sometimes in summer, it was a hundred and twenty degrees around here. Maybe more. Almost unendurable, she thought, the heat and the tight-closed culture, yet she felt an affinity for this soil, a contentment that she hadn't experienced while living with Ted in the green hills of Vermont. She had grown up in northern Utah, but it was the redrock country that pulled her back, its brilliant soil and strangely eroded cliffs.

In the car, they imagined polygamy, sharing a man with other women, having sex with a different wife or wives night after night, and under the same roof. Ted stretched his arm out on the seat back and fingered the lobe of her ear. After all, they had made love with other partners. But what about the children? Vinnie and Ted had none. It saddened her to know that their genetic makeup had come to a halt, that there would never be another Lavinia, or a straight-backed, fuzzy-haired Theodore. She wished that she had asked her grandmother what it was like to share her father with the children in other families and other houses. She wished she had dared.

They drove to the ranger station to ask for a ride up to Lava Point tomorrow. They would leave the Landcruiser here because the hike was a descent, beginning at an upper point of the canyon, and ending down here at the canyon floor. An expert on Vermont granite, Ted was eager to try sandstone. For months, their apartment in snowy northern Utah had been scattered with maps and trail guides. He had selected the trail and convinced Vinnie that her elementary recreational hiking prepared her for this. Mountain climbing was next, he had told her. He hoped they could be summer guides, perhaps in the Tetons.

She hadn't told Ted she was afraid of falling. Wasn't everyone? Falling into an abyss is a common dream, she was sure of it. And once, when hiking with her brother, she had frozen on a simple rock face, unable to move, and had allowed him to help her descend the twenty feet or so. Going up is nothing, she thought. It's the looking down. But Ted seemed fearless. Coming from a large family of boys, he had been taught that toughness was godliness.

Before it got dark, Vinnie wanted to show him the canyon, how it was cut by the river, take a look at the Narrows where they would end up tomorrow—if all went well—and get a sense of the fantastic rock formations. They walked the trail without speaking. The shadows enriched the pigments and deepened the pockets and cracks in the stone walls. All carved naturally from pillowy sandstone and sedimentary rock and white and buff and pink stone, some as hard as marble, the cliffs loomed around them and bizarre formations bulged. Eroded a bit more since she was last here, but still the same. Her sixty years on earth seemed a pathetic comparison to all this. Not a lot of time left for her, and perhaps she gave more weight to each experience than necessary. But that wasn't possible here, not in this incredible landscape. She had missed it deeply and now it deserved all her attention. Even the gritty sand blowing in her hair was a gift. Eroded and wild, the landscape was not just red, but flesh-tinted peach and orange and salmon and vermilion, turkey red and rust, copper, maroon, deep wine, and blood. She led the way up toward the Virgin River.

"You're strong, Vinnie. You'll be good at climbing," Ted said.

"But I enjoy walking."

"We can join the Wasatch Mountain Club in Salt Lake, hang out with the old men of the mountains."

"Count me out."

It was hot still and her lungs felt like overfull balloons. Ted's expectations were impossible. They produced painful echoes: parents who expected her to live their beliefs; brothers who leaned on her subservience; and a sweetheart grandmother with whom trust was broken when Vinnie ran away to get married. Not for love, simply for escape. And now Ted, who had chosen to live with her in Utah, but who had all sorts of plans about her life. She had hoped that by returning, she could put to rest some of the anger and remember the love, but the people were all gone. There were only memories.

Along the trail, songbirds were still out, flitting then nestling, then darting off again, but the hawks were missing. "Maybe they've had their fill for the day," Ted said.

She touched his arm and stopped, motionless on the trail. Three mule deer grazing in the high grass near a stream twisted their necks in unison to take in Ted and Vinnie, then returned to their methodical munching.

Coming up on the river, they admired its languid movement, its dynamic erosive force. This soft liquid had formed the canyon, had ground away at the layers of sandstone, pushing pebbles against larger surfaces, scraping and weakening, opening cracks to the onrush of stones, the crash of boulders, the deepening of the channel, grinding out offshooting canyons, exposing them to the force of wind and rain, buffing it all with the finest of grains. Then, the forever river laying down new rock, virgin rock, from silt and particles and ground insects and fish bones and grated stones and mud and gravel and ooze.

She hoped to walk the riverside pathway up and around the bend to show Ted the Narrows, the section where unyielding hard walls squeeze the river to a fifty-foot width, where there is no pathway, only water-walking. Where sometimes in a flash flood coming from rainfall hitting the upper reaches, torrents could sweep through and float bodies and backpacks away without notice. But the light had changed. Lavender and lilac had deepened into purple and it was too dark to go farther.

Later, in her sleeping bag, zipped together with Ted's, she tucked her novel and flashlight under her pillow. Once, in the desert, she had read herself to sleep by the white light of the moon. Maybe it would be like that tonight, letting her slip in and out of consciousness like a wave lapping at the shore.

Ted pulled the trail map out of the end pocket of his duffel. He had marked their route with fluorescent pen and covered it with clear plastic to protect it from moisture. Back at the apartment, she had studied the pen-line trail crossing the narrowing contour lines showing increasing steepness. They would walk down, over, through, across ravines and arroyos, in between pinnacles and gorges, and arrive back here at the campground tomorrow night. She had traced it with her finger, and she knew there would be no return to the trailhead after they had committed to a descent through one of the narrow side-winding canyons. Consciously blotting descent from her mind, she fell asleep before the moon rose.

But in her sleep, she saw a one-hundred-foot pylon placed perpendicularly on an empty plaza. Hunched together with many persons, she was at the top, gripping the pylon with scraped arms. The descent wasn't slanted like a staircase but chipped out of cement. Cement that exposed its aggregate, the pebbles ragged. Her toe stubbed a stone and, looking for blood, she saw that she wore sandals that allowed her toes to hang out. People fought to descend ahead of her. It was critical to get down. Some danger lurked in the sky and she searched for eagles or condors or winged serpents. Below her, an old woman descended face outward, ridiculously awkward. Vinnie stopped breathing, then turned to face the pylon, determined not to look down, never to let that paralysis invade her stomach.

Jerked awake by the terror in her own voice, she saw the image of her body flattened and clinging to the pylon. Ted shook her gently, sat her up, spoke softly, held her tightly, cradled her body in a rocking motion.

WHEN THEY arrived at Lava Point the next morning, there were no other hikers. Still early in the spring and the air sparkled. Vinnie slipped on her backpack and down bag, just in case they were forced to spend a night on the trail. She looked at Ted, patting at his gear, strapped and hung from his body. His grin was wide, and fine sweat misted his face and twisted his hair into tiny gray spit curls all over his head, like his muscles and enthusiasm, ready to spring. He slung a climbing rope across his body and snapped a few carabiners into his belt loops.

She said, "I thought we were free climbing. Down, that is. With no ropes."

"An experienced hiker is always prepared. You know that."

She knew also that the spirit of canyoneering was to discover the canyon from the top down, as it was formed, and that there was more than one way to reach the bottom. But once committed, it would be almost impossible for them to climb out. What she said was, "I've always wanted to do this and I'm not stopping now."

Ted flashed her one of his brilliant smiles.

Gently at first, the descent angled in and down, and leveled out through a landscape bewitched. Everywhere were the effects of centuries of water action, of wind and sand grinding away at the sedimentary rock, filing edges off the harder layers and indenting and rounding softer layers into freestanding shapes no sculptor could create. When she stroked the grace of a turned sandstone knob, she saw that a swipe of rose had come off on her hand.

After half an hour, a couple of women power-walked past them with "How's it going, mates?" but that was it. Solitude. Every vista pleased her, surprising her as if she were seeing redrock country for the first time. Ted was in the lead, and walking behind, she noticed that the soil was so compacted during this stretch that the cleat marks of his hiking boots were barely visible. The inside wall along the trail had eroded away, revealing a cross section of layering. Green, the color of pistachio ice cream, lay between a gypsum gray and a henna bubbled with hunky pebbles. Ted pulled his camera out of his backpack to get a close-up. He had taken a teaching position at a private boys' school, and already he was planning a unit on southern Utah geology. Suspended overhead on an updraft, a hawk inspected them, waiting to see what desirable morsel they might uncover.

The dry air had heated up. They were making good time, but talking very little, as if their heads were too full. At about five thousand feet, hanging gardens sprouted out of water seepage between layers of buff-colored stone. Maidenhair fern trailed down the wall, and in between, velvet moss to lay your cheek against. They pulled cups off their belts and held them under the precious water drips to take the dusty sand taste from their mouths. Leaning their backs against the canyon wall, they sat down to rest, their arms dangling across their bent knees. The air smelled dry. The heat had an oven odor and it crisped the hair in her nostrils.

Patting her canteen to make sure it was still there, she was reminded that water is the most precious commodity in the desert. Never waste it. Never drink all of it. In case of emergency. A soundless movement caught her eye: a small lizard, its bumpy skin pink like the sand, skittering, then stopping dead, inching one way and another, then disappearing under an out-thrust ledge.

She said, "So how do you like it? Does it live up to your expectations?"

He pumped his arms straight up and laughed. "Dynamite," he said. He had taken off his sunglasses and Vinnie traced the squint lines coming out from his eyes with her finger. Smiling, he squeezed her bicep. "Nice muscles there, lady. You doing okay?"

She was aware that the steep part lay ahead, that up until now it had been like sight-seeing. Yet it seemed so peaceful. She felt protected by the rosy glow enveloping her, and the softness resting on her shoulders. She looked down at the sand and studied the indented line of the lizard's passing, decorated periodically by its clawed footprints placed alternately on either side of its trail. "You can't hear it or smell it, but it leaves its slither marks behind."

Ted measured the first pad of his little finger against the lizard's footprint, about the same size. They were silent, listening to the sound the stillness made. He stood up, brushed off the seat of his khaki shorts, and put on his pack. "We're making pretty good time. The canyon floor is only about another one thousand feet down."

"You mean, in elevation, right?"

He nodded and started on ahead.

The canyon became increasingly less open, with side crevices and what appeared to be trails all going off in various directions. No markers, and Ted kept looking up and around, consulting the horizon, it seemed. Very few trees and not much vegetation. As their descent got steeper, the spaces between the pinnacles narrowed. Crevices that never saw sunlight appeared and disappeared and formed again. Ted stepped across a shaft from one outcropping to another. She followed. Tiny threads of water wiggled in and out of the base of the formations, sometimes turning into baby streams.

At an unexpectedly wide place, they stopped to look around. Suddenly cold, Vinnie asked Ted to hold up for a minute while she put on a sweatshirt. Waiting, he pulled out his map and compass and studied a two-inch square, turning the map from side to top to side. It's possible to get lost, she thought, sometimes people become confused, like in a maze, and can't find their way out. But they had sleeping bags with them, and surely someone would come along the trail. If this was the main trail. "A great place for hide-and-seek," she said.

The path turned to the right around an elegant wall looking like pink-veined marble. Sand veining, she thought, laid down in streaks between millennia. Walking quickly, Vinnie wanted to keep the momentum going but Ted insisted on stopping to photograph the wall. With Vinnie in profile against it. Then a shot of Vinnie's hands spread out on its flatness. Then her finger tracing the veining. And when they moved on, the space widened, directing them into a natural amphitheater, the walls bleached by sun to a bone color.

Ted consulted the map. "I can't find this. It isn't here."

"Well, maybe we took a short cut. Anyway, let's stop for a bite."

It was like a bowl, this place they were in, and the sun poured down, filling it to the top. She pulled plastic-wrapped sandwiches from her pack and took a drink from her canteen. He handed her an orange slice and when she bit into it, juice squirted onto her rose sweatshirt and disappeared instantly as into a blotter.

"I'll bet my grandmother never saw any of this when she was a girl. There were no cars around here. I wonder if she had a horse." Vinnie told him about her grandmother coming north to live with her family when Vinnie was a little girl. How her grandmother longed to travel, to see some other place, and how she would take Vinnie with her to watch the trains go by.

She would hold tight to her grandmother's hand as they walked two blocks to the Union Pacific tracks where they waited like statues for the first vibration. They felt it first through the soles of their feet. She remembered how tall she stood in her flowered cotton dress with the Peter Pan collar, how close to her grandmother's thigh. And when the yellow Streamliner streaked by with its glass-domed dining car, they thought they saw people eating from plates on white linen cloths. Vinnie was certain she had seen red roses in silver bud vases. They stood as close as they dared, counting the cars and feeling the roar through their bodies. Even now, Vinnie treasured waking up in the middle of a silent night to a distant train whistle.

Ted said, "I think we should get moving. Find our way out of here."

Leaving the amphitheater, she saw some white blossoms spilling out of a moist crack in the trail. Silken, they hugged the soil, their green leaves in compact bunches against the pink sand.

"Evening primroses, I think."

"Lovely." She stroked the broad petals. The spent blossoms had shrunk in upon themselves and had blushed a deep rose, as if absorbing dye from the soil. She picked at the same-colored sand ground into the cuticles of her fingernails.

"Over here," he said. "It's a bit steep."

"More walking across crevasses?"

"Nothing you can't handle."

But the crevasses got wider. Ted hesitated. He offered to tie the rope around her waist, have her descend ahead of him, let her down slowly from the rope wound around an outcropping. She refused. Better to go behind him. Step where he stepped quickly, without having to think.

Ten minutes later, before she had recognized the slightest danger, she fell. Slipped somehow, as if something got caught in the cleat of her boot. Not hurt, she said, just scraped the palms of her hands. She looked up to see what had happened, and was surprised to see she had fallen about eight feet. Had they taken a wrong turn?

Ted's face was white. "You okay?"

She swung her arms, rolled her shoulders. "I'm fine. Really."

He brushed the sand off her shorts and poked at a small rip in her backpack. "We're lucky."

"Shall we go?"

"Just thought we'd catch our breath." With hands on hips, he stretched his torso from side to side, and leaned down to break off a twig of sage. He smelled it and handed it to her.

She rubbed a leaf between her fingers to release the scent, then stuck it in her pocket.

"The steep part's ahead." He had the map out again, tracing the tightening contour lines with the point of his knife. "When we get you into mountaineering, we can come down here with pitons and slings—"

"I'm not going to learn mountaineering," she said. "I can't do everything your way. I've done enough of that." Her voice trailed off.

Here, the sun had slipped behind the high canyon walls, deepening the colors and cooling the air, but Vinnie felt warmed. Moving into a narrow side canyon, she could hear the sound of her shorts scraping the walls. She stretched out her arms to touch the sides as the space widened. But immediately the trail descended. Broken chunks of sandstone crumbled underfoot like dried mud and skidded along under her boots.

"This way," he said, almost doubling back on the way they had come. "We mustn't miss this notch." His pace slowed as he looked up and around, getting his bearings. A harsh glance of light illuminated his face, making it look chiseled.

He shivered. Rubbed his arms. Sliding his backpack around, he pulled out his camera and photographed the notch from several angles.

"You're not worried, are you? Have we lost the trail?"

Ted didn't answer. Seemed not to have heard. Selecting a slit through the cliff on his right, he looked back to see if she was following.

"Like glue," she said.

Lowering himself with his hands, he descended a couple of feet, then off to the left, following a needle-like side canyon. Close behind, Vinnie felt strong, powerful even, her adrenalin rising.

Unexpectedly, Ted stopped. There was a dark oval of sweat between his shoulders. Quickly then, he jumped across air to a narrow salmon-colored ledge, then dropped down out of sight. His voice came from below. "You okay?"

"On my way." Vinnie jumped to the ledge, then turned inward toward the cliff to avoid looking down. But she couldn't take the next steps safely without looking out, ahead, and then down. She clung to the pillar-like stone behind her and inhaled deeply. Her legs weren't as long as his, and she would have to zig-zag, skinny along an outcropping, face-out, then drop six feet straight down. When she landed, she found him prepared, if necessary, to break her fall.

"Cool. Like tucking when you're skiing."

They were at the bottom of a shaft, a naturally formed depression surrounded by steep canyon walls. There appeared to be no way out. Looking up, she saw a jagged patch of sky, like a blue hole cut out of black paper. Something disturbed the air.

"This must be what a sinkhole is like," she said.

"Except that we have a way out unless I'm mistaken."

The smell of mold hung in the air. She heard dripping sounds, maybe only an oozing spring in a side wall, maybe more. Tentatively, she stamped her feet and heard the splash of water. With arms out, she turned around in a circle and bumped into Ted's backpack.

"What do you think?" she said.

"I wish we could photograph it but I don't think there's enough light." Still, he braced himself against the wall and snapped the ragged hole overhead. Unstable globules of mud fell off the wall as he moved away.

"I mean about the water." When she touched the wall, more dried bits of mud came off in her hands. It was as if the entire cavern had been carved from mud. She wondered if it might cave in, if this was it, and if she loved Ted enough to be buried with him here, forever. Could she give up her life gracefully at this point, with so many things undone, unsettled?

"Stay close," he said. "Let's not get separated." He pulled a flashlight from his pack and shone it around. A bat darted through the beam, scattering the dust motes. She breathed shallowly, not wanting to take in more air than necessary.

"Hang on to my pack and let's explore a little."

They splashed at first, then sloshed. She could feel the water creeping into her boots, then over the tops, seeping in through her socks.

"There's not supposed to be so much water in here," he said.

"Could there have been a rainstorm upstream, a flash flood maybe?"

He gave the back of her neck a squeeze with his free hand and flashed the light around and up and down.

When she lifted her feet to walk, they felt like blocks of ice. Accidents were not that uncommon around here. She knew that people had been trapped in high water on the river, and how would they know if that were happening now? If the river were backing up into the side canyons and pushing into this very cavern? Moldy and stagnant and dark. Certainly the water was rising, was going up her legs ever so slightly.

"So what's your theory in getting out of here?" she said.

"I'm not sure."

She asked for the map and the compass and pulled out her own small penlight. Pointing to a shaded area on the map, she said, "If we are here, we ought to be able to figure out an exit by orienting ourselves to the shape of that jagged hole up there."

"I'll hold the flashlight," he said.

She steadied the compass in the palm of her hand, changed the angle of her body, tipped her head back, turned ninety degrees to the right and said, "It has to be over there."

"Let's hurry."

Together they half-saw, half-felt their way around the irregular space. Sandstone granules and warts of clay flaked off the walls with every handprint, each brush of a shoulder.

"It must be here," he said.

Reading the cracks and angles like braille, they found an indentation, then a perpendicular chink, then a plane of smooth stone. She listened for his breathing, touched the rough weave of his pack next to her, then caught a dusty sliver of light ahead.

She stamped her feet. The stagnant black water was suddenly gone and they stepped now into puddles. And she could see mist ahead, as if they were coming out of a tunnel. Swinging around a bend, they moved slowly into a filtered ray of light, thin and pink, that made her think of peach fuzz. Then fragile airiness everywhere. The space had become an aisle, broad enough for two abreast.

They followed it like children as it meandered and widened and filled with air. First, water seepage underfoot, then a tiny rivulet here and there as the water gathered itself into a small stream, continuing downward ever so slightly. The river must be very near. Her spirits lightened as she skipped freely from sandstone plane to boulder to gravel, then to flat sand, aware of the sky increasing in size and space with every move. Little streams joined one another and bubbled over rocks, and when they looked behind them, she could scarcely recognize their exit from the wall.

And from ahead, the hum of water at work, gathering in its brooks and creeks and rivulets and rills, amassing its power in clear crystal flow. Its wavy pebbles under shallow water and its lapping borders were their pathway back.

Stunning. The sound and sight of it. Then, with Ted sharing a large plum-colored boulder at the river's edge, they sat in relief. Stared upstream and down, noticed the natural bends the river had chosen, marveled at the design. Finding her voice, she spoke of the relief of safety, and its opposite, dark undercurrent.

Picking their way along the river's edges, sometimes wading, they crossed and recrossed. Real water-walking. And Ted snapped photo after photo, catching every color change.

A gravel basin in the riverbed formed a small pool where they stopped to look at themselves and splash off their grimy faces and hands. With wet fingers, she rubbed the sand out of the corners of her eyes and studied her wavering reflection in the water pool. Her likeness was nothing, but the natural basin held wonder and shivered her skin. Made by the river, it was paved with stones and sand and mud collected by river, gravity, and wind, by ice and floodwater and the grating of stone against stone. To be laid down again at some point in future time in another basin, a waterfall, a sandbar. Perhaps to be uplifted and reshaped in another geologic age.

It was safe here. A cloistered spot, with the sound of pure water rinsing the river stones, exposing mirror bits of mica in the sand grains. And what if she died here? If the parts of her being—the days, the years, the struggles—all dissolved? What if her muscles and tendons just let go, and her bones fell into the warm sand, to bleach and settle in, the way of the Anasazi people who came here first? It's the living of the life, after all. Not the completion. She would find a gentle home here, softened by the brilliant soil of her ancestors.

Coyote Woman

SHARMAN APT RUSSELL

SHARMAN APT RUSSELL, 40, grew up in Phoenix, Arizona, where she "imprinted early on vistas that were dry, spacious, and dramatic." In 1981, she and her husband chose to settle and "root" in the rural Mimbres Valley of southwestern New Mexico. They built a small adobe, had two home births, irrigated from a traditional acequia, and explored their connections to the surrounding land community. They live in the Mimbres still. Sharman has considered her "dreams and the naiveté of certain dreams" in works such as Songs of the Fluteplayer: Seasons of Life in the Southwest *and* Kill the Cowboy: A Battle of Mythology in the New West. *Her new book,* When the World was Young: Love and Longing in American Archaeology, *will be out in 1996.*

A *VERSION* of this paper was presented to the Sonoran Historical Society on May 18, 2030. I would like to thank Rose Begay, the Saguaro Home for Senior Citizens, and the twelve members of my PhD committee.

THE APACHE GIRL HAD a choice: She could have her nose cut off with a sharp knife—missing bone but shearing through cartilage—or she could be banished to the mescal fields for the rest of her life.

The memoirs of Captain James Tevis (*Arizona in the '50s*, UNM Press) record her decision. In 1859, Tevis was the manager of the Butterfield Overland Stage Station at Apache Pass, a rock-strewn, dangerous, narrow canyon of thickly-grown cottonwood trees. In Tevis's words, Cochise's brother-in-law "came to me and said that his sister had gone wrong and that the law of the tribe left it to the elder member of the family to pass her sentence. This fell to him, and she either must have her nose cut off or be sent to the mescal grounds. He was troubled over this duty and came to talk with me about it. I told him to bring her in. . . . She was a very good-looking squaw, about fifteen years of age. I asked her which she preferred, to have her nose cut or to be banished from her people. She chose the latter, so she was taken south to end her days by gathering, digging, and roasting mescal. She only saw others of her tribe when the women went there each year to help with the harvest." Coyote Woman's version differs slightly. In her journals, written years after the event, she complains that the white man pushed her against the adobe wall of the station and ran a hand down her hip. At fifteen, this "good-looking squaw" had thick black hair and a full figure. Tevis himself writes that "he felt sorry for the girl and offered twenty horses for her release, but they refused and said that ten horses would buy the best squaw in the tribe; that it would ruin the morals of the tribe to do such a thing; and that her punishment would be a warning to the other squaws."

Twenty horses!

It is not hard to read between the lines. Cochise's brother-in-law had acted cannily in bringing his sister to the station manager and all might have ended well, for him and for her, if the strong-willed girl had been sensible.

Instead, "He smells like shit," she told her brother when he questioned her at the Apache camp. "His ears have hair in them." Later, after a few days in the mescal fields, the hair in the white man's ears didn't seem so bad. Coyote Woman even wondered what it would be like to breathe without a nose: would the air hiss going in and out like a little song all day and night?

By then, of course, her choice had been made.

THE MESCAL plant is a rosette of spiked fleshy leaves that sends out in the spring a phallic stem growing, in some cases, over twelve feet high. When the stalk's white flowers are ready to blossom, an oak stick is driven into the plant below the crown and pounded until the woody caudex dislodges. Along with the stalk, this head is baked in a pit, sun-dried, and beaten into long-lasting cakes. Digging the four-foot-deep pit can be onerous. Next the hole must be lined with rocks, over which a pile of wood is placed in criss-crossed layers. The wrong kind gives the mescal a bitter flavor, and finding the proper mix of ironwood and mesquite is another difficult chore. All this is a prelude to hours of strong-armed hacking, stripping, drying, and beating.

Dumped in the middle of the Sonoran Desert, Coyote Woman began her labor. As the youngest in a family of three wives and eight daughters, she was unaccustomed to household drudgery. Now for the first time, she had to work hard, in temperatures that rose to one hundred-and-twenty in the shade, digging and dragging and pounding and roasting. At night she fell sideways into her brush shelter, too exhausted to fix a meal of the mescal she detested. That season, Coyote Woman cured herself of laziness. She searched longer for wood and beat the agave better (so she imagined) than any outcast had ever searched or beaten before. She vowed that when the women came to take the harvest home, they would find little to do. Amazed, they would murmur and shake their heads. Their eyes would grow dark as she held out her hands and told of her repentance.

"Yes," Coyote Woman practiced humility under the burning sun. "I went with my cousin into the cold night. Yes, when I grew tired of him, I took another lover into the brush. I took the shaman's son, married to a rich widow of whom we made fun as we lay together. Yes, even after that, I was too proud to flatter the white man who would have given my brother twenty horses. I have been foolish!" She wailed in the empty brown desert. "But I am sorry now. I am sorry, and I have worked hard."

IN JUNE, the harvesters arrived. Their eyes did not grow dark when they saw Coyote Woman's cracked and bleeding palms, nor did they shake their heads with the understanding that comes between women. Rather, they ignored her, as tradition demanded. Four men came as well, to guard the camp againt raiding O'odham. These guards, who would be killed if caught speaking to a banished female, were even more aloof.

Coyote Woman accepted this. In a flush of pleasure, she relished the mere presence of human beings working beside her, of arms and elbows and legs and toes. She thrilled to hear their voices: the gossip of girls patting cakes or the grunt of women dragging a heavy mescal. Listening to the former, she learned that Cochise was on the warpath and that the pale *Pindolickees* fled before him like rabbits before a wolf. All over the country, soldiers were abandoning their forts and settlers their homes.

"We have seen the last of them," a girl crowed. "We've defeated the *Goddamnies.*"
The others laughed. One woman made a face.

"They have only gone to fight each other," she warned, "to a big war in their own land."

The girls laughed harder. It was fine if the *Pindolickees* left to kill more *Pindolickees*.

What a bold day for my tribe, Coyote Woman thought. She felt proud to be a Chiricahua. She knew the others would stay a half moon more and, in her heart, she believed they would relent and welcome her back. Wasn't that her own sister singing as she cut the outer leaves of an agave? Wasn't that her aunt using a headband to drag a plant to the roasting pit? At the last minute, they would come and praise her. They would say that she had been punished enough.

As for the men, Coyote Women felt nothing. For a day, perhaps two, she had expected her brother or cousin or the shaman's son to ride to the mescal fields and lift her up on a bay horse. Now the shaman's son came as a guard, and she was astounded at how puny he looked. He was a flat gray stone. He was spit from her mouth. She didn't mind. It was part of her plan to return with the women and remain among them unmarried and manless.

One late afternoon, as distant mountains darkened lavender to purple, Coyote Woman brought in ironwood and found the camp making ready to leave. All night she waited for someone to approach her. She sent long looks to her sister, who (she remembered suddenly) had always been jealous of her hair and breasts. She hovered humbly near her aunt until the early morning hour, before dawn, when the whole bunch of them moved out—weaving a path through prickly pear. Only one person looked back, his gesture barely seen in the half light. Coyote Woman understood then what she had not once suspected before.

The tribe had no intention of letting her return.

Running to climb a hill so as to keep in sight the plodding figures, Coyote Woman watched the Apaches leave on horses laden with dried cake. "The *Pindolickees* will return," she screamed in prophecy. "Piss-ants! Stink-beetles! The Americans will return and eat you up!"

Like that, her humility vanished. All day, she raged about the abandoned campsite, burning the few supplies the women had left. Did they think she would sell herself for pieces of cloth? For the sound of a human voice once a year?

"I don't need you!" Coyote Woman snarled at the desert. "Sons of bitches!" she wailed, and she swore she would never use a digging stick again.

THAT SEASON, Coyote Woman went crazy and refused to eat of the plants that surrounded her. Ferociously hungry, craving meat, she began to make traps, a slingshot, a mulberry bow with stone-tipped arrows. Hunting obsessively, she believed that she was a warrior and that like a warrior she must dress in loincloth and observe a warrior's taboos. Her voice dropped into a deeper register. Her stride lengthened. She built a sweat bath. She killed many deer.

As spring approached, she hallucinated that she was the President of the United States. From some memory, she pulled out a name that the Apaches had learned twenty years ago, and from a picture in the Butterfield Stage Station she constructed the idea of a curled moustache.

Purple aster dotted the desert, creosote bloomed yellow, and Coyote Woman rattled her saber stick and pointed a finger imperiously at quail. Embracing the white man's conceits, she spent long hours drawing maps in the sand: here is where the Apaches must live, here the Pimas, here the O'odham. She brought Cochise to his knees, gave him a dreary reservation, and forbade the custom of beating wives and daughters. When Cochise rebelled, she hit him with a hoe. When his daughters rebelled, she cut off their noses. Using the stars, larger maps in the sky, she planned a new world and sent her troops in every direction. She brought peace and justice! Her knife was a flaming sword! Her reputation was infinite!

That year, when the Apaches saw Coyote Woman, they hid their annoyance that she had done no work. Every night at a good distance from camp, they put out food for the ragged and savagely-thin creature. Every night Coyote Woman ignored their offerings and marched to their fire where as President James Polk she demanded tribute in the form of horses, slaves, and corn. It was bad luck to harm a crazy person. In the end, the harvesters left earlier than planned.

Coyote Woman did not notice. By now, she found it as reasonable to talk to a saguaro as a human being. She picked those plants that best responded to her changing mood. On inspection duty, she addressed limbless soldiers, their thick trunks fluted with respect. In a benign humor, she counseled those cacti whose arms lifted in supplication.

"Be brave," she said to these weeping-women, the wives of white men dead in battle. "The world is full of long-legged warriors. The second husband is often the best."

———

HOW LONG this went on, we will never know. Coyote Woman believed she was insane for at least two years and, in retrospect, she remembered this as a pleasant time. As James Polk, she had a larger dominion than she would ever know again.

Slowly, for an hour, then two, Coyote Woman returned to her senses. Sometimes, for whole afternoons, she would find herself a banished female living alone in the mescal fields. Gradually the lucid days began to outnumber the presidential ones. One morning she stood and touched her skinny body. It was all hers. Coyote Woman sighed, but she did not weep.

The circuitous route of fantasy had led to acceptance. That very day she put in a garden. Soon she was building a permanent house of ocotillo branches and mesquite poles, with a mud oven nearby for baking. She learned to use the desert plants, pounding into medicine the root of the cereus and smoking creosote for her aching feet. She explored the borders of her territory and discovered the ruins of a civilization far older than that which had exiled her. On one trip she also found and buried the body of another outcast, a leathery figure who had slit her throat in despair. To ward off this fate, Coyote Woman went beyond even her own expectations. She built a smelter and made jewelry from copper and turquoise. She wove exquisite baskets, sewed beautiful deerskin clothing, and dug again in the mescal fields. This time she harvested only enough to trade for what the women might bring. This time, when the Apaches came, Coyote Woman behaved with dignity.

Her tribe had divorced her; she married the desert.

In this season, her prophecy also came true. The Americans returned with a vengeance and began to eat the Apaches up. Amazingly, whole regiments of white men were now black. It happened, one girl said, in a war that caused each *Pindolickee* to split into two halves, dark and light, thus doubling their population.

The women who came to the mescal harvest spoke easily to Coyote Woman now and told her the tribal news. Her sister and aunt were dead of disease. Cochise had signed a peace treaty. The whole Chiricahua tribe lived on a reservation, bordered in straight lines.

FIFTEEN WINTERS passed, fifteen springs, fifteen summers. Coyote Woman thought her life would continue in this way, unchanging except for the change of season. She thought of her monotonous existence as one that fit well into the folds of the desert, a life of solitude, without surprise or trauma. In this frame of mind, her meeting with the coyote came as a shock.

He was a large animal, powerfully built, with luminous eyes and a pelt of rich yellow fur. On that first night, Coyote Woman woke to find him straddling her, his slanted eyes waiting for hers to open. His sharp teeth had worried away the coverings. Naturally she thought she had gone crazy again.

On the second night, she did not sleep but sat on her pallet in the brush house.

By the fifth night, she knew that the flirtatious creature was wholly unimaginary. She wondered if he were not the Trickster himself, the sex-hungry fellow who appeared in so many of her people's stories. Perhaps, truly, her visitor was a god.

Perhaps he was simply unusual.

In any case, she was not afraid of him.

For more than a moon, the big yellow coyote came to the exile every night. Then he disappeared inexplicably and forever. Still Coyote Woman believed she could distinguish his voice among the others that howled on the ridge in darkness. She could never be sure, of course, and she never knew why he had come at all.

Alone again, Coyote Woman felt angry and off balance. The whole thing seemed a startling non sequitur until two months later when she realized that her menstrual flow had stopped. Soon she began to spend the entire day eating. As her belly bloomed, she felt an extraordinary surge of energy. Hardly needing to sleep at night, she roamed the desert, seeing its pastels lit with an eerie, ultraviolet glow. Like some impatient guide, her stomach led her up mountains and hills, into caves, down ravines. Her arms and legs shot out from her trunk like so many bolts of lightning.

"I ran all the time," she wrote later in one of her letters to the sailor Nat Begay. "I felt like a mountain lion, leaping from rock to rock."

That summer, the harvest of the mescal plants presented a problem. The cardinal reason for banishment was lack of chastity; the cardinal rule of banishment was to be chaste. Coyote Woman knew it would be impolitic, even dangerous, to let the others see her in this condition. Stealthily she erected a second campsite in the hills and from there kept watch on the trails that led to the mescal fields. All through June and July she fretted.

Finally she saw that the Apaches weren't coming that year. She had no way of knowing they would never come again.

THE GESTATION of Coyote Woman's children took thirteen months, the last two irksome as the pups wiggled and fought in her womb. At last, one evening, she lay down to bear three yellow-furred daughters and two yellow-furred sons. The labor was painful. When it was over, Coyote Woman realized that her years in the desert had not been happy.

They were years in which she had survived. They were years in which she had worked hard to keep the loneliness from destroying her as it destroyed the other woman she had buried, desiccated in the heat, a knife in one hand. They were years in which she had nursed pride and anger against her brother and lover and the whole of her tribe. They were years in which she had forgotten that happiness existed, that it had a taste and a smell and a feeling. Now Coyote Woman remembered that feeling as she lay exhausted in a bed of soft grass, surrounded by the young coyotes who licked, sucked, poked, and pushed at her breasts.

Her breasts, oh, her breasts, blossoming with purpose.

Coyote Woman smiled.

Slower than other canines, but faster than humans, her children grew up. By the age of two, they could follow simple instructions. At five, they were awkward, gangly adolescents. In seven years, they had become full-grown adults.

Like all mothers, Coyote Woman thought them exceptional—and in truth they were great sleek animals with slanted yellow eyes full of intelligence. Eventually the girls mated with desert coyotes and the boys did the same. Still they did not leave their mother's campsite. Instead they brought their families home so that Coyote Woman could enjoy her grandchildren.

Of course she wondered what had happened to the rest of the Chiricahuas. Each summer she waited for their return and each summer she was disappointed. Had they all been killed? Was she the last of the *Tsoka-ne-nde*, Cochise's people?

Coyote Woman hoped not. Her desire for vengeance had died a long time ago. Her life, simply, was too full of love.

RAIN FELL and the ocotillo was ribboned with scarlet when a buffalo soldier came riding through the mescal fields on a bay horse. Coyote Woman had just warmed a stew of venison and cholla buds by placing hot rocks into a basket lined with pitch. As usual, one of her sons came to warn her of a stranger's approach. By now, O'odham and Pimas rode by the fields fairly often, along with soldiers, miners, and settlers. Intent on water and some further destination, they were easy to spot as they scurried like lizards from spring to spring.

This one, so her son indicated, was traveling north and would not be a problem.

"He's alone?" Coyote Woman paused over the stew.

Her son nodded.

Thoughtfully Coyote Woman went into her house of mesquite poles and yucca. In a moment she emerged wearing a deerskin skirt fringed with turquoise beads. Using a comb of saguaro rib, she brushed out her long black hair. Then she put on her good moccasins, the ones with laces tipped in copper. Finally, as some Pima did, she painted designs of white clay on her uncovered chest.

Her son sat on his haunches and cocked his head.

"I'm going to speak to this man," Coyote Woman told him.

The hairs on the coyote's neck rose.

"Don't argue with me," his mother said fondly and watched the animal lope away to gather his siblings. She knew she would have to hurry herself if she were to meet the stranger at the willow spring.

Early on, black men in the Southwest had been named "buffalo soldiers" in honor of their dark, tightly-curled hair. After a tour of building forts and fighting Apaches, some of these solders left their segregated regiments to settle down as farmers and ranchers. The one passing now through Coyote Woman's land was in fact a poet who made his living by gambling and horse-racing. When Coyote Woman appeared before him in all her finery, like some opium dream from the Chinese dens of Tucson, the buffalo soldier was suitably impressed. In her early forties, Coyote Woman was still "a good-looking squaw," a maturer version of the girl who had inflamed a cousin, the shaman's son, and James Tevis. Deliberately, she approached the black man; she had chosen a hill so that she could look down on him and his horse.

"I am a *Tsoka-ne-nde*, the sister-in-law of Cochise," Coyote Woman spoke in a firm voice.

Unfortunately the poet did not know Apache.

"What has happened to Cochise and his family?" Coyote Woman said in Spanish.

Cochise was a familiar name. With a universal gesture, the man drew a finger across his throat.

"Ai!" Coyote Woman gave a half-hearted cry. She had never much liked her famous brother-in-law. "And the rest of the Chiricahuas?" she asked.

It was 1886. The last Apache renegade had just been captured and put on a train to a watery, disease-ridden land called Florida. With the banishment of Geronimo, Daklugie, Chihuahua, Kanseah, Mangus, and all their wives and children, Coyote Woman's tribe was scattered to the winds.

The buffalo soldier tried to explain.

It was as if Coyote Woman already knew.

"Ai!" she cried again with real grief.

Nearby, her children heard and leapt from their hiding places. The bay reared in fright, and the poet experienced the visual shock that would later be titled "The Five Dragons of the Desert." The horse took off with a pack of coyotes nipping at its heels.

Coyote Woman returned to her home.

There she thought of her first year gathering the mescal when she had wept and dreamed of human contact. In the coming weeks, she found herself dreaming again. She knew now that she was no longer an outcast; there was nothing to be outcast from. Her entire tribe had been exiled from the very desert itself, and if she were to meet by chance another *Tsoka-ne-nde* it would be the meeting of two equals.

She was free, she realized, to leave the mescal fields.

COYOTE WOMAN'S memoir, printed by hand in three bound journals, ends here. There now appears one of those frustrating lacuna of history. Our next record of this remarkable woman is a series of letters written from 1900 to 1924 and sent to Nat Begay, a sailor and displaced Navajo from Los Angeles. These letters show how well the Apache adjusted to the twentieth century. One refers to a tin lizzy. Another concerns investments in real estate. Many deal with the "children" and Coyote Woman's annual trips from California to visit them in the enduring wilderness of the Sonoran Desert.

Abruptly, in 1925, the letters stop. Naval records reveal that a Navajo named Nathanial Begey, age sixty-three, died that year aboard the *Connecticut* in a freak Pacific storm. At that time Coyote Woman would have been eighty-one years old.

Our last glimpse comes from a nursing home in Tucson where a patient named Clara Polk died and left a legacy of one blurred photograph. In the early 1990s, former employees of the home identified the woman in the picture as Clara Polk herself. In 1936, "Clara" was admitted to the Saguaro Home for Senior Citizens with an advanced case of leukemia. During her eight years there, she remained—according to an informal obituary—"cheerful, imperious, and fond of card games."

Historian Rose Begay (no relation to Nat Begay) believes that Clara Polk is Coyote Woman's last transformation. Dr. Begay is convinced that other journals still exist, specifically from the shadowy period of 1924–35. Working under a grant from the National Endowment for the Humanities, Dr. Begay promises some exciting discoveries.

In any case, we can only remain grateful for what we have already been given—a story of the early twentieth century that many consider inspirational and a rare window into the past. The light it sheds onto this, our more mundane world, is faintly golden and redolent of hope. The scent carried on this breeze is an intriguing mix: turpentine creosote, musty fur, and the honied flowers of ironwood, blooming purple in the spring.

Effie's Garden

TERESA JORDAN

*TERESA JORDAN, 39, is a Wyoming native who left the state eighteen years ago when the
family ranch was sold, and has since moved close to twenty times. She and her husband, Hal
Cannon, recently settled onto a small piece of hay ground in Nevada, and "hope never to move
again." Truly a writer of the West, Teresa says it may be easier to define herself as a "Nevada
writer" as she "absorbs this state up into her bones." She has shared her views of the West in*
Cowgirls: Women of the American West, Riding the White Horse Home, *and*
Graining the Mare: The Poetry of Ranch Women, *a collection she compiled and edited.
Another such collection, this time of essays—*The Stories That Shape Us: Contemporary
Women Write About the West (Norton)—*will be released in 1994.*

IN WYOMING, THE ALTITUDE is high and the air is thin and clear. Even snakes
hold their breath without effort. Children grow tall and have chests as broad as pickups.
They move to the cities as soon as they are able; on the coasts they run forever and
never break sweat.

Things happen in the high clear air. Men watch their skin grow translucent and
their wrinkles carve so deeply that they can't grow beards anymore. Women watch
their eyes get bluer and bluer until they go blind and then they see just what they've
always seen: They see the endless sky. They walk on this sky, on the thin blue air.
They never need to eat. They are thin, of course, and their arms are incredibly long.
Their fingers grow so bony that their wedding rings fall off, and then they can't
remember if they married at all, or if they bore children.

Lanky dogs live at this altitude, and they lounge around the ungrassed yards. They
chew on the old bones of prospectors, and they get thinner as the water runs out.

Their urine is yellow before it dries up completely, and the sky is always blue. The only mineral people need is phosphorus, and they mine it in their yards.

An old women digs in her yard, plants rows of seed in hard ground without any water. Her name is Effie and her garden won't grow. The dogs die. Effie watches as their skins shrink back, little by little, like newspaper curling up in a fire and turning to ash, turning to dust. She watches as the bones whiten and the skeletons sink in on themselves. She listens as the cartilage and tendons dissipate, the bones fall with little bell-like clinks. Soon the wind scatters the toe nails and the smallest bones and scapulas. Effie watches the dogs, like the garden, ride away on the wind, grain by grain and particle by particle.

A few weeds grow in the yard, and the old woman sits and watches them die in the thin high air. She thinks about how nice weeds might look after all, and cactus, but even the cacti go the way of the bones. Their meaty, fleshy parts get harder and drier and their prickles scatter, making a small raspy sound. The dust turns whiter and whiter and Effie remembers drinking out of a glass. She remembers the feel of water on her lips: she wasn't as thin back then, she still needed to eat.

As Effie sits in her garden, she remembers once touching a man. He pressed against her, but she knew what happened to gardens in the thin high air, and she drew away. He lay down then, in the white dry yard. His bones lost the connections of gristle and tendon. They scattered, losing the shape of him, and he blew away particle by particle and dust bit by dust bit. Not even his shadow remained. Sometimes, late at night when the wind sounds the loneliest and the dust quits glowing, Effie can still feel a part of him pressing against her, hard as bone.

Like a horse, Effie never lies down to sleep. She used to lie down but the lightness of her body made no impression on the ground and it scared her. This is what death is like, she had thought, as the wind tugged at her skin. Now she sleeps sitting up. Wind can't touch her if she keeps her distance from the dust.

At night, she sees white horses racing. They are just wisps of moonlight, she is sure, and clouds of dust, yet she can hear the sound of their hooves connecting with the hollow earth beneath the dust, she can hear their leader snort. She watches as the horses circle her yard. Some animals, she has heard, rearrange the bones of their dead in a ritual manner, and she thinks sometimes that the horses are looking for bones. They are certainly looking for something. Sometimes they seem to be looking for her.

She sleeps upright, and even in dreams she sees horses. She watches them sway in their sleep, and she knows that they feed on moonlight rather than grass. The horses are as phosphorescent as bone, and they eye her through their inner lids. They know the things she has forgotten: the words to lullabies, the taste of water, the press of a tall man's thigh.

The wind blows and Effie ages. She is eighty years old, a hundred-and-two. She should be growing weaker, joining the piles of bone and the kisses of dust. She can remember less and less, but she still has her flinty strength. She rises sometimes and walks across the yard, pushes on the rickety fence posts and pounds them deeper into the alkali with a rock. She knows she should die but she chooses not to. She no longer needs bone, nothing needs bone up here. Life is a simple matter of wind and rearrangement.

When the dinosaurs return, she will be here, moving around her yard. When great fires sear the forests in the lower parts of the world, she will be here, pounding fence posts. When all the animals climb up her steep cliffs to let go of their gristle and bone, she will be here, alive as a sneeze of talcum, vital as a quick cloud of dust.

Acknowledgments